Standards Practice Book

For Home or School
Grade 2

INCLUDES:
- Home or School Practice
- Lesson Practice and Test Preparation
- English and Spanish School-Home Letters
- Dig Deeper and Connect Lessons
- Getting Ready for Grade 3 Lessons

MidAmerica Nazarene University
Mabee Library
Olathe, KS

 **HOUGHTON MIFFLIN HARCOURT**

Copyright © by Houghton Mifflin Harcourt Publishing Company.

All rights reserved. No part of this work may be reproduced or transmitted in any form or by any means, electronic or mechanical, including photocopying or recording, or by any information storage and retrieval system, without the prior written permission of the copyright owner unless such copying is expressly permitted by federal copyright law. Requests for permission to make copies of any part of the work should be addressed to Houghton Mifflin Harcourt Publishing Company, Attn: Contracts, Copyrights, and Licensing, 9400 South Park Center Loop, Orlando, Florida 32819.

Printed in the U.S.A.

ISBN 978-0-547-39261-5

If you have received these materials as examination copies free of charge, Houghton Mifflin Harcourt Publishing Company retains title to the materials and they may not be resold. Resale of examination copies is strictly prohibited.

Possession of this publication in print format does not entitle users to convert this publication, or any portion of it, into electronic format.

6 7 8 9 10 0982 15 14 13 12 11

4500318084 ^B C D E

Number and Place Value

Big Idea 1

1 Number Concepts

	School-Home Letter (English)	P1
	School-Home Letter (Spanish)	P2
1.1	Understand Place Value	P3
1.2	Expanded Form	P5
1.3	Different Ways to Write Numbers	P7
1.4	Different Names for Numbers	P9
1.5	**Problem Solving:** Make a List • Tens and Ones	P11
1.6	**Hands On:** Even and Odd Numbers	P13
1.7	**Algebra:** Compare and Order Numbers to 100	P15
	Extra Practice	P17

2 Numbers to 1,000

	School-Home Letter (English)	P19
	School-Home Letter (Spanish)	P20
2.1	Hundreds	P21
2.2	**Hands On:** Model 3-Digit Numbers	P23
2.3	Hundreds, Tens, and Ones	P25
2.4	Place Value to 1,000	P27
2.5	Different Forms of Numbers	P29
2.6	Different Ways to Show Numbers	P31
2.7	Count by 10s and 100s	P33
2.8	**Algebra:** Number Patterns	P35
2.9	**Problem Solving:** Make a Model • Compare Numbers	P37
2.10	**Algebra:** Compare Numbers	P39
2.11	**Algebra:** Order Numbers	P41
	Extra Practice	P43

iii

Big Idea 2: Addition, Subtraction, Multiplication, and Data

3 Basic Facts and Relationships

	School-Home Letter (English)	P45
	School-Home Letter (Spanish)	P46
3.1	Addition Facts	P47
3.2	Make-a-Ten Facts	P49
3.3	Add 3 Addends	P51
3.4	Relate Addition and Subtraction	P53
3.5	Fact Families	P55
3.6	Subtraction Facts	P57
3.7	Represent Addition and Subtraction	P59
3.8	**Problem Solving:** Write a Number Sentence • Basic Facts	P61
3.9	**Algebra:** Balance Number Sentences	P63
3.10	Equal and Not Equal	P65
	Extra Practice	P67

4 2-Digit Addition

	School-Home Letter (English)	P69
	School-Home Letter (Spanish)	P70
4.1	Break Apart Ones to Add	P71
4.2	Use Compensation	P73
4.3	Break Apart Addends as Tens and Ones	P75
4.4	Model Regrouping for Addition	P77
4.5	Model and Record 2-Digit Addition	P79
4.6	2-Digit Addition	P81
4.7	Practice 2-Digit Addition	P83
4.8	Rewrite 2-Digit Addition	P85
4.9	**Problem Solving:** Draw a Diagram • Addition	P87
4.10	Estimate Sums	P89
4.11	Find Sums for 3 Addends	P91
4.12	Represent Addition Problems	P93
	Extra Practice	P95

5 — 2-Digit Subtraction

	School-Home Letter (English)	P97
	School-Home Letter (Spanish)	P98
5.1	Break Apart Ones to Subtract	P99
5.2	Break Apart Numbers to Subtract	P101
5.3	Model Regrouping for Subtraction	P103
5.4	Model and Record 2-Digit Subtraction	P105
5.5	2-Digit Subtraction	P107
5.6	Practice 2-Digit Subtraction	P109
5.7	Rewrite 2-Digit Subtraction	P111
5.8	**Problem Solving:** Draw a Diagram • Subtraction	P113
5.9	Represent Subtraction Problems	P115
5.10	Solve Multistep Problems	P117
	Extra Practice	P119

6 — Data

	School-Home Letter (English)	P121
	School-Home Letter (Spanish)	P122
6.1	Take a Survey	P123
6.2	**Problem Solving:** Make a List • Surveys	P125
6.3	Pictographs	P127
6.4	Make Bar Graphs	P129
6.5	Use Bar Graphs	P131
6.6	Use Data	P133
	Extra Practice	P135

7 3-Digit Addition and Subtraction

	School-Home Letter (English)	P137
	School-Home Letter (Spanish)	P138
7.1	Break Apart 3-Digit Addends	P139
7.2	Record 3-Digit Addition: Regroup Ones	P141
7.3	Record 3-Digit Addition: Regroup Tens	P143
7.4	3-Digit Addition	P145
7.5	Practice 3-Digit Addition	P147
7.6	**Problem Solving:** Make a Model • 3-Digit Subtraction	P149
7.7	Record 3-Digit Subtraction: Regroup Tens	P151
7.8	Record 3-Digit Subtraction: Regroup Hundreds	P153
	Extra Practice	P155

8 Multiplication Concepts

	School-Home Letter (English)	P157
	School-Home Letter (Spanish)	P158
8.1	Skip Count on a Hundred Chart	P159
8.2	**Problem Solving:** Act It Out • Patterns	P161
8.3	**Algebra:** Extend Patterns	P163
8.4	Connect Addition and Multiplication	P165
8.5	**Hands On:** Model Multiplication	P167
8.6	Multiply with 2	P169
8.7	Multiply with 5	P171
	Extra Practice	P173

Measurement and Geometry

Big Idea 3

9 Length

	School-Home Letter (English)	P175
	School-Home Letter (Spanish)	P176
9.1	**Hands On:** Indirect Measurement	P177
9.2	Compare Lengths	P179
9.3	**Hands On:** Measure with Inch Models	P181
9.4	**Hands On:** Make and Use a Ruler	P183
9.5	Estimate Lengths	P185
9.6	**Hands On:** Measure with an Inch Ruler	P187
9.7	Estimate and Measure Length	P189
9.8	**Hands On:** Measure in Inches and Feet	P191
9.9	**Hands On:** Measure in Feet and Yards	P193
9.10	**Hands On:** Measure with a Centimeter Model	P195
9.11	**Hands On:** Measure with a Centimeter Ruler	P197
9.12	Make Reasonable Estimates	P199
9.13	**Hands On:** Centimeters and Meters	P201
9.14	**Problem Solving:** Act It Out • Length	P203
	9.14A **DIG DEEPER** Graph Measurements	P204a
	Extra Practice	P205

10 Weight, Mass, and Capacity

	School-Home Letter (English)	P207
	School-Home Letter (Spanish)	P208
10.1	**Hands On:** Ounces and Pounds	P209
10.2	**Hands On:** Grams and Kilograms	P211
10.3	**Hands On:** Cups and Quarts	P213
10.4	**Hands On:** Milliliters and Liters	P215
10.5	Choose the Unit	P217
10.6	**Problem Solving:** Act It Out • Measurement	P219
	Extra Practice	P221

vii

11 Money and Time

	School-Home Letter (English)	**P223**
	School-Home Letter (Spanish)	**P224**
11.1	Dimes, Nickels, and Pennies	**P225**
11.2	Half Dollars and Quarters	**P227**
11.3	Count Collections	**P229**
11.4	**Problem Solving:** Find a Pattern • Money	**P231**
11.5	One Dollar	**P233**
11.5A	**CONNECT** Problem Solving with Money	**P234a**
11.6	Telling Time	**P235**
11.7	Time to the Hour and Half Hour	**P237**
11.7A	**CONNECT** Hour Before and Hour After	**P238a**
11.7B	**CONNECT** Elapsed Time in Hours	**P238c**
11.8	Time to 5 Minutes	**P239**
11.9	Time to the Minute	**P241**
11.10	Units of Time	**P243**
	Extra Practice	**P245**

12 Geometry and Patterns

	School-Home Letter (English)	**P247**
	School-Home Letter (Spanish)	**P248**
12.1	Three-Dimensional Shapes	**P249**
12.2	Two-Dimensional Shapes	**P251**
12.3	Sort Two-Dimensional Shapes	**P253**
12.3A	**DIG DEEPER** Angles	**P254a**
12.3B	**DIG DEEPER** Angles in Shapes	**P254c**
12.4	Symmetry	**P255**
12.4A	**DIG DEEPER** Equal Parts	**P256a**
12.4B	**DIG DEEPER** Name Equal Parts	**P256c**
12.5	**Algebra:** Extend Growing Patterns	**P257**
12.6	**Problem Solving:** Find a Pattern • Number Patterns	**P259**
12.7	**Algebra:** Find a Rule: Growing Patterns	**P261**
12.8	**Algebra:** Explain Rules for Patterns	**P263**
12.9	**Algebra:** Find Missing Terms for Patterns	**P265**
	Extra Practice	**P267**

End-of-Year Resources

Getting Ready for Grade 3

These lessons review important skills and prepare you for Grade 3.

Lesson 1	Thousands	**P269**
Lesson 2	Place Value: 4-Digit Numbers	**P271**
Lesson 3	Different Forms of 4-Digit Numbers	**P273**
Lesson 4	**Algebra:** Compare 4-Digit Numbers	**P275**
Lesson 5	**Algebra:** Order 4-Digit Numbers	**P277**
Checkpoint		**P279**
Lesson 6	**Estimate Sums:** 2-Digit Addition	**P281**
Lesson 7	**Estimate Sums:** 3-Digit Addition	**P283**
Lesson 8	**Estimate Differences:** 2-Digit Subtraction	**P285**
Lesson 9	**Estimate Differences:** 3-Digit Subtraction	**P287**
Checkpoint		**P289**
Lesson 10	**Hands On:** Equivalent Amounts	**P291**
Lesson 11	Compare Amounts	**P293**
Lesson 12	Make Change to 50¢	**P295**
Lesson 13	Make Change to $1.00	**P297**
Lesson 14	Money Amounts Over $1.00	**P299**
Lesson 15	$5, $10, and $20 Bills	**P301**
Checkpoint		**P303**
Lesson 16	Multiply with 3	**P305**
Lesson 17	Multiply with 10	**P307**
Lesson 18	**Hands On:** Size of Shares	**P309**
Lesson 19	**Hands On:** Number of Equal Shares	**P311**
Lesson 20	Connect Subtraction and Division	**P313**
Checkpoint		**P315**

Chapter 1
School-Home Letter

Dear Family,

My class started Chapter 1 today. In this chapter, I will learn about place value of 2-digit numbers, even and odd numbers, and comparing numbers.

Love, _____

Vocabulary

digits 0, 1, 2, 3, 4, 5, 6, 7, 8, and 9 are digits.

is greater than 3 is greater than 2
> 3 > 2

is less than 12 is less than 18
< 12 < 18

even numbers 2, 4, 6, 8, 10 . . .

odd numbers 1, 3, 5, 7, 9 . . .

Home Activity

Give your child a group of 20 small objects, such as beans. Have your child count the objects and tell how many. Then have your child pair the objects and tell whether the number is *even* or *odd*. Repeat with a different number of beans.

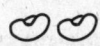

Literature

Look for this book at the library. Ask your child to point out math vocabulary words as you read the book together.

One Hundred Hungry Ants by Elinor J. Pinczes. Houghton Mifflin, 1993.

Capítulo 1

Carta para la casa

Querida familia:

Mi clase comenzó hoy el Capítulo 1. En este capítulo, aprenderé sobre el valor posicional de los números de 2 dígitos, números pares e impares y a comparar números.

Con cariño, _____

Vocabulario

dígitos 0, 1, 2, 3, 4, 5, 6, 7, 8 y 9 son dígitos.

es mayor que 3 es mayor que 2
> 3 > 2

es menor que 12 es menor que 18
< 12 < 18

números pares 2, 4, 6, 8, 10 . . .

números impares 1, 3, 5, 7, 9 . . .

Actividad para la casa

Dé a su hijo un grupo de 20 objetos pequeños, como frijoles. Pídale que cuente los objetos y diga cuántos hay. Luego pídale que los agrupe y diga si el número es *par* o *impar*. Repita con un distinto número de frijoles.

Literatura

Busquen este libro en la biblioteca. Pida a su hijo que señale palabras del vocabulario de matemáticas mientras leen juntos el libro.

One Hundred Hungry Ants
por Elinor J. Pinczes.
Houghton Mifflin, 1993.

Name _____

Lesson 1.1

Understand Place Value

Circle the value of the underlined digit.

1. 2̲3 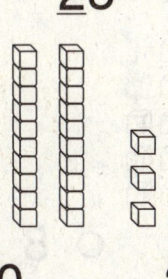 20 2	2. 4̲8 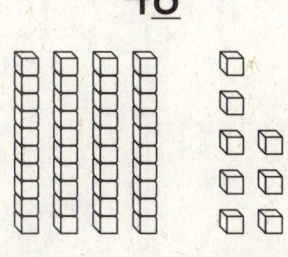 8 80	3. 1̲8 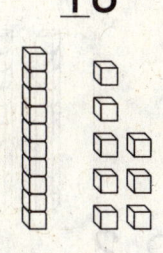 10 1
4. 4̲3 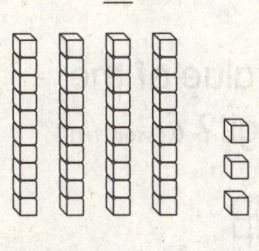 40 4	5. 5̲4 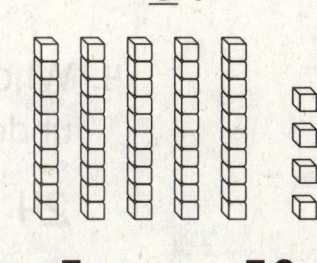 5 50	6. 6̲5 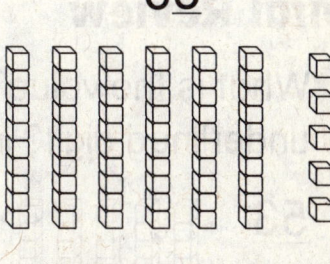 50 5
7. 7̲0 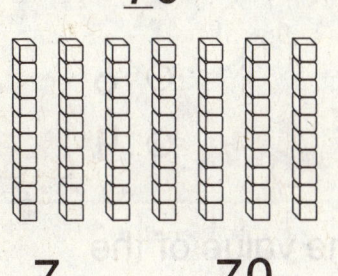 7 70	8. 3̲7 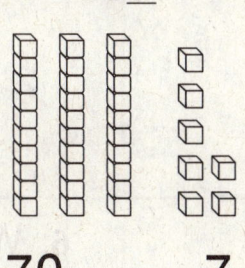 70 7	9. 2̲2 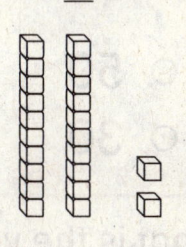 20 2

PROBLEM SOLVING REAL WORLD

Write the 2-digit number that matches the clues.

10. My number has a tens digit that is 8 more than the ones digit. Zero is not one of my digits.

My number is _____.

Chapter 1   three **P3**

Lesson Check

1. What is the value of the underlined digit?

   3<u>2</u>

   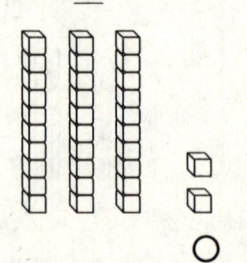

   ○ 2   ○ 20
   ○ 3   ○ 30

2. What is the value of the underlined digit?

   <u>2</u>8

   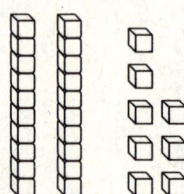

   ○ 80   ○ 8
   ○ 20   ○ 2

Spiral Review

3. What is the value of the underlined digit? (Lesson 1.1)

   <u>5</u>3

   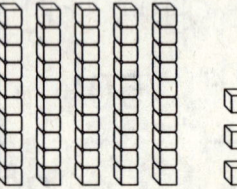

   ○ 50   ○ 8
   ○ 30   ○ 5

4. What is the value of the underlined digit? (Lesson 1.1)

   2<u>4</u>

   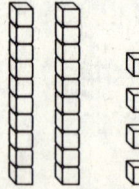

   ○ 40   ○ 6
   ○ 20   ○ 4

5. What is the value of the underlined digit? (Lesson 1.1)

   <u>4</u>7

   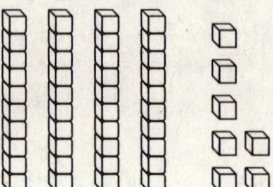

   ○ 4   ○ 40
   ○ 7   ○ 70

6. What is the value of the underlined digit? (Lesson 1.1)

   <u>5</u>5

   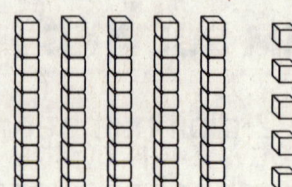

   ○ 50   ○ 6
   ○ 11   ○ 5

Lesson 1.2

Name _____

Expanded Form

Draw quick pictures to show the number.
Describe the number in two ways.

1. 68

   68 = ____ tens ____ ones
   68 = ____ + ____

2. 21

   21 = ____ tens ____ one
   21 = ____ + ____

3. 70

   70 = ____ tens ____ ones
   70 = ____ + ____

4. 53

   53 = ____ tens ____ ones
   53 = ____ + ____

5. 35

   35 = ____ tens ____ ones
   35 = ____ + ____

6. 47

   47 = ____ tens ____ ones
   47 = ____ + ____

PROBLEM SOLVING

7. Circle the ways to write the number shown by the model.

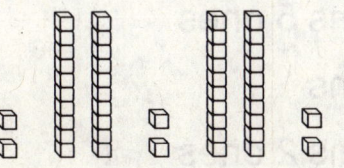

    4 tens 6 ones   40 + 6   64
    6 tens 4 ones   60 + 4   46

Chapter 1   five **P5**

Lesson Check

1. How many tens and ones are in the number 92?

   - ○ 9 tens
   - ○ 2 tens 9 ones
   - ○ 9 tens 2 ones
   - ○ 11 tens

2. How many tens and ones are in the number 45?

   - ○ 4 tens 5 ones
   - ○ 5 tens 4 ones
   - ○ 4 tens 0 ones
   - ○ 4 tens 9 ones

Spiral Review

3. What is the value of the underlined digit? (Lesson 1.1)

   4<u>9</u>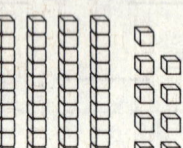

   - ○ 90
   - ○ 40
   - ○ 9
   - ○ 4

4. What is the value of the underlined digit? (Lesson 1.1)

   <u>3</u>4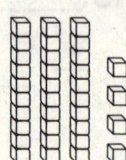

   - ○ 40
   - ○ 30
   - ○ 4
   - ○ 3

5. Which is another way to describe the number 76?

   (Lesson 1.2)

   - ○ 7 tens
   - ○ 6 tens 7 ones
   - ○ 7 tens 6 ones
   - ○ 7 tens 13 ones

6. Which is another way to describe the number 52?

   (Lesson 1.2)

   - ○ 7 tens 2 ones
   - ○ 2 tens 5 ones
   - ○ 5 tens
   - ○ 5 tens 2 ones

Different Ways to Write Numbers

Lesson 1.3

Name _____

Write the number another way.

1. 32

  ____ tens ____ ones

2. forty-one

  _____

3. 9 tens 5 ones

  _____

4. 80 + 3

  _____

5. 57

  ____ tens ____ ones

6. seventy-two

  ____ + ____

7. 60 + 4

  _____

8. 4 tens 8 ones

  _____

9. twenty-eight

  ____ + ____

10. 80

  ____ tens ____ ones

PROBLEM SOLVING

11. A number has the digit 3 in the ones place and the digit 4 in the tens place. Which of these is another way to write this number? Circle it.

    3 + 4   40 + 3   30 + 4

Chapter 1

seven P7

Lesson Check

1. What is another way to write this number?

   3 tens 9 ones

   ○ 93
   ○ 30 + 90
   ○ 90 + 3
   ○ 39

2. What is another way to write this number?

   eighteen

   ○ 8 + 1
   ○ 81
   ○ 10 + 8
   ○ 10 + 80

Spiral Review

3. Which is another way to write the number 47? (Lesson 1.3)

   ○ 70 + 4
   ○ 40 + 7
   ○ 4 + 7
   ○ 40 + 70

4. Which is another way to write the number 95? (Lesson 1.3)

   ○ 50 + 9
   ○ 90 + 50
   ○ fifty-nine
   ○ ninety-five

5. What is the value of the underlined digit? (Lesson 1.1)

   6<u>1</u>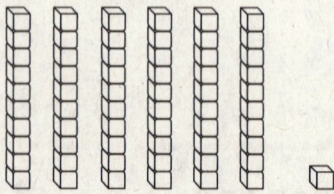

   ○ 1   ○ 7
   ○ 6   ○ 10

6. What is the value of the underlined digit? (Lesson 1.1)

   <u>1</u>7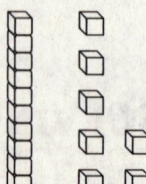

   ○ 1   ○ 10
   ○ 7   ○ 70

P8 eight

Name _____

Different Names for Numbers

Lesson 1.4

Write how many tens and ones.
Then write the number as tens plus ones.

1. 24

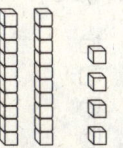
___ tens ___ ones
___ + ___

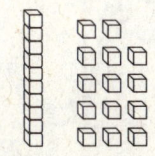
___ ten ___ ones
___ + ___

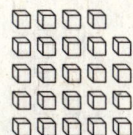
___ tens ___ ones
___ + ___

2. 36

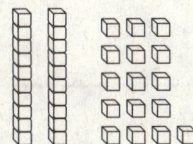
___ tens ___ ones
___ + ___

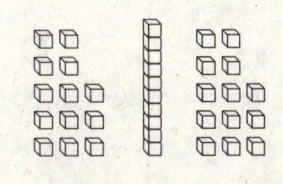
___ ten ___ ones
___ + ___

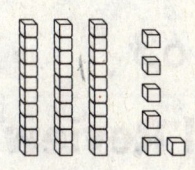
___ tens ___ ones
___ + ___

3. 45

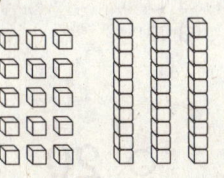
___ tens ___ ones
___ + ___

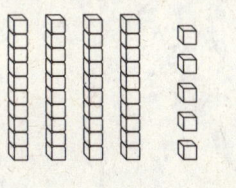
___ tens ___ ones
___ + ___

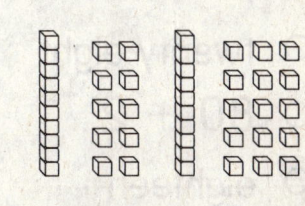
___ tens ___ ones
___ + ___

PROBLEM SOLVING  REAL WORLD

4. Toni has these blocks. Circle the blocks that she could use to show 34.

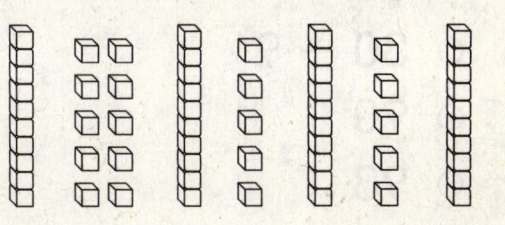

Chapter 1
nine P9

Lesson Check

1. What number is shown with the blocks?

   2 tens 13 ones

   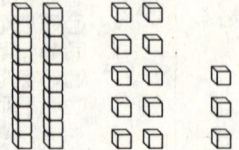

   ○ 33
   ○ 34
   ○ 43
   ○ 63

2. What number is shown with the blocks?

   1 ten 16 ones

   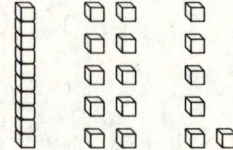

   ○ 16
   ○ 26
   ○ 31
   ○ 36

Spiral Review

3. Which is another way to write the number 82? (Lesson 1.3)

   ○ 20 + 8
   ○ twenty-eight
   ○ 80 + 2
   ○ eighteen

4. What is the value of the underlined digit? (Lesson 1.1)

   2<u>9</u>

   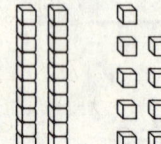

   ○ 2   ○ 20
   ○ 9   ○ 90

5. Which is another way to write 9 tens 3 ones? (Lesson 1.3)

   ○ 39
   ○ 30 + 9
   ○ 90
   ○ 93

6. How many tens and ones are in the number 50? (Lesson 1.2)

   ○ 0 tens 5 ones
   ○ 2 tens 3 ones
   ○ 5 tens 0 ones
   ○ 5 tens 5 ones

P10 ten

PROBLEM SOLVING
Lesson 1.5

Make a List • Tens and Ones

Make a list to solve.

1. Ann is grouping 38 rocks. She can put them into groups of 10 rocks or as single rocks. What are the different ways Ann can group the rocks?

Groups of 10 rocks	Single rocks

2. Mr. Grant needs 30 pieces of felt. He can buy them in packs of 10 or as single pieces. What are the different ways Mr. Grant can buy the felt?

Packs of 10 pieces	Single pieces

3. Ms. Sims is putting away 22 books. She can put them on the table in stacks of 10 or as single books. What are the different ways Ms. Sims can put away the books?

Stacks of 10 books	Single books

Chapter 1

Lesson Check

1. Mrs. Chang is packing 38 apples. She can pack them in bags of 10 or as single apples. What choice is missing from the list of ways Mrs. Chang can pack the apples?

   ○ 3 bags, 0 apples
   ○ 1 bag, 18 apples
   ○ 3 bags, 8 apples
   ○ 4 bags, 8 apples

Bags of 10 apples	Single apples
2	18
1	28
0	38

Spiral Review

2. What is the value of the underlined digit? (Lesson 1.1)

   5̲4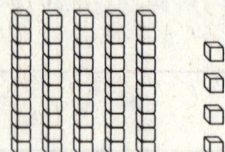

   ○ 50
   ○ 40
   ○ 5
   ○ 4

3. What number is shown with the blocks? (Lesson 1.4)

   2 tens 19 ones

   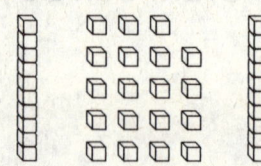

   ○ 21
   ○ 29
   ○ 34
   ○ 39

4. What is another way to write the number 62? (Lesson 1.3)

   ○ 2 tens 6 ones
   ○ 6 + 2
   ○ sixty-two
   ○ 20 + 6

5. What number can be written as 8 tens 6 ones? (Lesson 1.3)

   ○ 68
   ○ 86
   ○ 114
   ○ 140

Name _____

Even and Odd Numbers

**HANDS ON
Lesson 1.6**

Shade in the ten frames to show the number. Circle even or odd.

1. 15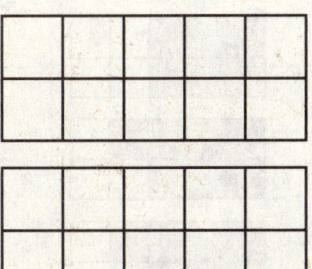
   even   odd

2. 18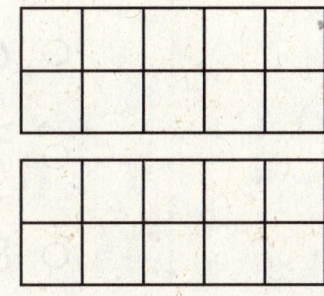
   even   odd

3. 11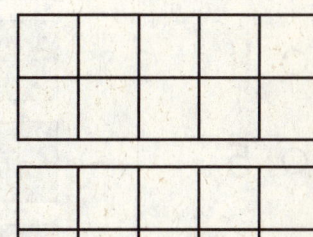
   even   odd

4. 27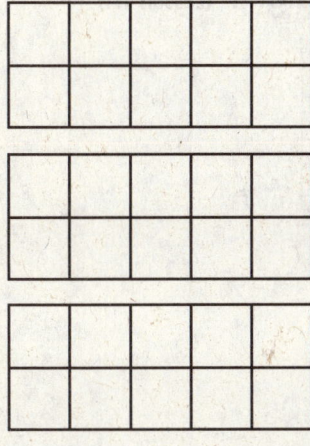
   even   odd

5. 23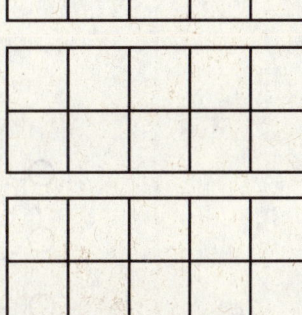
   even   odd

6. 30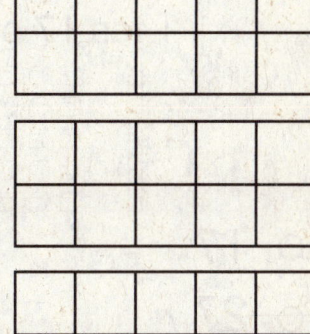
   even   odd

PROBLEM SOLVING

7. There are an odd number of girls and an even number of boys in Theo's class. Circle the choice that could tell about his class.

   9 girls and 10 boys

   10 girls and 11 boys

   8 girls and 12 boys

Chapter 1   thirteen P13

Lesson Check

1. Which of these numbers is an even number?
   - ○ 3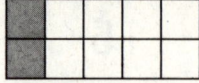
   - ○ 4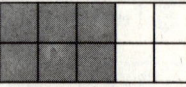
   - ○ 5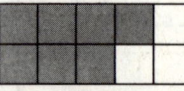
   - ○ 9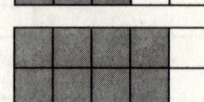

2. Which of these numbers is an odd number?
   - ○ 2
   - ○ 6
   - ○ 7
   - ○ 8

Spiral Review

3. What number is shown with the blocks? (Lesson 1.4)

   1 ten 17 ones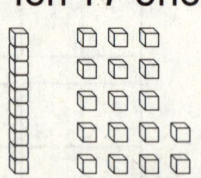
   - ○ 17
   - ○ 27
   - ○ 42
   - ○ 57

4. What is the value of the underlined digit? (Lesson 1.1)

   2<u>1</u>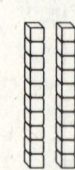
   - ○ 1
   - ○ 2
   - ○ 10
   - ○ 20

5. Which is another way to write 4 tens 3 ones? (Lesson 1.3)
   - ○ 7
   - ○ 34
   - ○ 43
   - ○ 47

6. Which is another way to write the number 59? (Lesson 1.3)
   - ○ 90 + 5
   - ○ 5 + 9
   - ○ 50 + 5
   - ○ 50 + 9

Lesson 1.7

Name _____

Algebra: Compare and Order Numbers to 100

Compare the numbers. Write >, <, or =.

1.	65 ◯ 56	2.	72 ◯ 72
3.	83 ◯ 85	4.	36 ◯ 26
5.	29 ◯ 27	6.	58 ◯ 59
7.	45 ◯ 45	8.	85 ◯ 81

Compare the numbers. Write > or <.
Then circle to show their order.

9. 26 ◯ 29 ◯ 34

least to greatest

greatest to least

10. 61 ◯ 58 ◯ 54

least to greatest

greatest to least

PROBLEM SOLVING — REAL WORLD

11. Ron has 81 cards. Tia has 82 cards. Ali has 80 cards. Compare the numbers. Write them in order.

_____ < _____ < _____

Chapter 1 fifteen **P15**

TEST PREP

Lesson Check

1. Which is true?
   - ○ 79 > 84
   - ○ 27 < 33
   - ○ 75 < 68
   - ○ 45 = 55

2. Which is true?
   - ○ 18 > 20
   - ○ 17 = 71
   - ○ 17 = 17
   - ○ 33 < 27

Spiral Review

3. Which is another way to write the number 76? (Lesson 1.3)
   - ○ 7 + 6
   - ○ 60 + 7
   - ○ 6 + 17
   - ○ 70 + 6

4. What is the value of the underlined digit? (Lesson 1.1)

   9<u>4</u>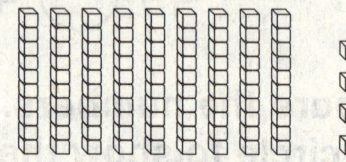
   - ○ 4
   - ○ 9
   - ○ 40
   - ○ 90

5. Which of these is an even number? (Lesson 1.6)
   - ○ 10
   - ○ 7
   - ○ 5
   - ○ 3

6. What number is shown with the blocks? (Lesson 1.4)

   6 tens 19 ones

   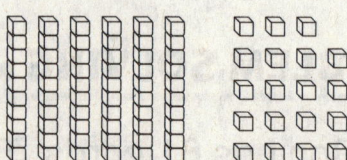
   - ○ 59
   - ○ 69
   - ○ 79
   - ○ 94

Name _____

Chapter 1 Extra Practice

Lesson 1.1 (pp. 13–16)
Circle the value of the underlined digit.

1. 5<u>7</u>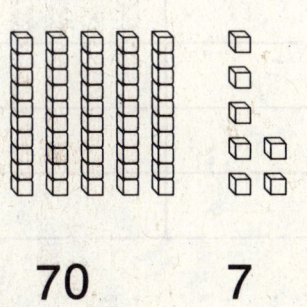

   70   7

2. <u>9</u>3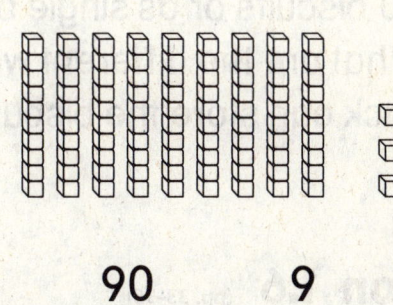

   90   9

Lesson 1.2 (pp. 17–20)
Draw quick pictures to show the number.
Describe the number in two ways.

1. 22

   22 = ____ tens ____ ones

   22 = ____ + ____

2. 67

   67 = ____ tens ____ ones

   67 = ____ + ____

Lesson 1.4 (pp. 25–28)
Write how many tens and ones.
Then write the number as tens plus ones.

1. 48

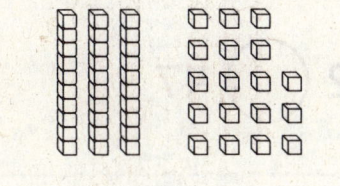 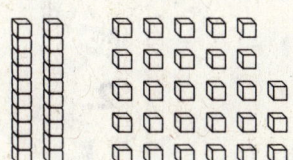 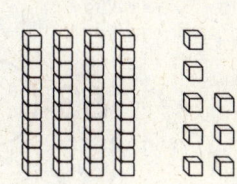

____ tens ____ ones   ____ tens ____ ones   ____ tens ____ ones

____ + ____   ____ + ____   ____ + ____

Lesson 1.5 (pp. 29–32)

Make a list to solve.

1. Jack baked 38 biscuits. He can store them in boxes of 10 biscuits or as single biscuits. What are the different ways Jack can store the biscuits?

Boxes of 10 biscuits	Single biscuits

Lesson 1.6 (pp. 33–36)

Shade in the ten frames to show the number. Circle **even** or **odd**.

1. 17

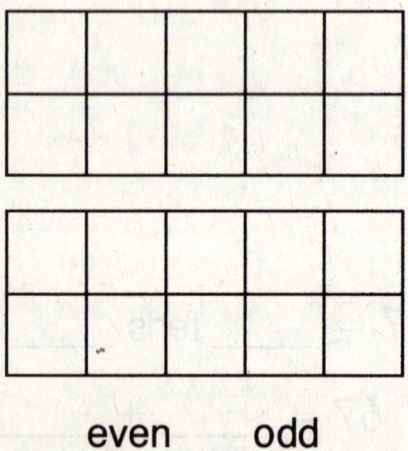

even   odd

2. 20

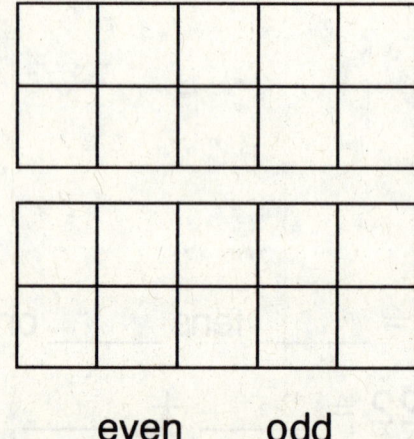

even   odd

Lesson 1.7 (pp. 37–40)

Compare the numbers. Write >, <, or =.

1. 63 ◯ 36

2. 42 ◯ 47

3. 18 ◯ 81

4. 76 ◯ 76

Chapter 2
School-Home Letter

Dear Family,

My class started Chapter 2 today. I will learn about place value of numbers to 1,000. I will also learn about comparing and ordering these numbers.

Love, _____

Vocabulary

hundred A group of 10 tens

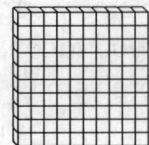

thousand A group of 10 hundreds

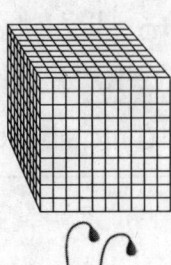

Home Activity

Have your child look through magazines for 3-digit numbers and cut them out. Work together to write a word problem using two of these numbers, gluing the cut-out numbers in place. Have your child solve the problem.

Charles collected __127__ leaves. Ann collected __240__ leaves. Who collected the greater number of leaves?

Literature

Reading math stories reinforces learning. Look for these books in the library.

A Place for Zero
by Angeline Sparagna LoPresti and Phyllis Hornung. Charlesbridge Publishing, 2003.

More or Less
by Stuart J. Murphy. HarperCollins, 2005.

Capítulo 2
Carta para la casa

Querida familia:
Mi clase comenzó hoy el Capítulo 2. Aprenderé sobre el valor posicional de los números hasta 1,000. También aprenderé a comparar y ordenar esos números.

Con cariño, _____

Vocabulario

centena un grupo de 10 decenas

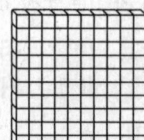

millar un grupo de 10 centenas

Actividad para la casa
Pida a su hijo que busque números de 3 dígitos en revistas y los recorte. Luego escriban un problema y péguenle dos de los números recortados. Pida a su hijo que resuelva el problema.

Carlos juntó ___127___ hojas.
Ana juntó ___240___ hojas.
¿Quién juntó más hojas?

Literatura
Leer cuentos de matemáticas refuerza el aprendizaje. Busquen estos libros en la biblioteca.

A Place for Zero
por Angeline Sparagna LoPresti y Phyllis Hornung. Charlesbridge Publishing, 2003.

More or Less
por Stuart J. Murphy. HarperCollins, 2005.

Name _____

Lesson **2.1**

Hundreds

Circle tens to make 1 hundred. Write the number in two ways.

1.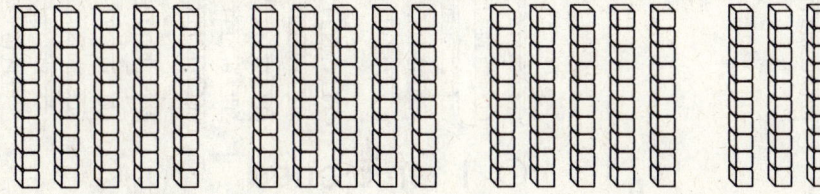

    ____ tens = ____ hundred ____ tens

2.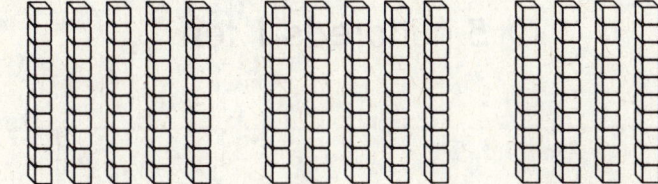

    ____ tens = ____ hundred ____ tens

3.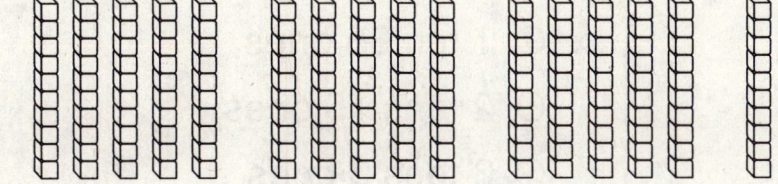

    ____ tens = ____ hundred ____ tens

PROBLEM SOLVING REAL WORLD

Solve. Write or draw to explain.

4. Millie has a box of 1 hundred cubes. She also has a bag of 70 cubes. How many trains of 10 cubes can she make?

    ____ trains of 10 cubes

Chapter 2   twenty-one **P21**

Lesson Check

1. Which is another way to show 12 tens?

   ○ 1 ten 2 ones
   ○ 2 tens 1 one
   ○ 2 hundreds 2 tens
   ○ 1 hundred 2 tens

2. Which is another way to show 15 tens?

   ○ 1 ten 5 ones
   ○ 5 tens 1 one
   ○ 1 hundred 5 tens
   ○ 5 hundreds 1 ten

Spiral Review

3. Which of these is an odd number? (Lesson 1.6)

   ○ 36
   ○ 24
   ○ 23
   ○ 14

4. Which is a way to show the number 35? (Lesson 1.4)

   ○ 1 ten 35 ones
   ○ 2 tens 15 ones
   ○ 3 tens 3 ones
   ○ 5 tens 3 ones

5. Which is another way to write the number 78? (Lesson 1.2)

   ○ 7 tens 8 ones
   ○ 8 tens 7 ones
   ○ 70 tens 8 ones
   ○ 7 tens 80 ones

6. Which is another way to show the number 55? (Lesson 1.3)

   ○ 505
   ○ 15 + 5
   ○ 50 tens 5 ones
   ○ 5 tens 5 ones

Name _____

Model 3-Digit Numbers

**HANDS ON
Lesson 2.2**

Write how many hundreds, tens, and ones.
Then draw quick pictures.

1. 118

Hundreds	Tens	Ones

2. 246

Hundreds	Tens	Ones

3. 143

Hundreds	Tens	Ones

4. 237

Hundreds	Tens	Ones

PROBLEM SOLVING

5. Write the number that matches the clues.
   - My number has 2 hundreds.
   - The tens digit is 9 more than the ones digit.

Hundreds	Tens	Ones

My number is _____.

Chapter 2

twenty-three **P23**

Lesson Check

1. What number is shown with the blocks?

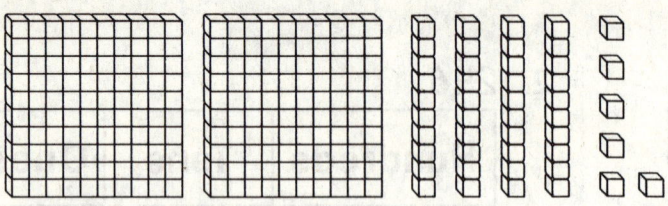

- ○ 246
- ○ 264
- ○ 462
- ○ 642

Spiral Review

2. Which is true? (Lesson 1.7)
   - ○ 45 < 23
   - ○ 23 > 45
   - ○ 23 = 45
   - ○ 45 > 23

3. Which is another way to write the number 59? (Lesson 1.3)
   - ○ 50 + 90
   - ○ 5 + 9
   - ○ 50 + 9
   - ○ 5 + 90

4. Which of these is an odd number? (Lesson 1.6)
   - ○ 11
   - ○ 12
   - ○ 18
   - ○ 20

5. What is a way to show the number 73? (Lesson 1.3)
   - ○ 3 tens 7 ones
   - ○ 7 tens 3 ones
   - ○ 70 tens 3 ones
   - ○ 30 tens 7 ones

Lesson 2.3

Name _____

Hundreds, Tens, and Ones

Write how many hundreds, tens, and ones. Write the number.

1.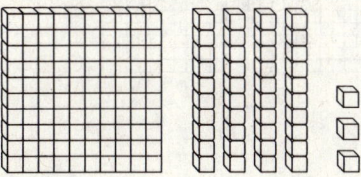

Hundreds	Tens	Ones

2.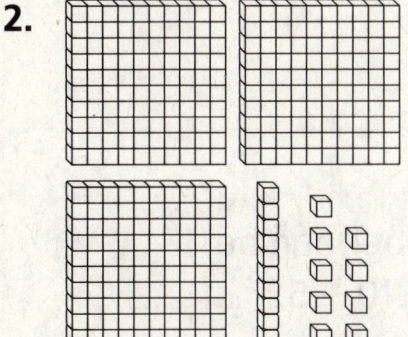

Hundreds	Tens	Ones

3.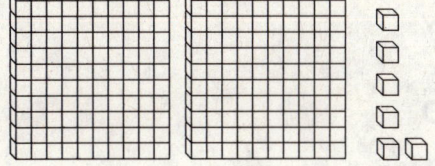

Hundreds	Tens	Ones

PROBLEM SOLVING · REAL WORLD

4. Write the number that matches the clues.

   I have 6 ones, 2 hundreds, and 3 tens.
   What number am I?

   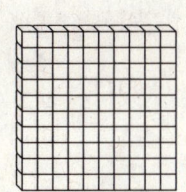 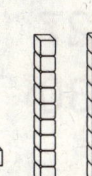 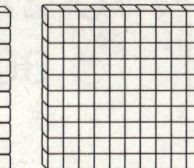

   _____

Chapter 2   twenty-five **P25**

Lesson Check

1. What number do the blocks show?

   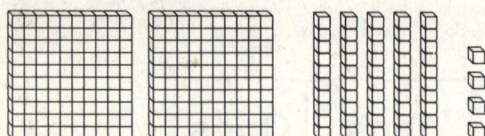

   ○ 245
   ○ 254
   ○ 425
   ○ 452

2. What number do the blocks show?

   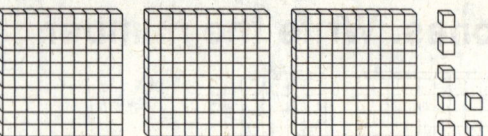

   ○ 307
   ○ 312
   ○ 317
   ○ 370

Spiral Review

3. Which is another way to write the number 83? (Lesson 1.3)

   ○ 80 + 3
   ○ 8 + 3
   ○ 8 + 30
   ○ 80 + 30

4. What number can be written as 40 + 5? (Lesson 1.2)

   ○ 4
   ○ 9
   ○ 45
   ○ 54

5. Which is true? (Lesson 1.7)

   ○ 24 > 48
   ○ 67 < 29
   ○ 54 = 45
   ○ 54 = 54

6. Which of these is an odd number? (Lesson 1.6)

   ○ 16
   ○ 24
   ○ 27
   ○ 30

Name _____

Lesson 2.4

Place Value to 1,000

Circle the value or the meaning of the underlined digit.

1. 3<u>3</u>7	3	30	300
2. 46<u>2</u>	200	20	2
3. <u>5</u>72	5	50	500
4. 56<u>7</u>	7 ones	7 tens	7 hundreds
5. <u>4</u>62	4 hundreds	4 ones	4 tens
6. <u>1</u>,000	1 ten	1 hundred	1 thousand

PROBLEM SOLVING  REAL WORLD

7. Write the 3-digit number that matches the clues.

   • My number has as many hundreds as ones.

   • It has 5 tens and 4 ones.

   My number is _____.

Chapter 2   twenty-seven   P27

Lesson Check

1. What is the value of the underlined digit?

    3̲15

    - ○ 3
    - ○ 30
    - ○ 33
    - ○ 300

2. What is the meaning of the underlined digit?

    64̲8

    - ○ 4 ones
    - ○ 4 hundreds
    - ○ 4 tens
    - ○ 4 thousands

Spiral Review

3. Which is another way to write the number 86? (Lesson 1.3)
    - ○ eighty-six
    - ○ eighty
    - ○ eighteen
    - ○ sixty-eight

4. Which is true? (Lesson 1.7)
    - ○ 15 > 67
    - ○ 34 < 15
    - ○ 67 < 34
    - ○ 15 < 34

5. Which is another way to show the number 26? (Lesson 1.4)
    - ○ 6 tens 2 ones
    - ○ 2 tens 2 ones
    - ○ 1 ten 16 ones
    - ○ 1 ten 6 ones

6. Which of these is an even number? (Lesson 1.6)
    - ○ 7
    - ○ 16
    - ○ 21
    - ○ 25

Name _____

Different Forms of Numbers

Lesson 2.5

Read the number and draw quick pictures.
Then write the number in different ways.

1. two hundred fifty-one

   ____ hundreds ____ tens ____ one

   _____ + _____ + _____

   _____

2. three hundred twelve

   ____ hundreds ____ ten ____ ones

   _____ + _____ + _____

   _____

3. two hundred seven

   ____ hundreds ____ tens ____ ones

   _____ + _____ + _____

   _____

PROBLEM SOLVING

Write the number another way.

4. 200 + 30 + 7

   _____

5. 895

   _____

Chapter 2

twenty-nine P29

Lesson Check

1. Which is another way to write the number 392?
   - ○ 200 + 90 + 3
   - ○ 200 + 30 + 9
   - ○ 300 + 90 + 2
   - ○ 300 + 19 + 2

2. Which is another way to write the number 271?
   - ○ 1 hundred 7 tens 2 ones
   - ○ 2 hundreds 1 ten 7 ones
   - ○ 2 hundreds 2 tens 7 ones
   - ○ 2 hundreds 7 tens 1 one

Spiral Review

3. What is the value of the underlined digit? (Lesson 1.1)

   5<u>6</u>

   - ○ 5
   - ○ 6
   - ○ 50
   - ○ 60

4. Which is true? (Lesson 1.7)
   - ○ 47 > 22
   - ○ 55 = 5
   - ○ 63 < 59
   - ○ 74 = 47

5. Which is another way to write the number 75? (Lesson 1.3)
   - ○ 7 + 5
   - ○ 70 + 5
   - ○ 7 + 50
   - ○ 70 + 50

6. What number can be written as 60 + 3? (Lesson 1.2)
   - ○ 6
   - ○ 9
   - ○ 36
   - ○ 63

Name _____

Lesson 2.6

Different Ways to Show Numbers

Write how many hundreds, tens, and ones.

1. 135

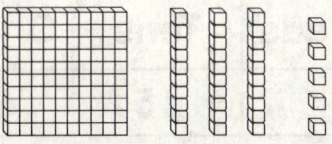

Hundreds	Tens	Ones

Hundreds	Tens	Ones

2. 216

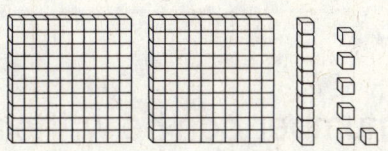   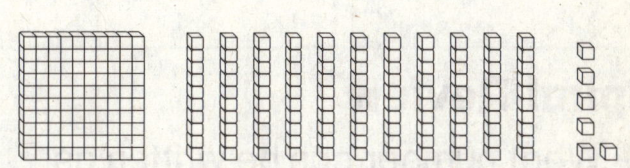

Hundreds	Tens	Ones

Hundreds	Tens	Ones

PROBLEM SOLVING

3. Write the number that these blocks show.

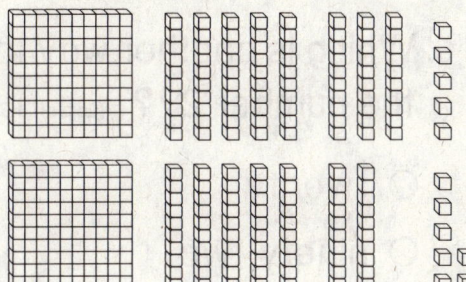

_____

Chapter 2 thirty-one **P31**

Lesson Check

1. Which of the following numbers can be shown with this number of hundreds, tens, and ones?

Hundreds	Tens	Ones
1	2	18

- ○ 128
- ○ 129
- ○ 138
- ○ 148

2. Which of the following numbers can be shown with this number of hundreds, tens, and ones?

Hundreds	Tens	Ones
2	15	6

- ○ 256
- ○ 266
- ○ 316
- ○ 356

Spiral Review

3. What number can be written as 6 tens 2 ones? (Lesson 1.3)

- ○ 26
- ○ 62
- ○ 206
- ○ 602

4. What number can be written as 30 + 2? (Lesson 1.2)

- ○ 302
- ○ 203
- ○ 32
- ○ 23

5. Which is true? (Lesson 1.7)

- ○ 67 > 75
- ○ 38 = 83
- ○ 15 < 12
- ○ 12 < 34

6. Which is another way to write the number 29? (Lesson 1.3)

- ○ twenty
- ○ ninety-two
- ○ two hundred nine
- ○ twenty-nine

Lesson 2.7

Name _____

Count by 10s and 100s

Write the number.

1. 10 more than 451
   _____

2. 10 less than 770
   _____

3. 100 more than 367
   _____

4. 100 less than 895
   _____

5. 10 less than 812
   _____

6. 100 more than 543
   _____

7. Count on by 10s.

   218, _____, _____, _____, 258, 268

8. Count back by 10s.

   379, _____, _____, _____, 339, 329

9. Count on by 100s.

   324, _____, _____, _____, 724, 824

PROBLEM SOLVING

Solve.

10. Sarah has 128 stickers. Alex has 10 fewer stickers than Sarah. How many stickers does Alex have?

    _____ stickers

Lesson Check

1. What number is 10 less than 526?
   - ○ 536
   - ○ 516
   - ○ 426
   - ○ 416

2. What number is 100 more than 487?
   - ○ 387
   - ○ 477
   - ○ 497
   - ○ 587

Spiral Review

3. Which is another way to show 14 tens? (Lesson 2.1)

   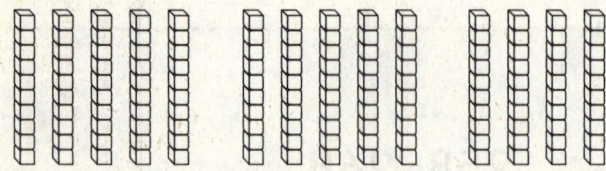

   - ○ 1 hundred 4 tens
   - ○ 1 hundred 9 tens
   - ○ 1 ten 4 ones
   - ○ 1 ten 9 ones

4. What is the value of the underlined digit? (Lesson 2.4)

   5<u>8</u>7

   - ○ 8
   - ○ 80
   - ○ 88
   - ○ 800

5. What number can be written as 30 + 5? (Lesson 1.2)
   - ○ 93
   - ○ 80
   - ○ 53
   - ○ 35

6. Which is another way to write 56? (Lesson 1.3)
   - ○ 506
   - ○ 50 + 60
   - ○ 50 + 6
   - ○ 500 + 6

Name _____

Algebra: Number Patterns

Lesson 2.8

Compare the digits to find the next two numbers.

1. 232, 242, 252, 262, ☐, ☐

   The next two numbers are _____ and _____.

2. 185, 285, 385, 485, ☐, ☐

   The next two numbers are _____ and _____.

3. 428, 528, 628, 728, ☐, ☐

   The next two numbers are _____ and _____.

4. 654, 664, 674, 684, ☐, ☐

   The next two numbers are _____ and _____.

5. 333, 433, 533, 633, ☐, ☐

   The next two numbers are _____ and _____.

PROBLEM SOLVING

6. What are the missing numbers in the pattern?

   431, 441, 451, 461, ☐, 481, 491, ☐

   The missing numbers are _____ and _____.

Chapter 2   thirty-five **P35**

Lesson Check

1. What is the next number in this pattern?

   453, 463, 473, 483, ▊

   - ○ 484
   - ○ 493
   - ○ 494
   - ○ 583

2. What is the next number in this pattern?

   295, 395, 495, 595, ▊

   - ○ 395
   - ○ 596
   - ○ 605
   - ○ 695

Spiral Review

3. Which is true? (Lesson 1.7)
   - ○ 26 > 16
   - ○ 45 < 24
   - ○ 88 > 98
   - ○ 34 < 14

4. What number can be written as 9 tens 1 one? (Lesson 1.3)
   - ○ 10
   - ○ 19
   - ○ 90
   - ○ 91

5. What is the value of the underlined digit? (Lesson 2.4)

   1̲95

   - ○ 1
   - ○ 10
   - ○ 100
   - ○ 1,000

6. Which is another way to show the number 43? (Lesson 1.4)
   - ○ 3 tens 4 ones
   - ○ 4 tens 3 ones
   - ○ 4 tens 13 ones
   - ○ 40 tens 3 ones

Name _____

PROBLEM SOLVING
Lesson 2.9

Make a Model • Compare Numbers

Draw quick pictures to model the problems. Then solve.

1. Lauryn has 128 marbles. Kristin has 118 marbles. Who has more marbles?

   _____

2. Nick has 189 trading cards. Kyle has 198 trading cards. Who has more cards?

   _____

3. A piano has 36 black keys and 52 white keys. Are there more black keys or white keys on a piano?

   _____

4. There are 253 cookies in a bag. There are 266 cookies in a box. Are there more cookies in the bag or in the box?

   _____

Chapter 2   thirty-seven

Lesson Check

1. Gina has 245 stickers. Which of these numbers is less than 245?
   - ○ 254
   - ○ 245
   - ○ 285
   - ○ 239

2. Carl's book has 176 pages. Which of these numbers is greater than 176?
   - ○ 203
   - ○ 168
   - ○ 139
   - ○ 174

Spiral Review

3. Which is another way to write the number 63? (Lesson 1.3)
   - ○ 60 + 3
   - ○ 6 + 3
   - ○ 30 + 6
   - ○ 30 + 60

4. Which is another way to write the number 58? (Lesson 1.2)
   - ○ 50 tens 8 ones
   - ○ 5 tens 8 ones
   - ○ 80 tens 5 ones
   - ○ 8 tens 5 ones

5. Which is true? (Lesson 1.7)
   - ○ 13 > 18
   - ○ 25 < 23
   - ○ 64 = 46
   - ○ 17 < 21

6. Which is another way to write the number 20? (Lesson 1.3)
   - ○ two
   - ○ twelve
   - ○ twenty
   - ○ two hundred

Name _____

Algebra: Compare Numbers

Lesson **2.10**

Compare. Write >, <, or =.

1. 123 ◯ 132

2. 137 ◯ 137

3. 229 ◯ 230

4. 164 ◯ 246

5. 310 ◯ 302

6. 1,000 ◯ 467

PROBLEM SOLVING

Solve. Draw or write to explain.

7. There are 165 pages in Matt's book.
   There are 186 pages in Kristen's book.
   Whose book has more pages?

   _____ book

Lesson Check

1. Which is true?

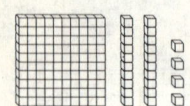 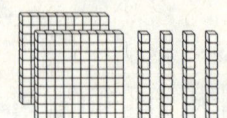

- ○ 124 > 240
- ○ 240 < 124
- ○ 124 = 240
- ○ 240 > 124

2. Which is true?

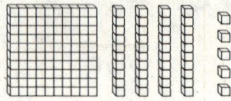 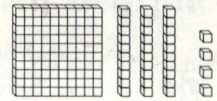

- ○ 145 > 134
- ○ 134 > 145
- ○ 134 = 145
- ○ 145 < 134

Spiral Review

3. What is the value of the underlined digit? (Lesson 1.1)

   8̲2

   - ○ 80
   - ○ 20
   - ○ 8
   - ○ 2

4. Which is another way to write the number 62? (Lesson 1.2)

   - ○ 2 tens 0 ones
   - ○ 20 tens 6 ones
   - ○ 6 tens 2 ones
   - ○ 60 tens 2 ones

5. Which is true? (Lesson 1.7)

   - ○ 73 > 67
   - ○ 53 > 76
   - ○ 29 > 30
   - ○ 37 > 61

6. What number can be written as 9 tens 8 ones? (Lesson 1.3)

   - ○ 10
   - ○ 17
   - ○ 89
   - ○ 98

Name _____

Algebra: Order Numbers

Lesson **2.11**

Compare the numbers. Write them in order from greatest to least. Write > or <.

Write the number for each model first.

1.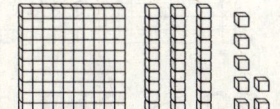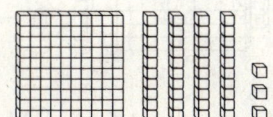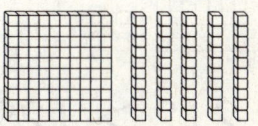

   _____ _____ _____
      greatest   least

2.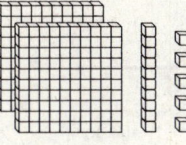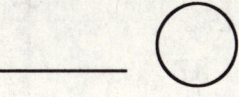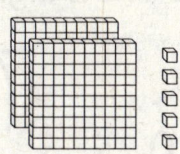

   _____ _____ _____
      greatest   least

PROBLEM SOLVING REAL WORLD

3. Maurice has more than 154 cards. He has fewer than 192 cards. How many cards might he have? Write that number in the box.

   154 > ☐ > 192

Chapter 2   forty-one **P41**

Lesson Check

1. Which is true?

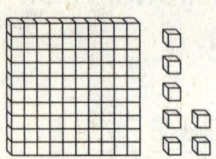 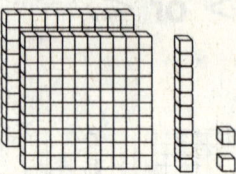 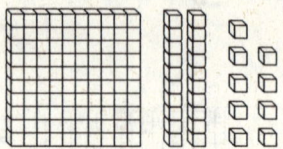

- ○ 212 > 129 > 107
- ○ 129 > 212 > 107
- ○ 107 > 129 > 212
- ○ 212 > 107 > 129

Spiral Review

2. What is the value of the underlined digit? (Lesson 1.1)

    7<u>8</u>

    - ○ 80
    - ○ 70
    - ○ 8
    - ○ 7

3. Which number makes this true? (Lesson 1.7)

    45 > ____

    - ○ 46
    - ○ 54
    - ○ 65
    - ○ 35

4. Which is another way to write 68? (Lesson 1.3)

    - ○ 60 + 8
    - ○ 80 + 6
    - ○ 60 + 80
    - ○ 6 + 8

5. What number can be written as 4 tens 2 ones? (Lesson 1.3)

    - ○ 6
    - ○ 24
    - ○ 42
    - ○ 52

Name _____

Chapter 2 Extra Practice

Lesson 2.2 (pp. 53 – 56) ....

Write how many hundreds, tens, and ones. Draw quick pictures.

1. 214

Hundreds	Tens	Ones

2. 125

Hundreds	Tens	Ones

Lesson 2.3 (pp. 57 – 60) ....

Write how many hundreds, tens, and ones. Write the number.

1.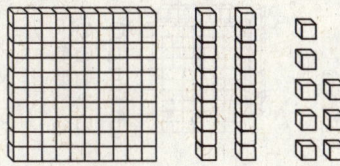

Hundreds	Tens	Ones

_____

Lesson 2.5 (pp. 65 – 68) ....

Read the number and draw quick pictures. Then write the number in different ways.

1. two hundred sixty-nine

____ hundreds ____ tens ____ ones

_____ + _____ + _____

_____

2. three hundred seventeen

____ hundreds ____ ten ____ ones

_____ + _____ + _____

_____

Lesson 2.8 (pp. 77–80)
Compare the digits to find the next two numbers.

1. 577, 587, 597, 607, ▩, ▩

   The next two numbers are _____ and _____.

2. 494, 594, 694, 794, ▩, ▩

   The next two numbers are _____ and _____.

Lesson 2.10 (pp. 85–88)
Compare. Write >, <, or =.

1.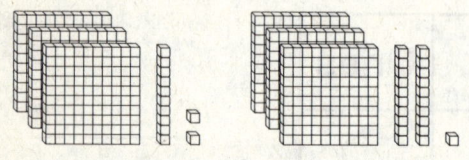

   312 ◯ 321

2.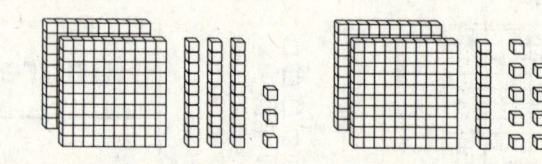

   233 ◯ 219

Lesson 2.11 (pp. 89–92)
Compare the numbers. Write them in order from greatest to least. Write > or <.

Write the number for each model first.

1.

_____ ◯ _____ ◯ _____

greatest   least

P44   forty-four

Chapter 3
School-Home Letter

Dear Family,

My class started Chapter 3 today. In this chapter, we will use different ways to practice our basic addition and subtraction facts.

Love, _____

Vocabulary

sum $4 + 5 = 9$
The sum is **9**.

difference $12 - 4 = 8$
The difference is **8**.

fact family A group of related facts
$3 + 5 = 8$ $8 - 5 = 3$
$5 + 3 = 8$ $8 - 3 = 5$

is not equal to ($\neq$) $5 \neq 4$
5 is not equal to 4.

Home Activity

Write 5 addition problems (with sums through 10) on individual slips of paper. Write their sums on separate slips. Have your child choose a sum and then match it to the correct addition problem. Repeat until all the problems have been matched correctly with sums.

Literature

Reading math stories reinforces ideas. Look for these books at the library.

Cats Add Up
by Marilyn Burns and Dianne Ochiltree.
Cartwheel Books, 1998.

Each Orange Had 8 Slices
by Paul Giganti.
HarperTrophy, 1999.

Capítulo 3

Carta para la casa

Querida familia:

Mi clase comenzó hoy el Capítulo 3. En este capítulo, usaremos diferentes modos de practicar nuestras operaciones básicas de suma y resta.

Con cariño, _____

Vocabulario

suma $4 + 5 = 9$
La suma da **9**.

diferencia $12 - 4 = 8$
La diferencia es **8**.

familia de operaciones Un grupo de operaciones relacionadas
$3 + 5 = 8 \quad 8 - 5 = 3$
$5 + 3 = 8 \quad 8 - 3 = 5$

no es igual a ($\neq$) $5 \neq 4$
5 no es igual a 4.

Actividad para la casa

Escriba 5 problemas de suma (con sumas hasta 10) en diferentes pedazos de papel. Escriba los totales en papeles diferentes. Pida a su hijo que elija un total y lo empareje con el problema de suma que le corresponda. Repita los pasos hasta que todos los problemas concuerden con los totales.

Literatura

Leer cuentos de matemáticas refuerza los conceptos. Busquen estos libros en la biblioteca.

Cats Add Up
por Marilyn Burns y Dianne Ochiltree. Cartwheel Books, 1998.

Each Orange Had 8 Slices
por Paul Giganti. HarperTrophy, 1999.

Name _____

Lesson 3.1

Addition Facts

Write the sums.

1. $9 + 1 = $ ___

   $1 + 9 = $ ___

2. $7 + 6 = $ ___

   $6 + 7 = $ ___

3. $8 + 0 = $ ___

   $5 + 0 = $ ___

4. ___ $= 7 + 9$

   ___ $= 9 + 7$

5. $4 + 4 = $ ___

   $4 + 5 = $ ___

6. $9 + 9 = $ ___

   $9 + 8 = $ ___

7. $8 + 8 = $ ___

   $8 + 7 = $ ___

8. $10 + 10 = $ ___

   $10 + 9 = $ ___

9. ___ $= 6 + 3$

   ___ $= 3 + 6$

10. $6 + 6 = $ ___

    $6 + 7 = $ ___

11. ___ $= 7 + 0$

    ___ $= 9 + 0$

12. $5 + 5 = $ ___

    $5 + 6 = $ ___

13. $8 + 5 = $ ___

    $5 + 8 = $ ___

14. $8 + 2 = $ ___

    $2 + 8 = $ ___

15. $7 + 4 = $ ___

    $4 + 7 = $ ___

PROBLEM SOLVING

Solve. Write or draw to explain.

16. Jason has 7 puzzles. Quincy has the same number of puzzles as Jason. How many puzzles do they have altogether?

    ___ puzzles

Chapter 3   forty-seven **P47**

Lesson Check

1. What is the sum?

    8 + 7 = ___

    ○ 15
    ○ 14
    ○ 12
    ○ 11

2. What is the sum?

    2 + 9 = ___

    ○ 7
    ○ 11
    ○ 12
    ○ 13

Spiral Review

3. Which number can be written as 400 + 3? (Lesson 2.5)

    ○ 304
    ○ 403
    ○ 430
    ○ 434

4. Which number is 100 more than 276? (Lesson 2.7)

    ○ 176
    ○ 286
    ○ 376
    ○ 672

5. Which group of numbers is in order from greatest to least? (Lesson 2.11)

    ○ 402, 302, 502
    ○ 218, 220, 198
    ○ 634, 591, 519
    ○ 386, 591, 535

6. Which is true? (Lesson 2.10)

    ○ 127 > 142
    ○ 142 < 127
    ○ 127 = 142
    ○ 127 < 142

Name _____

Lesson 3.2

Make-a-Ten Facts

Write the sum. Show the make-a-ten fact you used.

1. 9 + 7 = ____
    /\
   1 6

   10 + ____ = ____

2. 8 + 5 = ____

   10 + ____ = ____

3. 8 + 6 = ____

   10 + ____ = ____

4. 3 + 9 = ____

   10 + ____ = ____

5. 8 + 7 = ____

   10 + ____ = ____

6. 6 + 5 = ____

   10 + ____ = ____

7. 7 + 6 = ____

   10 + ____ = ____

8. 5 + 9 = ____

   10 + ____ = ____

PROBLEM SOLVING

Solve. Write or draw to explain.

9. There are 9 children on the bus. Then 8 more children get on the bus. How many children are on the bus now?

   ____ children

Chapter 3

forty-nine P49

Lesson Check

1. Which has the same sum as 8 + 7?
   - ○ 10 + 3
   - ○ 10 + 4
   - ○ 10 + 5
   - ○ 10 + 6

2. Which has the same sum as 7 + 5?
   - ○ 10 + 1
   - ○ 10 + 2
   - ○ 10 + 3
   - ○ 10 + 4

Spiral Review

3. Which number can be written as 200 + 10 + 7? (Lesson 2.5)
   - ○ 207
   - ○ 210
   - ○ 217
   - ○ 271

4. Which of these is an odd number? (Lesson 1.6)
   - ○ 2
   - ○ 4
   - ○ 6
   - ○ 7

5. Which group of numbers is listed in order from least to greatest? (Lesson 2.11)
   - ○ 256, 319, 322
   - ○ 571, 582, 578
   - ○ 439, 501, 384
   - ○ 186, 237, 225

6. Which is another way to write the number 47? (Lesson 1.3)
   - ○ 4 tens 7 ones
   - ○ 7 tens 4 ones
   - ○ 4 + 7
   - ○ 40 + 70

Name _____

Lesson 3.3

Add 3 Addends

Solve two ways. Circle the two addends you add first.

1. $2 + 3 + 7 =$ ___ $2 + 3 + 7 =$ ___

2. $5 + 3 + 3 =$ ___ $5 + 3 + 3 =$ ___

3. $4 + 5 + 4 =$ ___ $4 + 5 + 4 =$ ___

4. $4 + 4 + 4 =$ ___ $4 + 4 + 4 =$ ___

5.
```
  5        5
  4        4
+ 5      + 5
```

6.
```
  6        6
  3        3
+ 4      + 4
```

PROBLEM SOLVING

Solve. Write or draw to explain.

7. Amber has 2 red crayons, 5 blue crayons, and 4 yellow crayons. How many crayons does she have in all?

_____ crayons

Chapter 3

fifty-one P51

Lesson Check

1. Which has the same sum as 2 + 4 + 6?
   - ○ 2 + 9
   - ○ 4 + 7
   - ○ 5 + 6
   - ○ 6 + 6

2. Which has the same sum as 5 + 4 + 2?
   - ○ 6 + 6
   - ○ 5 + 7
   - ○ 5 + 6
   - ○ 6 + 4

Spiral Review

3. Which is true? (Lesson 2.10)
   - ○ 264 < 246
   - ○ 688 > 648
   - ○ 234 = 233
   - ○ 825 < 725

4. Which number has 6 hundreds, 2 tens, and 5 ones? (Lesson 2.5)
   - ○ 256
   - ○ 526
   - ○ 605
   - ○ 625

5. Which of these is an even number? (Lesson 1.6)
   - ○ 1
   - ○ 4
   - ○ 7
   - ○ 9

6. What number should be next in the pattern? (Lesson 2.8)

   42, 52, 62, 72, ____
   - ○ 82
   - ○ 85
   - ○ 92
   - ○ 102

Name _____

Lesson 3.4

Relate Addition and Subtraction

Write the sum and difference for the related facts.

1. $9 + 6 =$ ____
   $15 - 6 =$ ____

2. $8 + 5 =$ ____
   $13 - 5 =$ ____

3. $9 + 9 =$ ____
   $18 - 9 =$ ____

4. $4 + 10 =$ ____
   $14 - 10 =$ ____

5. $7 + 5 =$ ____
   $12 - 5 =$ ____

6. $6 + 8 =$ ____
   $14 - 6 =$ ____

7. $10 + 3 =$ ____
   $13 - 3 =$ ____

8. $8 + 8 =$ ____
   $16 - 8 =$ ____

9. $6 + 4 =$ ____
   $10 - 4 =$ ____

10. $7 + 9 =$ ____
    $16 - 9 =$ ____

11. $9 + 4 =$ ____
    $13 - 9 =$ ____

12. $8 + 7 =$ ____
    $15 - 7 =$ ____

PROBLEM SOLVING  REAL WORLD

Solve. Write or draw to explain.

13. There are 13 children on the bus. Then 5 children get off the bus. How many children are on the bus now?

    ____ children

Chapter 3

fifty-three **P53**

Lesson Check

1. Which fact is related to this subtraction fact?

    $$15 - 6 = 9$$

    ○ $9 + 6 = 15$
    ○ $3 + 3 = 6$
    ○ $6 + 6 = 12$
    ○ $3 + 6 = 9$

2. Which fact is related to this addition fact?

    $$5 + 7 = 12$$

    ○ $5 - 2 = 3$
    ○ $15 - 5 = 10$
    ○ $7 - 5 = 2$
    ○ $12 - 7 = 5$

Spiral Review

3. Which is another way to write 4 hundreds? (Lesson 2.2)

    ○ 4
    ○ 40
    ○ 400
    ○ 440

4. What number should be next in the pattern? (Lesson 2.8)

    65, 75, 85, 95, _____

    ○ 100
    ○ 105
    ○ 115
    ○ 120

5. What number is 10 more than 237? (Lesson 2.7)

    ○ 227
    ○ 247
    ○ 337
    ○ 347

6. Which is another way to write the number 110? (Lesson 2.5)

    ○ 100 + 100
    ○ 1 hundred 1 ten 1 one
    ○ 11 hundreds
    ○ 100 + 10

Name _____

Lesson 3.5

Fact Families

Complete the fact family.

1. (7, 4, 3)   4 + 3 = ___   7 − ___ = 4
   ___ + ___ = ___   ___ − ___ = ___

2. (5, 0, 5)   0 + 5 = ___   5 − 5 = ___
   ___ + ___ = ___   ___ − ___ = ___

3. (10, 6, 4)   6 + 4 = ___   10 − ___ = 6
   ___ + ___ = ___   ___ − ___ = ___

4. (15, 7, 8)   7 + 8 = ___   15 − ___ = 7
   ___ + ___ = ___   ___ − ___ = ___

5. (12, 3, 9)   3 + 9 = ___   12 − 9 = ___
   ___ + ___ = ___   ___ − ___ = ___

PROBLEM SOLVING  REAL WORLD

6. Circle 3 numbers that can be used to make a fact family. Write the facts for that fact family.

   4   7

   11   13

   ___ + ___ = ___   ___ − ___ = ___
   ___ + ___ = ___   ___ − ___ = ___

Chapter 3   fifty-five P55

Lesson Check

1. Which fact completes the fact family?

5 + 2 = 7	7 − 2 = 5
2 + 5 = 7	

   - ○ 5 − 2 = 3
   - ○ 7 − 4 = 3
   - ○ 7 − 1 = 6
   - ○ 7 − 5 = 2

2. Which fact completes the fact family?

6 + 5 = 11	11 − 5 = 6
	11 − 6 = 5

   - ○ 5 + 6 = 11
   - ○ 11 − 7 = 4
   - ○ 11 + 5 = 16
   - ○ 7 + 4 = 11

Spiral Review

3. Which group of numbers is listed in order from least to greatest? (Lesson 2.11)
   - ○ 211, 221, 201
   - ○ 201, 221, 211
   - ○ 201, 211, 221
   - ○ 211, 201, 221

4. What is the value of the underlined digit? (Lesson 2.4)

   $\underline{4}91$

   - ○ 4
   - ○ 40
   - ○ 400
   - ○ 900

5. Which is another way to write 20 + 6? (Lesson 1.2)
   - ○ 14
   - ○ 26
   - ○ 206
   - ○ 602

6. Which is another way to write 76? (Lesson 1.3)
   - ○ six
   - ○ sixty-seven
   - ○ seven
   - ○ seventy-six

Name _____

Subtraction Facts

Lesson 3.6

Write the difference.

1. $15 - 9 = $ ___
2. $13 - 8 = $ ___
3. ___ $= 13 - 5$
4. $14 - 7 = $ ___
5. $10 - 8 = $ ___
6. $12 - 7 = $ ___
7. ___ $= 10 - 7$
8. $16 - 7 = $ ___
9. $13 - 3 = $ ___
10. $11 - 5 = $ ___
11. $13 - 6 = $ ___
12. ___ $= 12 - 9$
13. $16 - 9 = $ ___
14. ___ $= 11 - 9$
15. $12 - 8 = $ ___
16. $14 - 8 = $ ___
17. $17 - 10 = $ ___
18. $12 - 5 = $ ___
19. $15 - 7 = $ ___
20. $14 - 9 = $ ___
21. $17 - 9 = $ ___

PROBLEM SOLVING  REAL WORLD

Solve. Write or draw to explain.

22. Mr. Li has 16 pencils. He gives 9 pencils to some students. How many pencils does Mr. Li have now?

___ pencils

Chapter 3　　　　　　　　　　　　　　　　　　　fifty-seven P57

Lesson Check

1. What is the difference?

    13 − 6 = ___

    ○ 6
    ○ 7
    ○ 8
    ○ 9

2. What is the difference?

    12 − 3 = ___

    ○ 5
    ○ 6
    ○ 7
    ○ 9

Spiral Review

3. What is the value of the underlined digit? (Lesson 2.4)

    6<u>2</u>5

    ○ 2
    ○ 10
    ○ 20
    ○ 200

4. Which is true? (Lesson 1.7)

    ○ 72 > 80
    ○ 72 < 72
    ○ 72 = 72
    ○ 72 < 67

5. Which is another way to write 2 hundreds, 5 tens, 3 ones?

    (Lesson 2.6)

    ○ 235
    ○ 253
    ○ 352
    ○ 532

6. Which of these is an odd number? (Lesson 1.6)

    ○ 23
    ○ 32
    ○ 46
    ○ 64

Name _____

Lesson 3.7

Represent Addition and Subtraction

Complete the bar model to solve.

1. Sara has 4 yellow beads and 3 green beads. How many beads does Sara have?

   | 4 yellow beads | 3 green beads |

   _____ beads in all

   _____ beads

2. Adam had 12 trucks. He gave 4 trucks to Ed. How many trucks does Adam have now?

   | _____ trucks left | 4 trucks to Ed |

   12 trucks in all

   _____ trucks

3. Grandma has 14 red roses and 7 pink roses. How many more red roses than pink roses does she have?

   | 14 red roses |
   | 7 pink roses | _____ |

   _____ more red roses

Chapter 3   fifty-nine **P59**

Lesson Check

1. Abby has 16 grapes. Jason has 9 grapes. How many more grapes does Abby have than Jason?

   - ○ 7
   - ○ 8
   - ○ 15
   - ○ 25

16 grapes
9 grapes

Spiral Review

2. Which is true? (Lesson 1.7)

   - ○ 78 > 89
   - ○ 99 = 9
   - ○ 16 < 11
   - ○ 44 > 39

3. What is the difference? (Lesson 3.6)

   18 − 9 = ___

   - ○ 6
   - ○ 9
   - ○ 10
   - ○ 27

4. Which is another way to write 300 + 20 + 5? (Lesson 2.5)

   - ○ 55
   - ○ 235
   - ○ 325
   - ○ 523

5. Which is true? (Lesson 2.10)

   - ○ 156 > 146
   - ○ 156 < 146
   - ○ 156 = 146
   - ○ 146 > 156

PROBLEM SOLVING
Lesson 3.8

Write a Number Sentence • Basic Facts

Write a number sentence to show the problem.

1. Calvin has 9 dimes. Jordan gives him 3 more dimes. How many dimes does Calvin have now?

   ___ ◯ ___ ◯ ___

   _____ dimes

2. Erika picks 12 flowers. Five of the flowers are red. The rest of the flowers are yellow. How many flowers are yellow?

   ___ ◯ ___ ◯ ___

   _____ yellow flowers

3. There are 6 children on the swings and 4 children at the slide. How many children are there in all?

   ___ ◯ ___ ◯ ___

   _____ children

4. Mr. Hayes has 13 apples and 7 pears. How many more apples than pears does he have?

   ___ ◯ ___ ◯ ___

   _____ more apples

Chapter 3   sixty-one P61

Lesson Check

1. Kyle read 5 pages in the morning. He read 8 pages in the afternoon. How many pages did Kyle read in all?

   Which number sentence can be used to solve the problem?

   - ○ 5 − 3 = 2
   - ○ 8 − 5 = 3
   - ○ 5 + 8 = 13
   - ○ 3 + 10 = 13

2. Kiley has 3 dolls. Jasmine has 4 dolls. How many dolls in all do they have?

   Which number sentence can be used to solve the problem?

   - ○ 3 + 4 = 7
   - ○ 3 + 6 = 9
   - ○ 4 − 3 = 1
   - ○ 3 − 2 = 1

Spiral Review

3. Which is another way to write 74? (Lesson 1.3)

   - ○ 70 + 40
   - ○ 40 + 7
   - ○ 7 + 4
   - ○ 70 + 4

4. Which shows skip counting by tens? (Lesson 2.7)

   - ○ 10, 11, 12, 13, 14
   - ○ 10, 20, 30, 40, 50
   - ○ 10, 12, 14, 16, 18
   - ○ 10, 15, 20, 25, 30

5. Which of these is an odd number? (Lesson 1.6)

   - ○ 2
   - ○ 9
   - ○ 12
   - ○ 24

6. Which group of numbers is listed in order from least to greatest? (Lesson 2.11)

   - ○ 302, 452, 481
   - ○ 220, 235, 215
   - ○ 635, 591, 748
   - ○ 591, 686, 535

Name _____

Lesson 3.9

Algebra: Balance Number Sentences

Write the number that will complete the number sentence.

1. $3 + 6 = 4 + \boxed{}$

2. $8 + 5 = \boxed{} + 6$

3. $7 + 1 = 5 + \boxed{}$

4. $\boxed{} + 5 = 6 + 4$

5. $8 + 2 = \boxed{} + 5$

6. $9 + \boxed{} = 6 + 6$

7. $\boxed{} + 1 = 6 + 3$

8. $3 + 8 = \boxed{} + 9$

9. $3 + \boxed{} = 7 + 5$

10. $\boxed{} + 7 = 8 + 6$

11. $9 + 6 = \boxed{} + 8$

12. $5 + \boxed{} = 8 + 4$

13. $9 + \boxed{} = 3 + 7$

14. $9 + 7 = 8 + \boxed{}$

PROBLEM SOLVING  REAL WORLD

Write two numbers that will complete the number sentence.

15. $5 + \boxed{} = \boxed{} + 2$

16. $\boxed{} + 7 = 5 + \boxed{}$

Chapter 3

sixty-three

Lesson Check

1. What number completes the number sentence?

    $8 + 5 = \square + 6$

    - ○ 6
    - ○ 7
    - ○ 13
    - ○ 19

2. What number completes the number sentence?

    $4 + 7 = \square + 6$

    - ○ 5
    - ○ 6
    - ○ 11
    - ○ 17

Spiral Review

3. Which is another way to write seventeen? (Lesson 1.3)
    - ○ 1
    - ○ 7
    - ○ 17
    - ○ 71

4. Which group of numbers is listed in order from least to greatest? (Lesson 2.11)
    - ○ 278, 326, 319
    - ○ 457, 382, 460
    - ○ 183, 192, 191
    - ○ 353, 361, 415

5. Which is true? (Lesson 2.10)
    - ○ 105 < 95
    - ○ 568 > 564
    - ○ 123 = 132
    - ○ 785 > 875

6. Which number should be next in the pattern? (Lesson 2.8)

    85, 95, 105, 115, ___

    - ○ 116
    - ○ 118
    - ○ 120
    - ○ 125

Name _____

Lesson 3.10

Equal and Not Equal

Write = or ≠ to make the number sentence true.

1. 4 + 2 ◯ 5 + 1
2. 7 + 5 ◯ 6 + 6
3. 15 − 6 ◯ 16 − 7
4. 8 + 4 ◯ 9 + 2
5. 8 − 1 ◯ 11 − 3
6. 12 − 5 ◯ 10 − 3
7. 9 + 0 ◯ 0 + 9
8. 7 + 2 ◯ 6 + 5
9. 10 − 4 ◯ 9 − 5
10. 14 − 7 ◯ 6 + 1
11. 9 + 6 ◯ 8 + 6
12. 7 − 3 ◯ 2 + 2

PROBLEM SOLVING

13. Circle all the cards that make the number sentence true.

 = 14

| 5 + 4 + 5 | 7 + 7 |
| 9 + 5 | 7 + 9 |

Chapter 3

sixty-five **P65**

Lesson Check

1. Which makes the number sentence true?

    17 − 8 = ___

    ○ 10 − 1
    ○ 4 + 4
    ○ 8 − 1
    ○ 2 + 5

2. Which makes the number sentence true?

    5 + 5 = ___

    ○ 6 + 3
    ○ 10 − 5
    ○ 4 + 7
    ○ 15 − 5

Spiral Review

3. Which is another way to write 80 + 9? (Lesson 1.2)

    ○ 8
    ○ 9
    ○ 89
    ○ 98

4. Which is another way to write 56? (Lesson 1.3)

    ○ 50 tens 6 ones
    ○ 60 tens 5 ones
    ○ 6 tens 5 ones
    ○ 5 tens 6 ones

5. What is the value of the underlined digit? (Lesson 2.4)

    <u>7</u>58

    ○ 7
    ○ 70
    ○ 700
    ○ 750

6. Which is another way to write 30 + 7? (Lesson 1.2)

    ○ 10
    ○ 37
    ○ 73
    ○ 307

Name _____

Chapter 3 Extra Practice

Lessons 3.1 – 3.3 (pp. 109 – 120)
Write the sum.

1. 6 + 6 = ___
   6 + 7 = ___

2. ___ = 7 + 4
   ___ = 4 + 7

3. 2 + 0 = ___
   8 + 0 = ___

4. 6 + 9 = ___
   10 + ___ = ___

5. 7 + 5 = ___
   10 + ___ = ___

6. 4 + 6 + 4 = ___

7. 4 + 5 + 3 = ___

8. 2 + 7 + 3 = ___

9. 2 + 2 + 8 = ___

Lesson 3.5 (pp. 125 – 128)
Complete the fact family.

1.    7 + 8 = ___   15 − ___ = 7

   ___ + ___ = ___   ___ − ___ = ___

2. (13, 4, 9)   4 + 9 = ___   13 − ___ = 4

   ___ + ___ = ___   ___ − ___ = ___

sixty-seven P67

Lesson 3.6 (pp. 129–131)
Write the difference.

1. $9 - 3 =$ ___
2. ___ $= 12 - 5$
3. $16 - 8 =$ ___
4. ___ $= 14 - 6$
5. $11 - 8 =$ ___
6. $12 - 6 =$ ___

Lesson 3.8 (pp. 137–140)
Write a number sentence to show the problem.

1. There were 14 birds in the tree. Some birds flew away. Then there were 5 birds in the tree. How many birds flew away?

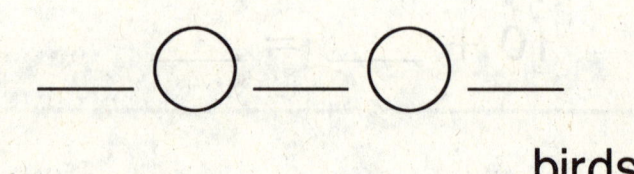

___ birds

Lesson 3.9 (pp. 141–144)
Write the number that will complete the number sentence.

1. $8 + 5 = 9 + \square$
2. $4 + 7 = \square + 5$
3. $5 + \square = 7 + 7$
4. $\square + 4 = 7 + 2$

Lesson 3.10 (pp. 145–148)
Write = or ≠ to make each number sentence true.

1. $7 + 9 \bigcirc 8 + 8$
2. $14 - 6 \bigcirc 12 - 7$
3. $6 + 5 \bigcirc 4 + 9$
4. $10 - 5 \bigcirc 13 - 8$

P68 sixty-eight

Chapter 4

School-Home Letter

Dear Family,

My class started Chapter 4 this week. In this chapter, I will learn how to solve addition problems with 2-digit addends using different strategies. I will also learn how to estimate sums.

Love, _____

Vocabulary

estimate To tell about how many

regroup To make a group of 10 ones and trade it for a ten

Home Activity

Pretend you are going on a treasure hunt. Using small pieces of paper, make a path in a small area. Each piece of paper should have an addition problem on it for your child to solve. At the end of the path, place a treasure of some kind.

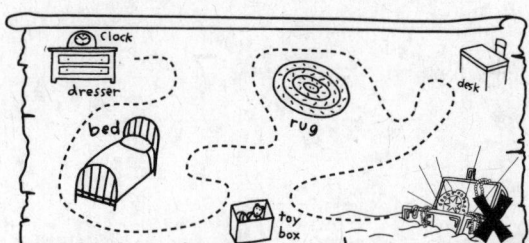

Literature

Reading math stories reinforces ideas. Look for these books at the library.

A Collection for Kate by Barbara Derubertis. Kane Press, 1999.

Mission: Addition by Loreen Leedy. Holiday House, 1997.

Capítulo 4

Carta para la casa

Querida familia:

Esta semana, mi clase comenzó el Capítulo 4. En este capítulo, aprenderé a resolver problemas de suma con sumandos de dos dígitos usando diferentes estrategias. También aprenderé a estimar sumas.

Con cariño, _____

Vocabulario

estimar decir qué cantidad hay aproximadamente

reagrupar formar un grupo de 10 unidades y convertirlo en una decena

Actividad para la casa

Jueguen a buscar un tesoro. Con pequeños trozos de papel, haga un camino en un espacio pequeño. Cada trozo de papel deberá tener un problema de suma para que su hijo lo resuelva. Al final del camino, coloque algún tipo de "tesoro".

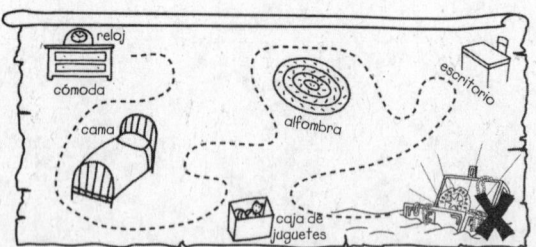

Literatura

Leer cuentos de matemáticas refuerza los conceptos. Busquen estos libros en la biblioteca.

Una colección para Kate por Barbara Derubertis. Kane Press, 1999.

Mission: Addition por Loreen Leedy. Holiday House, 1997.

Name _____

Lesson 4.1

Break Apart Ones to Add

**Break apart ones to make a ten.
Then add and write the sum.**

1. 62 + 9 = ____
2. 27 + 7 = ____
3. 28 + 5 = ____
4. 17 + 8 = ____
5. 57 + 6 = ____
6. 23 + 9 = ____
7. 39 + 7 = ____
8. 26 + 5 = ____
9. 13 + 8 = ____
10. 18 + 7 = ____
11. 49 + 8 = ____
12. 27 + 5 = ____
13. 39 + 4 = ____
14. 18 + 8 = ____

PROBLEM SOLVING  REAL WORLD

Solve. Write or draw to explain.

15. Jimmy had 18 toy airplanes. His mother bought him 7 more toy airplanes. How many toy airplanes does he have now?

____ toy airplanes

Chapter 4   seventy-one **P71**

Lesson Check

1. What is the sum?

    26 + 7 = ___

    - 96
    - 78
    - 33
    - 19

2. What is the sum?

    15 + 8 = ___

    - 7
    - 10
    - 13
    - 23

Spiral Review

3. Which group of numbers are in order from least to greatest? (Lesson 2.11)

    - 156, 158, 153
    - 214, 218, 216
    - 342, 345, 347
    - 415, 423, 208

4. Which of the following is another way to write 72? (Lesson 1.3)

    - 2 tens 7 ones
    - 7 tens 2 ones
    - 20 + 7
    - 70 + 20

5. What is the sum? (Lesson 3.3)

    4 + 5 + 4 =

    - 13
    - 12
    - 11
    - 10

6. Which of the following is another way to write 281? (Lesson 2.5)

    - 1 hundred 2 tens 8 ones
    - 1 hundred 8 tens 2 ones
    - 2 hundreds 1 ten 8 ones
    - 2 hundreds 8 tens 1 one

Name _____

Lesson **4.2**

Use Compensation

Show how to make one addend the next ten.
Complete the new addition sentence.

1. 15 + 37 = ? 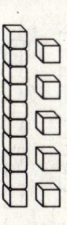 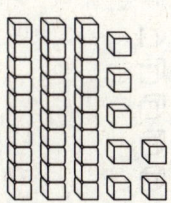   ___ + ___ = ___

2. 22 + 49 = ? 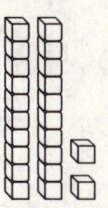 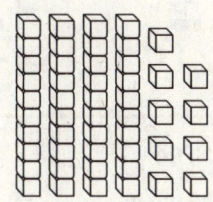   ___ + ___ = ___

3. 38 + 26 = ? 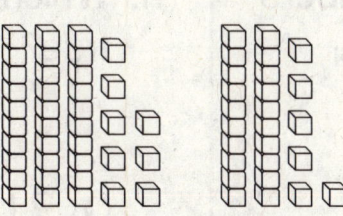   ___ + ___ = ___

4. 27 + 47 = ? 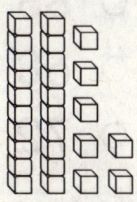 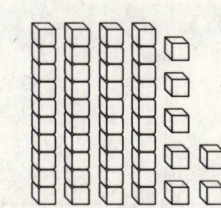   ___ + ___ = ___

PROBLEM SOLVING REAL WORLD

Solve. Write or draw to explain.

5. The oak tree at the school was 34 feet tall.
   Then it grew 18 feet taller.
   How tall is the oak tree now?

   _____ feet tall

Lesson Check

1. What is the sum?

    18 + 25 = ?

    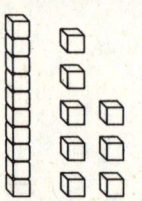 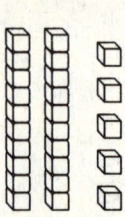

    ○ 43 ○ 31
    ○ 33 ○ 17

2. What is the sum?

    27 + 24 = ?

    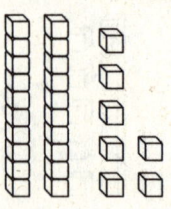 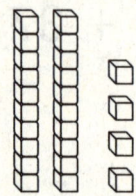

    ○ 41 ○ 51
    ○ 43 ○ 59

Spiral Review

3. Which of the following numbers is an even number? (Lesson 1.6)

    ○ 27
    ○ 14
    ○ 11
    ○ 5

4. Which number makes this true? (Lesson 1.7)

    72 > ___

    ○ 91
    ○ 83
    ○ 68
    ○ 72

5. Which is a related subtraction fact for 7 + 6 = 13? (Lesson 3.4)

    ○ 13 − 6 = 7
    ○ 7 − 1 = 6
    ○ 7 − 6 = 1
    ○ 13 + 6 = 19

6. What is the sum? (Lesson 3.1)

    2 + 8 = ___

    ○ 0
    ○ 6
    ○ 8
    ○ 10

Name _____

Lesson 4.3

Break Apart Addends as Tens and Ones

Break apart the addends. Solve for the total sum.

1. 18 → ___ + ___
   +21 → ___ + ___

   ___ + ___ = ___

2. 33 → ___ + ___
   +49 → ___ + ___

   ___ + ___ = ___

3. 72 → ___ + ___
   +18 → ___ + ___

   ___ + ___ = ___

PROBLEM SOLVING

Solve. Write or draw to explain.

4. Christopher has 28 baseball cards. Justin has 18 baseball cards. How many baseball cards do they have altogether?

_____ baseball cards

Chapter 4 seventy-five **P75**

Lesson Check

1. What is the sum?

    27
    + 12

    - ○ 15
    - ○ 19
    - ○ 29
    - ○ 39

2. What is the sum?

    17
    + 35

    - ○ 40
    - ○ 42
    - ○ 52
    - ○ 59

Spiral Review

3. What is the value of the underlined digit? (Lesson 1.1)

    2<u>5</u>

    - ○ 5
    - ○ 7
    - ○ 50
    - ○ 55

4. What number has 12 tens? (Lesson 2.1)

    - ○ 10
    - ○ 12
    - ○ 100
    - ○ 120

5. Which group of numbers are in order from greatest to least? (Lesson 2.11)

    - ○ 408, 402, 411
    - ○ 420, 418, 435
    - ○ 594, 591, 587
    - ○ 586, 575, 591

6. What number will make this true? (Lesson 3.10)

    $12 - 4 = 5 + \blacksquare$

    - ○ 2
    - ○ 3
    - ○ 7
    - ○ 8

Name _____

Lesson 4.4

Model Regrouping for Addition

Write how many tens and ones in the sum.
Write the sum.

1. Add 63 and 9.

   ____ tens ____ ones
   ____

2. Add 25 and 58.

   ____ tens ____ ones
   ____

3. Add 58 and 18.

   ____ tens ____ ones
   ____

4. Add 64 and 26.

   ____ tens ____ ones
   ____

5. Add 17 and 77.

   ____ tens ____ ones
   ____

6. Add 16 and 39.

   ____ tens ____ ones
   ____

PROBLEM SOLVING REAL WORLD

Solve. Write or draw to explain.

7. Cathy has 43 leaves in her collection. Jane has 38 leaves. How many leaves do they have altogether?

   ____ leaves

Chapter 4   seventy-seven **P77**

Lesson Check

1. Add 27 and 48. What is the sum?

Tens	Ones
(illustration)	(illustration)

   - ○ 27
   - ○ 48
   - ○ 65
   - ○ 75

Spiral Review

2. What is the sum? (Lesson 3.1)

   $7 + 7 =$ _____

   - ○ 14
   - ○ 13
   - ○ 12
   - ○ 11

3. Which of these is an odd number? (Lesson 1.6)

   - ○ 6
   - ○ 12
   - ○ 21
   - ○ 22

4. Which of the following numbers will complete this number sentence? (Lesson 3.9)

   $6 + 8 = 7 +$ _____

   - ○ 21
   - ○ 14
   - ○ 9
   - ○ 7

5. What is the sum?

   (Lesson 3.3)

   $5 + 3 + 4 =$ _____

   - ○ 9
   - ○ 12
   - ○ 14
   - ○ 16

Lesson 4.5

Name _____

Model and Record 2-Digit Addition

Draw quick pictures help you to solve.
Write the sum.

1. | Tens | Ones |
    |------|------|
    | ☐ | |
    | 3 | 8 |
    | +1 | 7 |

Tens	Ones

2. | Tens | Ones |
    |------|------|
    | ☐ | |
    | 5 | 8 |
    | +2 | 6 |

Tens	Ones

3. | Tens | Ones |
    |------|------|
    | ☐ | |
    | 4 | 2 |
    | +3 | 7 |

Tens	Ones

4. | Tens | Ones |
    |------|------|
    | ☐ | |
    | 5 | 3 |
    | +3 | 8 |

Tens	Ones

PROBLEM SOLVING  REAL WORLD

Solve. Write or draw to explain.

5. There were 37 children at the park on Saturday and 25 children at the park on Sunday. How many children were at the park on those two days?

    _____ children

Lesson Check

1. What is the sum?

Tens	Ones
☐	
3	4
+ 2	8

   - ○ 44
   - ○ 52
   - ○ 54
   - ○ 62

2. What is the sum?

Tens	Ones
☐	
4	3
+ 2	7

   - ○ 64
   - ○ 65
   - ○ 70
   - ○ 74

Spiral Review

3. Which is a different way to show the number 47? (Lesson 1.3)
   - ○ 7 tens 4 ones
   - ○ 4 tens 7 ones
   - ○ 4 tens 4 ones
   - ○ 1 ten 7 ones

4. Which is true? (Lesson 1.7)
   - ○ 38 < 42
   - ○ 27 > 29
   - ○ 45 < 36
   - ○ 59 = 48

5. Mia and Jeff have 18 marbles. Mia has 9 marbles. How many marbles does Jeff have? (Lesson 3.8)
   - ○ 11
   - ○ 10
   - ○ 9
   - ○ 8

6. What is the difference? (Lesson 3.6)

   13 − 5 = _____
   - ○ 7
   - ○ 8
   - ○ 9
   - ○ 18

Name _____

Lesson 4.6

2-Digit Addition

Regroup if you need to. Write the sum.

1.
```
  4 | 7
+ 2 | 5
```

2.
```
  3 | 3
+ 1 | 8
```

3.
```
  2 | 8
+ 6 | 4
```

4.
```
  1 | 3
+ 6 | 5
```

5.
```
  1 | 7
+ 2 | 6
```

6.
```
  3 | 6
+ 5 | 3
```

7.
```
  5 | 8
+ 2 | 5
```

8.
```
  3 | 7
+ 4 | 9
```

9.
```
  5 | 2
+ 2 | 9
```

10.
```
  6 | 6
+ 2 | 4
```

11.
```
  7 | 4
+ 1 | 4
```

12.
```
  3 | 7
+ 3 | 7
```

PROBLEM SOLVING

Solve. Write or draw to explain.

13. Angela drew 16 flowers on her paper in the morning. She drew 25 more flowers in the afternoon. How many flowers did she draw in all?

_____ flowers

Lesson Check

1. What is the sum?

    ```
      2 | 1
    + 3 | 7
    ```

    - ○ 16
    - ○ 18
    - ○ 56
    - ○ 58

2. What is the sum?

    ```
      3 | 8
    + 5 | 2
    ```

    - ○ 90
    - ○ 86
    - ○ 80
    - ○ 76

Spiral Review

3. What is the next number in the pattern? (Lesson 2.8)

    103, 203, 303, 403, ____

    - ○ 433
    - ○ 500
    - ○ 503
    - ○ 613

4. What number completes this number sentence? (Lesson 3.9)

    6 + 5 = ____ + 3

    - ○ 14
    - ○ 11
    - ○ 8
    - ○ 7

5. Which number is 100 more than 265? (Lesson 2.7)

    - ○ 165
    - ○ 275
    - ○ 305
    - ○ 365

6. Which of the following is another way to write 42? (Lesson 1.3)

    - ○ 402
    - ○ 40 + 2
    - ○ 400 + 2
    - ○ 40 tens 2 ones

Name _____

Practice 2-Digit Addition

Lesson 4.7

Write the sum.

1.
```
   58
+ 17
----
```

2.
```
   44
+ 86
----
```

3.
```
   36
+ 13
----
```

4.
```
   49
+ 72
----
```

5.
```
   58
+ 87
----
```

6.
```
   32
+ 59
----
```

7.
```
   77
+ 58
----
```

8.
```
   45
+ 45
----
```

9.
```
   54
+ 28
----
```

PROBLEM SOLVING — REAL WORLD

Solve. Write or draw to explain.

10. There are 45 books on the shelf. There are 37 books on the table. How many books in all are on the shelf and the table?

_____ books

Chapter 4   eighty-three P83

Lesson Check

1. What is the sum?

    $$\begin{array}{r}56\\+\ 35\\\hline\end{array}$$

    ○ 91
    ○ 81
    ○ 51
    ○ 21

2. What is the sum?

    $$\begin{array}{r}74\\+\ 15\\\hline\end{array}$$

    ○ 61
    ○ 69
    ○ 89
    ○ 91

Spiral Review

3. What is the value of the underlined digit? (Lesson 2.4)

    5̲26

    ○ 600
    ○ 500
    ○ 50
    ○ 5

4. Julia picked 8 flowers. Then she picked 4 more flowers. How many flowers does she have now? (Lesson 3.8)

    ○ 4
    ○ 12
    ○ 13
    ○ 16

5. What is the difference? (Lesson 3.6)

    11 − 6 = ____

    ○ 17
    ○ 15
    ○ 7
    ○ 5

6. What is another way to write the number 83? (Lesson 1.2)

    ○ 80 + 3
    ○ 80 + 30
    ○ 30 + 8
    ○ 8 + 3

Lesson 4.8

Name _____

Rewrite 2-Digit Addition

Rewrite the numbers. Then add.

1. 27 + 19
2. 36 + 23
3. 31 + 29
4. 48 + 23

   +_____   +_____   +_____   +_____

5. 53 + 12
6. 69 + 13
7. 24 + 38
8. 46 + 37

   +_____   +_____   +_____   +_____

PROBLEM SOLVING

Use the table to solve the problem.

9. How many pages in all did Sasha and Kara read?

   _____ pages

Pages Read This Week	
Child	Number of Pages
Sasha	62
Kara	29
Juan	50

Chapter 4   eighty-five **P85**

Lesson Check

1. What is the sum of 39 + 17?

　　　+ _____

   ○ 66
   ○ 56
   ○ 50
   ○ 22

2. What is the sum of 28 + 16?

　　　+ _____

   ○ 44
   ○ 42
   ○ 34
   ○ 18

Spiral Review

3. Which of the following is another way to write 60 + 4? (Lesson 1.3)

   ○ 46
   ○ 64
   ○ 100
   ○ 604

4. What number will make this true? (Lesson 3.10)

   $11 - 6 = 2 + \square$

   ○ 7
   ○ 6
   ○ 5
   ○ 3

5. Which is true? (Lesson 1.7)

   ○ 34 < 29
   ○ 51 > 48
   ○ 60 < 59
   ○ 45 > 67

6. What number can be written as 3 hundreds 7 tens 5 ones? (Lesson 2.3)

   ○ 753
   ○ 573
   ○ 375
   ○ 357

Name _____

Draw a Diagram • Addition

**PROBLEM SOLVING
Lesson 4.9**

Complete the bar model to solve.

1. Jacob counts 37 ants on the sidewalk and 11 ants on the grass. How many ants does Jacob count altogether?

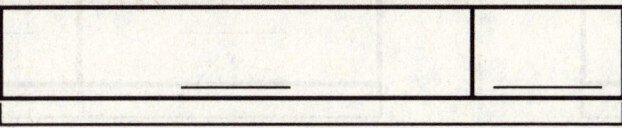

_____ ants

2. There are 14 bees in the hive and 17 bees in the garden. How many bees are there in all?

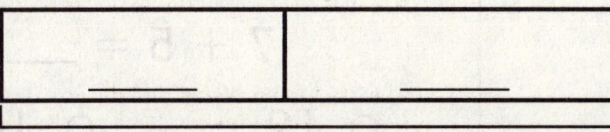

_____ bees

3. There are 28 flowers in Sasha's garden. 16 flowers are yellow and the rest are white. How many white flowers are in Sasha's garden?

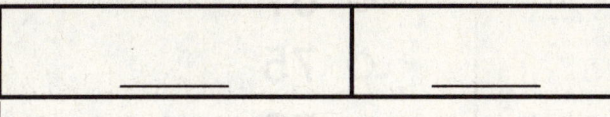

_____ white flowers

Chapter 4 eighty-seven **P87**

Lesson Check

1. Sean and Abby have 23 markers altogether. Abby has 14 markers. How many markers does Sean have?

   ○ 9   ○ 7
   ○ 8   ○ 6

2. Mrs. James has 22 students in her class. Mr. Williams has 24 students in his class. How many students are in the two classes?

   ○ 42   ○ 51
   ○ 46   ○ 56

Spiral Review

3. What is the difference? (Lesson 3.6)

   15 − 9 = ___

   ○ 24   ○ 7
   ○ 14   ○ 6

4. What is the sum? (Lesson 3.2)

   7 + 5 = ___

   ○ 12   ○ 10
   ○ 11   ○ 9

5. Which number makes this true? (Lesson 2.10)

   ___ < 283

   ○ 327
   ○ 290
   ○ 238
   ○ 283

6. What is the next number in the pattern? (Lesson 2.8)

   29, 39, 49, 59, ___

   ○ 49
   ○ 69
   ○ 75
   ○ 79

Name _____

Estimate Sums

Lesson 4.10

**Estimate the sum.
Circle the better choice.**

1. 37 + 48 = ■

   greater than 100

   less than 100

2. 23 + 35 = ■

   greater than 50

   less than 50

3. 21 + 18 = ■

   greater than 20

   less than 20

4. 19 + 27 = ■

   greater than 20

   less than 20

5. 86 + 43 = ■

   greater than 100

   less than 100

6. 13 + 21 = ■

   greater than 50

   less than 50

7. 45 + 35 = ■

   greater than 50

   less than 50

8. 80 + 10 = ■

   greater than 100

   less than 100

9. 4 + 6 = ■

   greater than 20

   less than 20

PROBLEM SOLVING

10. In the store, there are 40 goldfish, 31 clownfish, and 38 angelfish. Estimate the total number of clownfish and angelfish. Circle the better choice.

    greater than 50

    less than 50

Chapter 4

eighty-nine P89

Lesson Check

1. Which is the best estimate for the sum?

    18 + 23 = ■

    ○ less than 20
    ○ less than 50
    ○ greater than 50
    ○ greater than 100

2. Which is the best estimate for the sum?

    18 + 53 = ■

    ○ less than 20
    ○ less than 50
    ○ greater than 50
    ○ greater than 100

Spiral Review

3. What number will complete the number sentence? (Lesson 3.9)

    8 + 3 = 5 + ☐

    ○ 16
    ○ 11
    ○ 7
    ○ 6

4. Which is another way to write 84? (Lesson 1.3)

    ○ 4 tens 8 ones
    ○ 6 tens 4 ones
    ○ 8 tens 4 ones
    ○ 8 tens 8 ones

5. What is the value of the underlined digit? (Lesson 2.4)

    7<u>8</u>3

    ○ 800
    ○ 80
    ○ 78
    ○ 8

6. What is the sum? (Lesson 3.3)

    3 + 4 + 6 = ■

    ○ 13
    ○ 10
    ○ 9
    ○ 7

Name _____

Lesson 4.11

Find Sums for 3 Addends

Add.

1.
```
  2 3
  2 0
+ 2 5
```

2.
```
  1 5
  2 2
+ 3 8
```

3.
```
  1 3
  5 2
+ 3 4
```

4.
```
  2 7
  4 0
+ 1 9
```

5.
```
  3 1
  4 5
+ 2 4
```

6.
```
  3 4
  1 1
+ 2 8
```

7.
```
  4 2
  3 6
+ 1 1
```

8.
```
  1 8
  2 2
+ 3 4
```

9.
```
  5 3
  1 9
+ 2 5
```

PROBLEM SOLVING  REAL WORLD

Solve.

10. Liam has 24 yellow pencils, 15 red pencils, and 9 blue pencils. How many pencils does he have altogether?

_____ pencils

Chapter 4   ninety-one **P91**

Lesson Check

TEST PREP

1. What is the sum?

    $$\begin{array}{r} 22 \\ 31 \\ +16 \\ \hline \end{array}$$

    ○ 69
    ○ 79
    ○ 83
    ○ 96

2. What is the sum?

    $$\begin{array}{r} 17 \\ 26 \\ +30 \\ \hline \end{array}$$

    ○ 47
    ○ 56
    ○ 63
    ○ 73

Spiral Review

3. What number is 10 more than 127? (Lesson 2.7)

    ○ 117
    ○ 137
    ○ 227
    ○ 277

4. Which of the following is true? (Lesson 1.7)

    ○ 36 < 24
    ○ 33 > 44
    ○ 48 < 50
    ○ 29 > 31

5. Bob tosses 8 horseshoes. Liz tosses 9 horseshoes. How many horseshoes do they toss altogether? (Lesson 3.8)

    ○ 15
    ○ 17
    ○ 18
    ○ 27

6. Which of the following is another way to write 315? (Lesson 2.5)

    ○ 1 hundred 3 tens 5 ones
    ○ 3 hundreds 1 ten 5 ones
    ○ 3 hundreds 5 tens 1 one
    ○ 5 hundreds 1 ten 3 ones

Name _____

Lesson 4.12

Represent Addition Problems

Write a number sentence for the problem. Solve.

1. Emily and her friends went to the park. They saw 15 robins and 9 blue jays. How many birds did they see in all?

   _____   _____ birds

2. Joe has 13 fish in one tank. He has 8 fish in another tank. How many fish does Joe have in all?

   _____   _____ fish

PROBLEM SOLVING

Solve.

3. There are 21 children in Kathleen's class. 12 of the children are girls. How many children in her class are boys?

   _____ boys

Chapter 4   ninety-three **P93**

Lesson Check

1. Clare has 14 blocks. Jasmine has 6 blocks. How many blocks do they have in all?
   - ○ 8
   - ○ 19
   - ○ 20
   - ○ 22

2. Matt finds 16 acorns at the park. Trevor finds 18 acorns. How many acorns do they find in all?
   - ○ 38
   - ○ 34
   - ○ 32
   - ○ 22

Spiral Review

3. What number will make this true? (Lesson 3.9)

   $6 + 8 = 7 + \square$
   - ○ 21
   - ○ 14
   - ○ 9
   - ○ 7

4. What is the sum? (Lesson 3.3)

   $4 + 3 + 6 = \underline{}$
   - ○ 13
   - ○ 10
   - ○ 9
   - ○ 7

5. Which number makes this true? (Lesson 2.10)

   $481 < \underline{}$
   - ○ 481
   - ○ 398
   - ○ 184
   - ○ 490

6. Which is an even number? (Lesson 1.6)
   - ○ 9
   - ○ 14
   - ○ 17
   - ○ 21

Name _____

Chapter 4 Extra Practice

Lessons 4.1 – 4.2 (pp. 157 – 164)
Break apart ones to add. Write the sum.

1. 42 + 9 = ____
2. 38 + 7 = ____

Show how to make one addend the next ten.
Complete the new addition sentence.

3. 22 + 49 = ?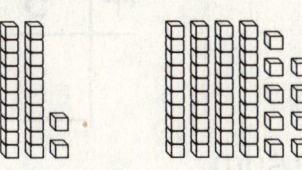

____ + ____ = ____

Lesson 4.3 (pp. 165 – 168)
Break apart the addends. Solve for the total sum.

1. 18 ⟶ ____ + ____
   + 26 ⟶ ____ + ____

   ____ + ____ = ____

Lesson 4.4 (pp. 169 – 172)
Write how many tens and ones in the sum.
Write the sum.

1. Add 45 and 29.

Tens	Ones

____ tens ____ ones

____

2. Add 13 and 48.

Tens	Ones

____ tens ____ ones

____

3. Add 38 and 18.

Tens	Ones

____ tens ____ ones

____

Lesson 4.5 – 4.6 (pp. 173 – 180)
Draw quick pictures to help you solve. Write the sum.

1.

Tens	Ones
4	6
+ 3	8

Tens	Ones

2.

Tens	Ones
3	2
+ 5	7

Tens	Ones

Regroup if you need to. Write the sum.

3.
```
   5 | 8
 + 1 | 7
```

4.
```
   4 | 3
 + 2 | 7
```

5.
```
   3 | 3
 + 5 | 8
```

Lessons 4.11 – 4.12 (pp. 197 – 204)
Add.

1.
```
   50
   25
 + 19
```

2.
```
   26
   21
 + 31
```

3.
```
   64
   17
 + 22
```

Write a number sentence for the problem. Solve.

4. Tony has 24 blue marbles and 18 red marbles. How many marbles does he have in all?

____ marbles

Chapter 5 School-Home Letter

Dear Family,

We started Chapter 5 this week. In this chapter, I will learn how to solve 2-digit subtraction problems using different strategies.

Love, _____

Vocabulary

minus sign a symbol used in a subtraction problem

difference the answer to a subtraction problem

$$7 - 4 = 3$$
↑
difference

Home Activity

Write 2-digit numbers, such as 56, 67, and 89, each on a separate index card. Use a pencil and a paper clip to make a pointer for the spinner. Have your child choose a card, spin the pointer, and subtract the number on the spinner from the number on the card.

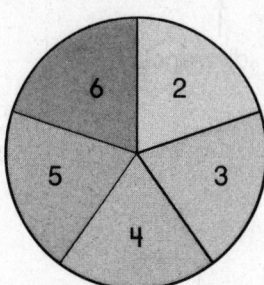

Literature

Look for these books at the library. Read them with your child to reinforce learning.

The Action of Subtraction by Brian P. Cleary. Millbrook Press, 2006.

The Shark Swimathon by Stuart J. Murphy. HarperCollins, 2001.

Capítulo 5

Carta para la casa

Querida familia:

Mi clase comenzó esta semana el Capítulo 5. En este capítulo, aprenderé a resolver problemas de resta de números de 2 dígitos usando estrategias diferentes.

Con cariño, _____

Vocabulario

signo de menos símbolo que se usa en un problema de resta

diferencia la respuesta a un problema de resta

7 − 4 = 3
        ↑
   diferencia

Actividad para la casa

Escriba números de 2 dígitos, como 56, 67 y 89, cada uno en una tarjeta. Con un lápiz y un clip, haga una flecha giratoria para la rueda. Pida a su hijo que elija una tarjeta, gire la flecha, y reste el número en que se detenga en la rueda del número de la tarjeta.

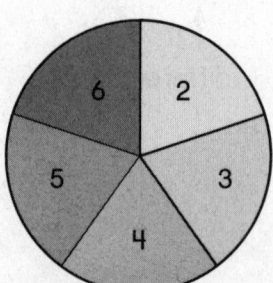

Literatura

Busquen estos libros en la biblioteca. Léalos con su hijo para reforzar el aprendizaje.

The Action of Subtraction por Brian P. Cleary. Millbrook Press, 2006.

The Shark Swimathon por Stuart J. Murphy. HarperCollins, 2001.

P98 ninety-eight

Name _____

Lesson 5.1

Break Apart Ones to Subtract

Break apart ones to subtract.
Write the difference.

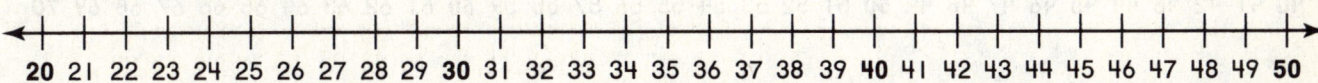

1. $36 - 7 =$ ___
2. $35 - 8 =$ ___
3. $37 - 9 =$ ___
4. $41 - 6 =$ ___
5. $44 - 5 =$ ___
6. $33 - 7 =$ ___
7. $32 - 4 =$ ___
8. $31 - 6 =$ ___
9. $46 - 9 =$ ___
10. $43 - 5 =$ ___

PROBLEM SOLVING

Solve. Write or draw to explain.

11. Beth had 44 marbles. She gave 9 marbles to her brother. How many marbles does she have now?

    ____ marbles

Lesson Check

1. What is the difference?

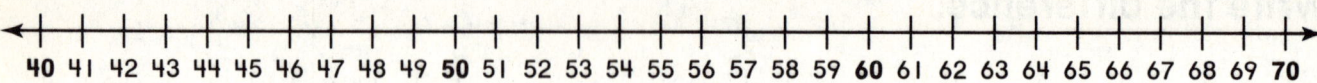

58 − 9 = ___

- ○ 67
- ○ 51
- ○ 49
- ○ 41

Spiral Review

2. What is the difference? (Lesson 3.6)

   14 − 6 = ___
   - ○ 7
   - ○ 8
   - ○ 9
   - ○ 10

3. What is the sum? (Lesson 3.3)

   3 + 6 + 2 = ___
   - ○ 11
   - ○ 10
   - ○ 9
   - ○ 5

4. What is the sum? (Lesson 4.1)

   64 + 7 = ___
   - ○ 81
   - ○ 73
   - ○ 71
   - ○ 68

5. What is the sum? (Lesson 4.2)

   56 + 18 = ___
   - ○ 74
   - ○ 72
   - ○ 64
   - ○ 62

Lesson 5.2

Break Apart Numbers to Subtract

Break apart the number you are subtracting. Write the difference.

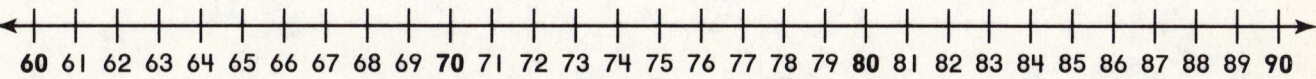

1. 81 − 14 = ___
2. 84 − 16 = ___
3. 77 − 14 = ___
4. 83 − 19 = ___
5. 81 − 17 = ___
6. 88 − 13 = ___
7. 84 − 19 = ___
8. 86 − 18 = ___
9. 84 − 17 = ___
10. 76 − 15 = ___
11. 86 − 22 = ___
12. 82 − 19 = ___

PROBLEM SOLVING

Solve. Write or draw to explain.

13. Mr. Pearce bought 43 plants. He gave 14 plants to his sister. How many plants does Mr. Pearce have now?

    ___ plants

Lesson Check

1. What is the difference?

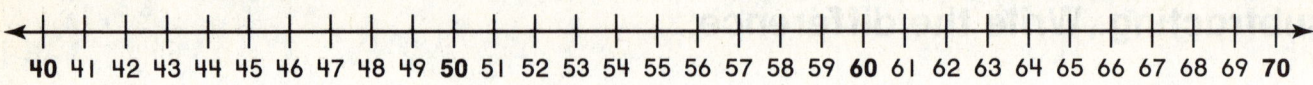

$63 - 19 =$ _____

- ○ 82
- ○ 56
- ○ 44
- ○ 36

Spiral Review

2. What is the sum? (Lesson 4.3)

$$\begin{array}{r} 14 \\ +\ 23 \\ \hline \end{array}$$

- ○ 11
- ○ 37
- ○ 31
- ○ 47

3. Which is true? (Lesson 1.7)

- ○ $47 < 51$
- ○ $82 > 90$
- ○ $65 < 56$
- ○ $34 > 42$

4. Which number completes this number sentence? (Lesson 3.9)

$7 + 4 =$ _____ $+ 9$

- ○ 20
- ○ 11
- ○ 3
- ○ 2

5. John has 7 kites. Annie has 4 kites. How many kites do they have in all? (Lesson 3.8)

- ○ 12
- ○ 11
- ○ 7
- ○ 3

P102 one hundred two

Lesson 5.3

Model Regrouping for Subtraction

**Write how many tens and ones.
Write the difference.**

1. Subtract 9 from 35.

Tens	Ones

   _____ tens _____ ones

   _____

2. Subtract 14 from 52.

Tens	Ones

   _____ tens _____ ones

   _____

3. Subtract 17 from 46.

Tens	Ones

   _____ tens _____ ones

   _____

4. Subtract 28 from 63.

Tens	Ones

   _____ tens _____ ones

   _____

PROBLEM SOLVING  REAL WORLD

Solve. Write or draw to explain.

5. Mr. Ortega made 51 cookies. He gave 14 cookies away. How many cookies does he have now?

   _____ cookies

Chapter 5   one hundred three **P103**

Lesson Check

1. Subtract 9 from 36. What is the difference?

   ○ 45
   ○ 27
   ○ 26
   ○ 7

2. Subtract 28 from 45. What is the difference?

   ○ 73
   ○ 37
   ○ 23
   ○ 17

Spiral Review

3. Which number completes this number sentence? (Lesson 3.9)

   ___ + 6 = 8 + 3

   ○ 2
   ○ 4
   ○ 5
   ○ 11

4. What is the sum? (Lesson 3.3)

   4 + 4 + 6 = ___

   ○ 14
   ○ 13
   ○ 12
   ○ 11

5. What is the sum? (Lesson 4.2)

   38 + 35 = ___

   ○ 63   ○ 73
   ○ 67   ○ 76

6. Which number is an even number? (Lesson 1.6)

   ○ 41   ○ 27
   ○ 32   ○ 9

Name _____

Lesson 5.4

Model and Record 2-Digit Subtraction

**Draw quick pictures to solve.
Write the difference.**

1.

Tens	Ones
☐	☐
4	3
− 1	7

Tens	Ones

2.

Tens	Ones
☐	☐
3	8
− 2	9

Tens	Ones

3.

Tens	Ones
☐	☐
5	2
− 3	7

Tens	Ones

4.

Tens	Ones
☐	☐
3	5
− 1	9

Tens	Ones

PROBLEM SOLVING  REAL WORLD

Solve.

5. Kendall has 63 stickers. Her sister has 57 stickers. How many more stickers does Kendall have than her sister?

_____ more stickers

Chapter 5   one hundred five **P105**

Lesson Check

1. What is the difference?

Tens	Ones
☐	☐
4	7
−1	8

   ○ 55   ○ 29
   ○ 31   ○ 19

2. What is the difference?

Tens	Ones
☐	☐
3	3
−2	9

   ○ 16   ○ 8
   ○ 12   ○ 4

Spiral Review

3. What is the difference? (Lesson 3.6)

   $10 - 6 = \_\_\_$

   ○ 5   ○ 3
   ○ 4   ○ 2

4. What is the sum? (Lesson 4.2)

   $16 + 49 = \_\_\_$

   ○ 53   ○ 67
   ○ 65   ○ 75

5. What is the sum? (Lesson 4.1)

   $28 + 8 = \_\_\_$

   ○ 36
   ○ 20
   ○ 18
   ○ 10

6. Which of the following numbers is an odd number? (Lesson 1.6)

   ○ 15
   ○ 18
   ○ 24
   ○ 30

Name _____

2-Digit Subtraction

Lesson 5.5

Regroup if you need to.
Write the difference.

1.
```
   4 | 7
 - 2 | 8
 ----|----
     |
```

2.
```
   3 | 3
 - 1 | 8
 ----|----
     |
```

3.
```
   2 | 8
 - 1 | 4
 ----|----
     |
```

4.
```
   6 | 6
 - 1 | 9
 ----|----
     |
```

5.
```
   7 | 7
 - 2 | 6
 ----|----
     |
```

6.
```
   5 | 8
 - 3 | 4
 ----|----
     |
```

7.
```
   5 | 2
 - 2 | 5
 ----|----
     |
```

8.
```
   8 | 7
 - 4 | 9
 ----|----
     |
```

PROBLEM SOLVING

Solve. Write or draw to explain.

9. Mrs. Paul bought 32 erasers. She gave 19 erasers to students. How many erasers does she still have?

_____ erasers

Chapter 5   one hundred seven **P107**

Lesson Check

1. What is the difference?

   ```
   4 | 8
 - 3 | 9
   ```

   - ○ 9
   - ○ 10
   - ○ 11
   - ○ 19

2. What is the difference?

   ```
   8 | 4
 - 6 | 6
   ```

   - ○ 48
   - ○ 38
   - ○ 28
   - ○ 18

Spiral Review

3. Which is another way to write the number 54? (Lesson 1.4)
   - ○ 5 + 4
   - ○ 50 + 4
   - ○ 4 tens 5 ones
   - ○ 5 tens 4 tens

4. Which of the following has the same sum as 8 + 7? (Lesson 3.2)
   - ○ 10 + 2
   - ○ 10 + 3
   - ○ 10 + 5
   - ○ 10 + 6

5. 27 boys and 23 girls go on a field trip to the museum. How many children go to the museum in all? (Lesson 4.9)
   - ○ 40
   - ○ 44
   - ○ 50
   - ○ 54

6. There are 17 sandwiches at the picnic. Then 9 sandwiches are eaten. How many sandwiches are there now? (Lesson 3.8)
   - ○ 6
   - ○ 8
   - ○ 12
   - ○ 26

Name _____

Lesson 5.6

Practice 2-Digit Subtraction

Write the difference.

1.
```
  5 0
- 1 8
```

2.
```
  4 3
- 1 7
```

3.
```
  7 5
- 1 8
```

4.
```
  2 2
-   6
```

5.
```
  6 0
- 3 5
```

6.
```
  4 2
- 3 4
```

7.
```
  2 1
-   8
```

8.
```
  3 9
- 2 7
```

9.
```
  6 1
- 3 7
```

PROBLEM SOLVING · REAL WORLD

Solve. Write or draw to explain.

10. Julie has 42 sheets of paper. She gives 17 sheets to Kari. How many sheets of paper does Julie have now?

_____ sheets of paper

Chapter 5   one hundred nine **P109**

Lesson Check

1. What is the difference?

    $$\begin{array}{r} 73 \\ -\ 47 \\ \hline \end{array}$$

    - ○ 24
    - ○ 26
    - ○ 34
    - ○ 36

2. What is the difference?

    $$\begin{array}{r} 54 \\ -\ 13 \\ \hline \end{array}$$

    - ○ 31
    - ○ 37
    - ○ 39
    - ○ 41

Spiral Review

3. What is the sum of 9 + 9?

    (Lesson 3.1)

    - ○ 20
    - ○ 18
    - ○ 9
    - ○ 0

4. What is the difference for 14 − 7? (Lesson 3.6)

    - ○ 21
    - ○ 13
    - ○ 7
    - ○ 6

5. What is the sum? (Lesson 4.2)

    36 + 25 = _____

    - ○ 61
    - ○ 54
    - ○ 51
    - ○ 11

6. What is the sum? (Lesson 3.3)

    7 + 2 + 3 = _____

    - ○ 6
    - ○ 11
    - ○ 12
    - ○ 14

P110 one hundred ten

Name _____

Lesson 5.7

Rewrite 2-Digit Subtraction

Rewrite the numbers. Then subtract.

1. 35 − 19
2. 47 − 23
3. 55 − 28

4. 22 − 15
5. 61 − 32
6. 70 − 37

PROBLEM SOLVING

Solve.

7. Jimmy went to the toy store. He saw 23 wooden trains and 41 plastic trains. How many more plastic trains than wooden trains did he see?

_____ more plastic trains

Chapter 5   one hundred eleven **P111**

Lesson Check

1. What is the difference for 43 − 17?

   − ___

   ○ 16   ○ 36
   ○ 26   ○ 60

2. What is the difference for 50 − 16?

   − ___

   ○ 66   ○ 34
   ○ 46   ○ 24

Spiral Review

3. Which of the following numbers completes this number sentence? (Lesson 3.9)

   $7 + 6 = \underline{} + 9$

   ○ 22   ○ 5
   ○ 13   ○ 4

4. Which of the following is true? (Lesson 1.7)

   ○ 59 > 50
   ○ 46 > 51
   ○ 38 < 35
   ○ 70 < 58

5. Which of the following has the same sum as 5 + 9? (Lesson 3.2)

   ○ 10 + 6
   ○ 10 + 5
   ○ 10 + 4
   ○ 10 + 3

6. Which of the following numbers is an odd number? (Lesson 1.6)

   ○ 6
   ○ 21
   ○ 30
   ○ 48

Name _____

Draw a Diagram • Subtraction

PROBLEM SOLVING
Lesson 5.8

Label the bar model. Then solve.

1. Megan picked 34 flowers. Some of the flowers are yellow and 18 flowers are pink. How many of the flowers are yellow?

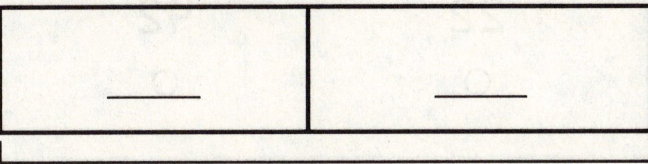

_____ yellow flowers

2. Alex had 45 toy cars. He put 26 toy cars in a box. How many toy cars are not in the box?

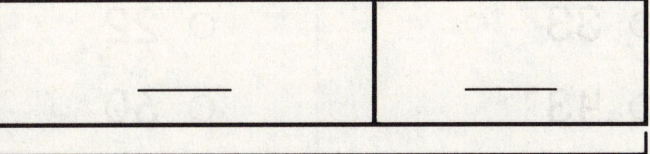

_____ toy cars

3. Mr. Kane makes 43 pizzas. 28 of the pizzas are small. The rest are large. How many pizzas are large?

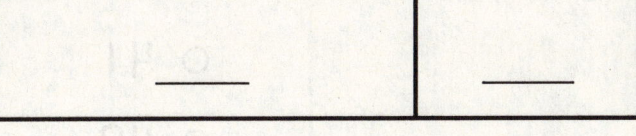

_____ large pizzas

Chapter 5 one hundred thirteen P113

Lesson Check

1. There were 39 pumpkins at the store. Then 17 of the pumpkins were sold. How many pumpkins are still at the store?

   ○ 12   ○ 22   ○ 42   ○ 56

Spiral Review

2. Ashley had 26 markers. Her friend gave her 17 more markers. How many markers does Ashley have now? (Lesson 4.12)

   ○ 17   ○ 33
   ○ 26   ○ 43

3. What is the sum? (Lesson 4.7)

   $$\begin{array}{r} 46 \\ +\ 24 \\ \hline \end{array}$$

   ○ 22   ○ 70
   ○ 60   ○ 72

4. Which of the numbers makes this number sentence true?
   (Lesson 3.9)

   $3 + \underline{} = 9 + 4$

   ○ 6
   ○ 10
   ○ 16
   ○ 18

5. What is the sum? (Lesson 4.1)

   $34 + 5 = \underline{}$

   ○ 39
   ○ 41
   ○ 49
   ○ 51

Name _____

Represent Subtraction Problems

Lesson 5.9

Write a number sentence for the problem. Solve.

1. 29 children rode their bikes to school. After some of the children rode home, there were 8 children with bikes still at school. How many children rode their bikes home?

   _____

   ____ children

2. 32 children were on the school bus. Then 24 children got off the bus. How many children were still on the bus?

   _____

   ____ children

PROBLEM SOLVING  **REAL WORLD**

Solve.

3. There were 21 children in the library. After 7 children left the library, how many children were still in the library?

   ____ children

Lesson Check

1. Cindy had 42 beads. She used some beads for a bracelet. She has 14 beads left. How many beads did she use for the bracelet?
   - ○ 22
   - ○ 28
   - ○ 32
   - ○ 56

2. Jake had 36 baseball cards. He gave 17 cards to his sister. How many baseball cards does Jake have now?
   - ○ 19
   - ○ 21
   - ○ 23
   - ○ 41

Spiral Review

3. What is the sum? (Lesson 3.1)

   $6 + 7 =$ ____
   - ○ 11
   - ○ 12
   - ○ 13
   - ○ 15

4. What is the difference? (Lesson 3.6)

   $16 - 9 =$ ____
   - ○ 11
   - ○ 9
   - ○ 8
   - ○ 7

5. Which of these is another way to write 67? (Lesson 1.2)
   - ○ 60 + 7
   - ○ 70 + 6
   - ○ 6 + 7
   - ○ 60 + 70

6. Which of the following has the same sum as 6 + 8? (Lesson 3.2)
   - ○ 10 + 2
   - ○ 10 + 3
   - ○ 10 + 4
   - ○ 10 + 5

Name _____

Lesson 5.10

Solve Multistep Problems

Label the bar models for the steps you do to solve the problem.

1. Greg has 60 building blocks. His sister gives him 17 more blocks. He uses 38 blocks to make a tower. How many blocks are not used in the tower?

   ____ blocks

2. Jenna has a train of 26 connecting cubes and a train of 37 connecting cubes. She gives 15 cubes to a friend. How many cubes does Jenna have now?

   ____ cubes

3. Thomas had 25 books on a shelf. He took 7 books off the shelf and put 12 other books on the shelf. How many books are on the shelf now?

   ____ books

Chapter 5

one hundred seventeen P117

Lesson Check

1. Sara has 18 crayons. Max has 19 crayons. How many more crayons do they need to get to have 50 crayons in all?

   ○ 13   ○ 31
   ○ 23   ○ 37

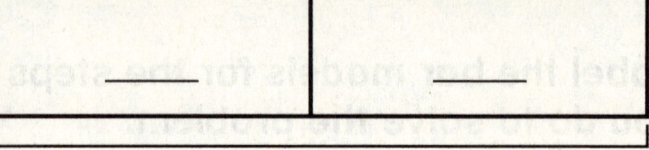

Spiral Review

2. Which number completes this number sentence? (Lesson 3.9)

   ___ + 8 = 9 + 3

   ○ 4
   ○ 12
   ○ 17
   ○ 20

3. What is the sum? (Lesson 3.3)

   5 + 4 + 5 = ___

   ○ 6
   ○ 12
   ○ 14
   ○ 16

4. Which of the following is true? (Lesson 1.7)

   ○ 32 = 23
   ○ 65 > 70
   ○ 92 < 88
   ○ 46 > 37

5. Which of the following is another way to write 30 + 8? (Lesson 1.3)

   ○ 11
   ○ 22
   ○ 38
   ○ 83

Chapter 5 Extra Practice

Lessons 5.1 – 5.2 (pp. 213 – 220)

Break apart the number you are subtracting.
Write the difference.

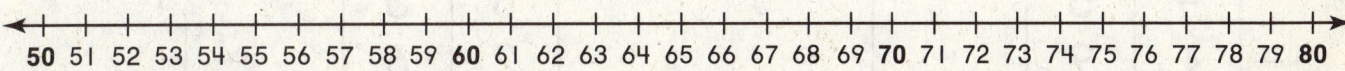

1. 73 − 7 = ____

2. 65 − 7 = ____

3. 64 − 8 = ____

4. 75 − 18 = ____

5. 72 − 12 = ____

6. 74 − 19 = ____

Lesson 5.3 (pp. 221 – 224)

Write how many tens and ones.
Write the difference.

1. Subtract 7 from 52.

____ tens ____ ones

____

2. Subtract 8 from 41.

____ tens ____ ones

____

3. Subtract 6 from 34.

____ tens ____ ones

____

Lesson 5.4 (pp. 225–228)
Draw quick pictures to solve.
Write the difference.

1. | Tens | Ones |
   |------|------|
   | ☐ | ☐ |
   | 4 | 5 |
   | − 1 | 9 |

Tens	Ones

2. | Tens | Ones |
   |------|------|
   | ☐ | ☐ |
   | 5 | 3 |
   | − 2 | 6 |

Tens	Ones

Lessons 5.5 – 5.6 (pp. 229–235)
Write the difference.

1. 7 | 3
  − 2 | 8

2. 9 | 5
  − 4 | 7

3. 6 0
  − 4 8

4. 4 9
  − 2 4

Lesson 5.10 (pp. 249–252)
Label the bar models. Solve the problem.

1. Ryan buys a pack of 30 stickers. His mom gives him 14 stickers. How many more stickers does he need to have 62 stickers in all?

____ more stickers

P120 one hundred twenty

Chapter 6
School-Home Letter

Dear Family,

My class started Chapter 6 this week. In this chapter, I will learn about taking surveys, making graphs, and interpreting the data.

Love, _____

Vocabulary

pictograph A graph that uses pictures to show data

Apples Sold				
Eric	●	●		
Deb	●	●	●	●
Alex	●			

Key: Each ● stands for 2 apples.

bar graph A graph that uses bars to show data

Home Activity

Take your child on a walk in your neighborhood. Help your child make a tally chart to record how many people you see driving, walking, and biking. Then talk with your child about the information that is in your tally chart.

How People Are Moving	
How Moving	Tally
driving	||||| ||
walking	||||
biking	||

Literature

Reading math stories reinforces learning. Look for these books at the library.

Tables and Graphs of Healthy Things by Joan Freese. Gareth Stevens Publishing, 2008.

Lemonade for Sale by Stuart J. Murphy Harper Collins, 1998.

Capítulo 6
Carta para la casa

Querida familia:

Mi clase comenzó hoy el Capítulo 6. En este capítulo, aprenderé a realizar encuestas, hacer gráficas e interpretar datos.

Con cariño, _____

Vocabulario

pictografía Una gráfica que usa ilustraciones para mostrar los datos

Manzanas vendidas				
Eric	●	●		
Deb	●	●	●	●
Alex	●			

Clave: Cada ● representa 2 manzanas.

gráfica de barras Una gráfica que usa barras para mostrar los datos

Actividad para la casa

Lleve a pasear a su hijo por el vecindario. Ayúdelo crear una tabla de conteo para anotar cuántas personas ven manejando, caminando y montando bicicleta. Luego conversen sobre la información que hay en la tabla de conteo.

Cómo se mueve la gente	
Se mueven	Conteo
manejando	|||| ||
caminando	||||
en bicicleta	||

Literatura

Leer cuentos de matemáticas refuerza los conceptos. Busquen estos libros en la biblioteca.

Tables and Graphs of Healthy Things por Joan Freese. Gareth Stevens Publishing, 2008.

Lemonade for Sale por Stuart J. Murphy. Harper Collins, 1998.

Name _____

Lesson 6.1

Take a Survey

1. Take a survey. Ask 10 classmates how they got to school. Use tally marks to show their answers.

How We Got to School	
Way	**Tally**
walk	
bus	
car	
bike	

2. Use the tally chart. Record the data in the chart below.

How We Got to School	
Way	**Number**
walk	
bus	
car	
bike	

3. How many classmates rode the bus to school?

   _____ classmates

4. How many classmates rode in a car to school?

   _____ classmates

5. Which way did the fewest classmates get to school? _____

6. Which way did the most classmates get to school? _____

7. Did more classmates get to school by walking or by riding bikes? _____

   How many more? _____ more classmates

Chapter 6   one hundred twenty-three **P123**

Lesson Check

Use the tally chart.

1. Which color had the fewest votes?
   - ○ blue
   - ○ green
   - ○ red
   - ○ yellow

Favorite Color	
Color	Tally
blue	|||
green	𝍲 ||||
red	𝍲 ||
yellow	𝍲	

Spiral Review

2. What number completes the number sentence? (Lesson 3.9)

   $3 + 6 = \square + 4$
   - ○ 4
   - ○ 5
   - ○ 9
   - ○ 13

3. What is the sum? (Lesson 4.1)

   $33 + 8 = \underline{}$
   - ○ 25
   - ○ 31
   - ○ 41
   - ○ 42

4. What is the sum? (Lesson 3.1)

   $0 + 9 = \underline{}$
   - ○ 0
   - ○ 5
   - ○ 8
   - ○ 9

5. What number is 10 more than 155? (Lesson 2.7)
   - ○ 145
   - ○ 156
   - ○ 165
   - ○ 255

Name _____

PROBLEM SOLVING
Lesson 6.2

Make a List • Surveys

Jackson took a survey of his class. He asked this question.
Which is your favorite winter activity, sledding, skiing, or ice skating?
He wrote the votes on the board.
Which winter activity did the most classmates choose?

sledding	skiing	ice skating	skiing
skiing	ice skating	sledding	sledding
sledding	sledding	skiing	ice skating
ice skating	sledding	sledding	skiing

1. Complete the tally chart for the data above.

Activity	Tally	Total

2. Which activity did the most children choose?

   _____

3. Write a question about your chart.
   Have a classmate use your chart to answer the question.

   _____

   _____

   _____

Chapter 6　　　　　　　　　　　　　　　　one hundred twenty-five **P125**

Lesson Check

1. Taryn took a survey of her classmates. She made this chart. How many more classmates chose a zebra than a giraffe?

Favorite Zoo Animal		
Animal	Tally	Total
giraffe	|||	3
elephant	‖‖‖ |||	8
zebra	‖‖‖ ‖‖‖		11
lion	‖‖‖		6

    ○ 3
    ○ 8
    ○ 11
    ○ 14

Spiral Review

2. Carson has 25 crayons. Loren has 18 crayons. How many crayons do they have in all? (Lesson 4.9)

    ○ 13
    ○ 33
    ○ 43
    ○ 53

3. Which is another way to write 28? (Lesson 1.2)

    ○ 20 + 2
    ○ 20 + 8
    ○ 80 + 2
    ○ 80 + 8

4. Al has 25 trading cards. He gave 16 cards to Bob. How many cards does Al have now? (Lesson 5.5)

    ○ 9
    ○ 19
    ○ 26
    ○ 41

5. What is the sum? (Lesson 4.11)

    23
    21
    +14

    ○ 69
    ○ 68
    ○ 59
    ○ 58

Lesson 6.3

Name _____

Pictographs

1. Use the tally chart to complete the pictograph.
   Draw a ☺ for every 2 children.

Favorite Cookie	
Cookie	Tally
chocolate	|||||	
oatmeal	||||
peanut butter	||||| |||||

Favorite Cookie					
chocolate					
oatmeal					
peanut butter					

Key: Each ☺ stands for 2 children.

2. How many children chose chocolate? _____ children

3. Which cookie did the fewest children choose? _____

Use the pictograph.

4. How many cars does Aaron have?

   _____ cars

5. How many more cars does Kim have than Thomas?

   _____ more cars

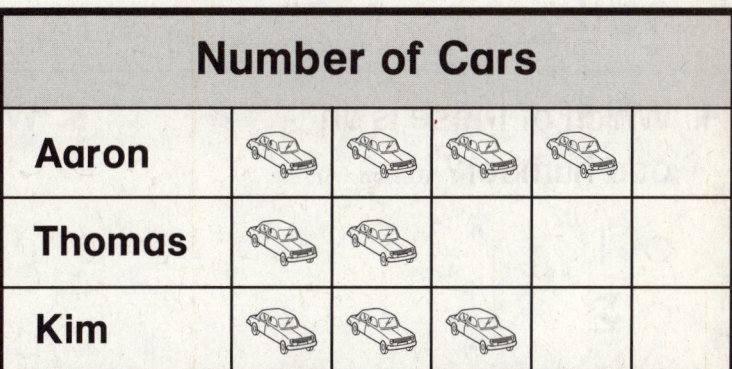

Key: Each 🚗 stands for 5 cars.

6. How many cars in all do the three children have? _____ cars

Chapter 6   one hundred twenty-seven   **P127**

Lesson Check

Use the pictograph.

1. How many more rainy days were there in April than in May?
   ○ 2
   ○ 4
   ○ 6
   ○ 12

Number of Rainy Days

March	☂	☂	☂	☂	☂
April	☂	☂	☂	☂	
May	☂	☂			

Key: Each ☂ stands for 2 days.

Spiral Review

2. What is the sum? (Lesson 4.2)

   $17 + 24 = $ ___
   ○ 31
   ○ 33
   ○ 41
   ○ 42

3. What number is 100 more than 345? (Lesson 2.7)
   ○ 245
   ○ 355
   ○ 445
   ○ 455

4. Which of these is an odd number? (Lesson 1.6)
   ○ 1
   ○ 2
   ○ 4
   ○ 6

5. What is the difference? (Lesson 5.1)

   $35 - 8 = $ ___
   ○ 43
   ○ 37
   ○ 33
   ○ 27

Name _____

Lesson 6.4

Make Bar Graphs

Maria asked her friends to tell her how many hours they practice soccer each week.

- Jessie practices for 3 hours.
- Victor practices for 2 hours.
- Samantha practices for 5 hours.
- David practices for 6 hours.

Complete the bar graph for the data.

1. Write a title and labels.

2. Draw bars in the graph to show the data.

Hours Playing Soccer Each Week											
Jessie											
Victor											
Samantha											
David											

0 1 2 3 4 5 6 7 8 9 10

3. Which friend practices soccer for the most hours each week? _____

4. Which friends practice soccer for fewer than 4 hours each week?

_____

Chapter 6   one hundred twenty-nine **P129**

Lesson Check
Use the bar graph.

1. How many more people voted for summer than for spring?
   - ○ 2
   - ○ 3
   - ○ 5
   - ○ 8

Favorite Season

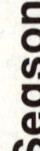

Spiral Review

2. Felix walked for 28 minutes. Ray walked for 17 minutes. How many more minutes did Felix walk than Ray? (Lesson 5.9)
   - ○ 1 more minute
   - ○ 11 more minutes
   - ○ 12 more minutes
   - ○ 45 more minutes

3. Which is another way to write 6 tens 5 ones? (Lesson 1.3)
   - ○ 6 + 5
   - ○ 50 + 6
   - ○ 60 + 5
   - ○ 60 + 50

4. Which is true? (Lesson 2.10)
   - ○ 334 = 343
   - ○ 438 > 538
   - ○ 101 = 110
   - ○ 207 < 270

5. What is the difference? (Lesson 3.4)

   $7 + 9 = 16$
   $16 - 7 = \_\_$
   - ○ 7
   - ○ 9
   - ○ 11
   - ○ 13

Name _____

Lesson 6.5

Use Bar Graphs

Ava made a bar graph to show the favorite flowers of her classmates.

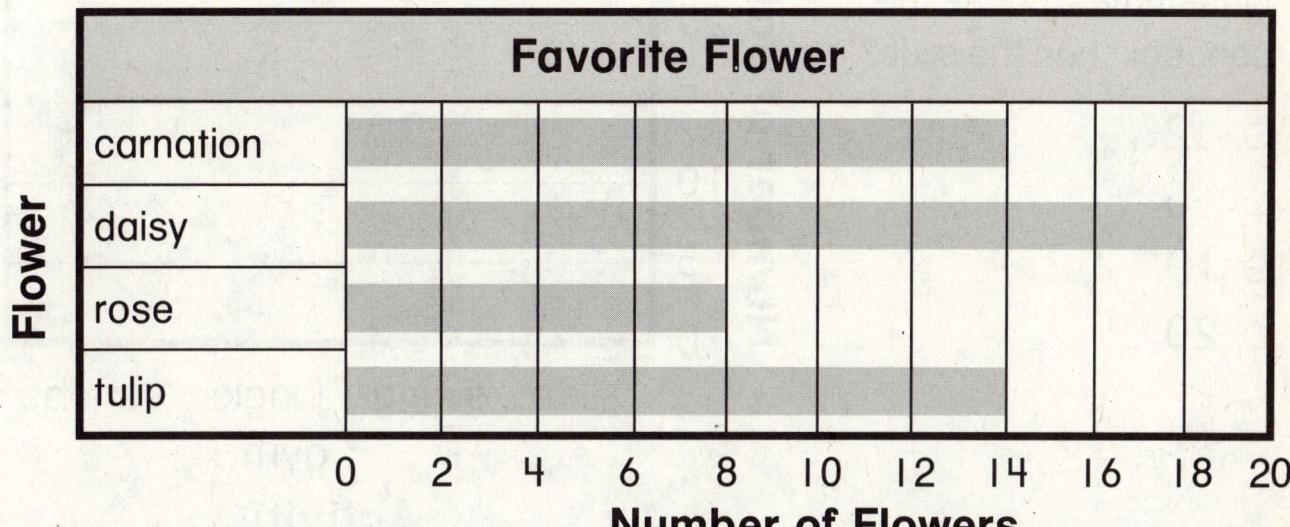

1. Which flower had the most votes?

   _____

2. Which flower had the fewest votes?

   _____

3. How many classmates voted for a daisy?

   ____ classmates

4. How many more classmates voted for a carnation than for a rose?

   ____ more classmates

5. How many more classmates voted for a tulip than for a rose?

   ____ more classmates

6. Which flower had 8 votes?

   _____

7. Which two flowers had the same number of votes?

   _____

8. How many fewer classmates voted for a rose than for a daisy?

   ____ fewer classmates

Lesson Check
Use the bar graph.

1. How many more classmates chose the sandbox than the slide?
   - ○ 2
   - ○ 5
   - ○ 10
   - ○ 20

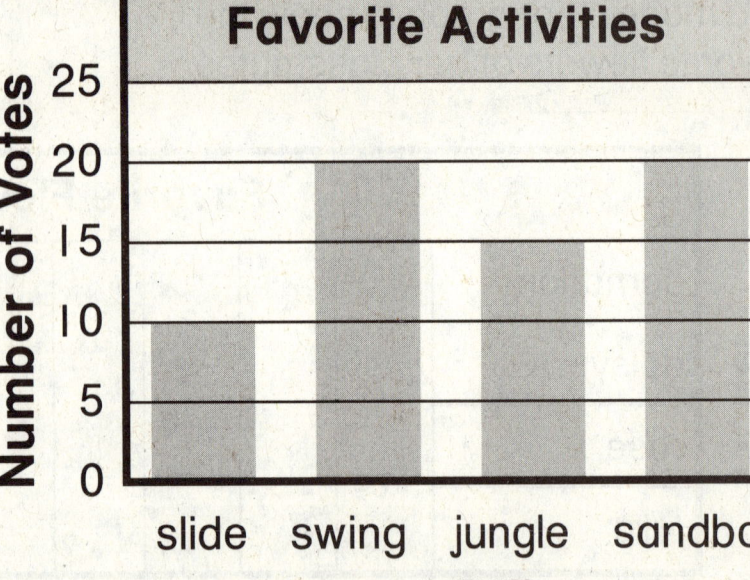

Spiral Review

2. Which is another way to write the number 83? (Lesson 2.5)
   - ○ 80 + 30
   - ○ 80 + 3
   - ○ 30 + 8
   - ○ 8 + 3

3. Which has the same sum as 6 + 1 + 4? (Lesson 3.3)
   - ○ 7 + 5
   - ○ 6 + 4
   - ○ 6 + 3
   - ○ 10 + 1

4. What number should be next in the pattern? (Lesson 2.8)

   118, 218, 318, 418, ___
   - ○ 518
   - ○ 428
   - ○ 420
   - ○ 419

5. What is the sum? (Lesson 4.6)

   27
   + 33
   - ○ 50
   - ○ 54
   - ○ 60
   - ○ 61

Name _____

Lesson 6.6

Use Data

Jan took two surveys. She made these charts.

Grade 2 Class Favorite Sport	
Sport	**Tally**
soccer	||||| |||
baseball	||||
football	|||||
basketball	||||| ||

Grade 5 Class Favorite Sport	
Sport	**Tally**
soccer	|||
baseball	||||| ||||
football	||||
basketball	|||||

1. In which class did more children choose basketball?

   _____

2. In which class did fewer children choose soccer?

   _____

3. How many more children chose baseball in Grade 5 than in Grade 2?

   ____ more children

4. How many children in all are in the Grade 2 class?

   ____ children

5. In which class did 5 children choose football?

   _____

6. How many fewer children chose soccer in Grade 5 than in Grade 2?

   ____ fewer children

Lesson Check

Use the pictographs.

1. How many more apples did Max pick than Shelly on Tuesday?
   - ○ 1
   - ○ 2
   - ○ 4
   - ○ 20

Apples Picked by Shelly					
Monday	🍎	🍎			
Tuesday	🍎	🍎	🍎	🍎	

Key: Each 🍎 stands for 2 apples.

Apples Picked by Max					
Monday	🍎	🍎	🍎	🍎	
Tuesday	🍎	🍎	🍎	🍎	🍎

Key: Each 🍎 stands for 2 apples.

Spiral Review

2. What is the value of the underlined digit? (Lesson 2.4)

   6<u>8</u>5

   - ○ 800
   - ○ 80
   - ○ 68
   - ○ 8

3. Which group of numbers is listed in order from least to greatest? (Lesson 2.11)
   - ○ 402, 422, 412
   - ○ 412, 402, 422
   - ○ 412, 422, 402
   - ○ 402, 412, 422

4. Which makes the number sentence true? (Lesson 3.10)

   12 − 5 = ___
   - ○ 5 + 7
   - ○ 12 + 5
   - ○ 3 + 4
   - ○ 12 − 6

5. Which is true? (Lesson 2.10)
   - ○ 327 < 372
   - ○ 327 > 372
   - ○ 327 = 372
   - ○ 372 < 327

Chapter 6 Extra Practice

Lesson 6.2 (pp. 265-268)

Emily took a survey.
She asked this question.
Which is your favorite ice-cream flavor, vanilla, chocolate, or strawberry?
She wrote down the votes.

vanilla	strawberry
vanilla	strawberry
strawberry	vanilla
strawberry	chocolate
chocolate	strawberry

1. Complete the tally chart for the data above.

2. Which flavor did the most children choose?

   _____

Favorite Ice-Cream Flavor

Flavor	Tally	Total

Lesson 6.3 (pp. 269-271)

1. Use the tally chart to complete the pictograph.
   Draw ● for every 2 books.

Number of Books Read

Name	Tally
Maya	IIII
Gabe	HHT HHT
Tia	HHT III

Number of Books Read

Maya					
Gabe					
Tia					

Key: Each ● stands for 2 books.

Lesson 6.4 (pp. 273-276)

Robin is making a bar graph to show the colors of her beads.
Robin has 5 red beads, 7 blue beads, 8 yellow beads, and 5 green beads.

1. Write a title and labels for the graph.
2. Draw bars in the graph to show the data.

Bead Colors

	0	1	2	3	4	5	6	7	8	9	10
red											
blue											
yellow											
green											

Lessons 6.5 – 6.6 (pp. 277-284)

Use the bar graphs for the two classes.

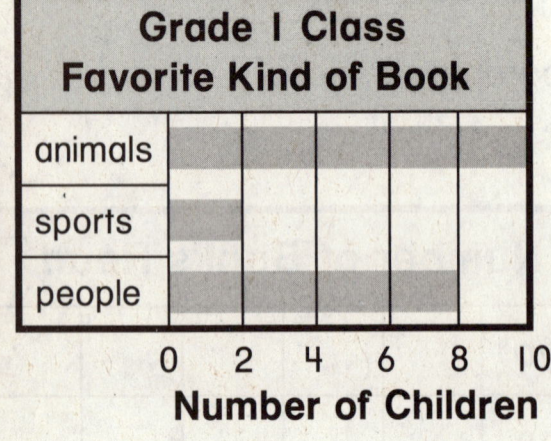
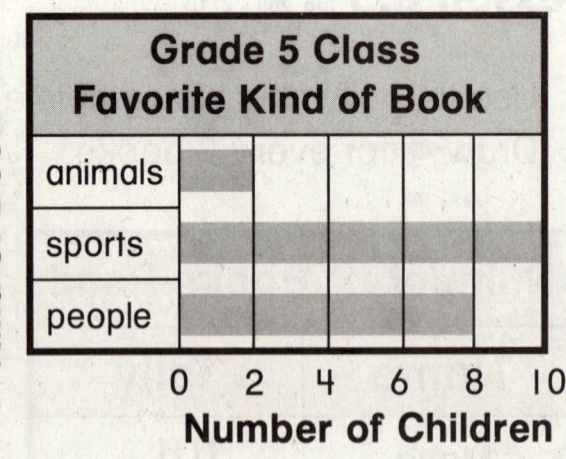

1. In which class did more children choose sports? _____

2. How many children in all voted in the Grade 1 class? _____ children

P136   one hundred thirty-six

Chapter 7 School-Home Letter

Dear Family,

My class started Chapter 7 this week. I will learn how to add and subtract 3-digit numbers, including regrouping ones, tens, and hundreds.

Love, _____

Vocabulary

addends Numbers added together in addition problems

7 + 2 = 9
↑   ↑
addends

sum Answer to an addition problem

7 + 2 = 9
        ↑
        sum

difference Answer to a subtraction problem

Home Activity

Write addition and subtraction problems with two 3-digit numbers for your child. Write some problems where regrouping is needed and other problems where regrouping is not needed.

```
  462       796
+ 341     − 578
```

Literature

Reading math stories reinforces learning. Look for these books at the library.

A Collection for Kate by Barbara Derubertis. Kane Press, 1999.

The Action of Subtraction by Brian P. Cleary. Millbrook Press, 2006.

Capítulo 7

Carta para la casa

Querida familia:

Mi clase comenzó esta semana el Capítulo 7. Aprenderé a sumar y restar números de 3 dígitos, incluyendo la reagrupación de unidades, decenas y centenas.

Con cariño, _____

Vocabulario

sumandos números que se suman unos a otros en problemas de suma

$$7 + 2 = 9$$
sumandos (↑ ↑ sobre 7 y 2)

suma resultado de un problema de suma

$$7 + 2 = 9$$
suma (↑ sobre 9)

diferencia resultado de un problema de resta

Actividad para la casa

Escriba problemas de suma y resta de 3 dígitos para resolverlos con su hijo. Escriba algunos problemas que necesiten reagrupación y otros que no la necesiten.

$$\begin{array}{r} 462 \\ +341 \\ \hline \end{array} \qquad \begin{array}{r} 796 \\ -578 \\ \hline \end{array}$$

Literatura

Leer cuentos de matemáticas refuerza el aprendizaje. Busquen estos libros en la biblioteca.

A Collection for Kate
por Barbara Derubertis.
Kane Press, 1999.

The Action of Subtraction
por Brian P. Cleary.
Millbrook Press, 2006.

Lesson 7.1

Name _____

Break Apart 3-Digit Addends

**Break apart the addends.
Find the total sum.**

1. 518 ⟶ ____ + ____ + ____
   +221 ⟶ ____ + ____ + ____

   ____ + ____ + ____ = ____

2. 438 ⟶ ____ + ____ + ____
   +142 ⟶ ____ + ____ + ____

   ____ + ____ + ____ = ____

3. 324 ⟶ ____ + ____ + ____
   +239 ⟶ ____ + ____ + ____

   ____ + ____ + ____ = ____

PROBLEM SOLVING REAL WORLD

Solve. Write or draw to explain.

4. There are 126 crayons in the bucket. A teacher puts 144 more crayons in the bucket. How many crayons are in the bucket now?

   _____ crayons

Chapter 7

Lesson Check

1. What is the sum?

    218
    + 145

    ○ 263
    ○ 363
    ○ 463
    ○ 541

2. What is the sum?

    664
    + 223

    ○ 441
    ○ 881
    ○ 887
    ○ 888

Spiral Review

3. What is the sum? (Lesson 4.2)

    $19 + 21 = ?$

    ○ 41
    ○ 40
    ○ 39
    ○ 38

4. Which is a related subtraction fact? (Lesson 3.4)

    $9 + 6 = 15$

    ○ $15 - 9 = 6$
    ○ $9 - 6 = 3$
    ○ $6 + 9 = 15$
    ○ $9 - 3 = 6$

5. The pet store has 25 goldfish and 33 betta fish. How many fish are there in all? (Lesson 4.7)

    ○ 8
    ○ 48
    ○ 58
    ○ 68

6. Which is another way to write $300 + 40 + 9$? (Lesson 1.2)

    ○ 349
    ○ 394
    ○ 439
    ○ 493

Name _____

Record 3-Digit Addition: Regroup Ones

Lesson 7.2

Write the sum.

1.

Hundreds	Tens	Ones
	☐	
1	4	8
+ 2	3	4

2.

Hundreds	Tens	Ones
	☐	
3	2	1
+ 3	1	8

3.

Hundreds	Tens	Ones
	☐	
4	1	9
+ 1	7	

4.

Hundreds	Tens	Ones
	☐	
6	0	2
+ 2	5	8

PROBLEM SOLVING

Solve. Write or draw to explain.

5. In the garden, there are 258 yellow daisies and 135 white daisies. How many daisies are in the garden altogether?

_____ daisies

Chapter 7

Lesson Check

1. What is the sum?

    $$435 + 146$$

    - ○ 311
    - ○ 371
    - ○ 571
    - ○ 581

2. What is the sum?

    $$436 + 306$$

    - ○ 712
    - ○ 730
    - ○ 742
    - ○ 7,312

Spiral Review

3. There are 12 goats and 8 sheep. How many more goats than sheep are there? Which number sentence can be used to solve this problem? (Lesson 3.8)

    - ○ $8 - 2 = 6$
    - ○ $12 + 8 = 20$
    - ○ $20 - 8 = 12$
    - ○ $12 - 8 = 4$

4. Which is another way to write four hundred seventy-eight? (Lesson 2.5)

    - ○ 478
    - ○ 487
    - ○ $400 + 80 + 7$
    - ○ $400 + 70 + 80$

5. What is the sum? (Lesson 4.1)

    $$26 + 7 = \underline{\quad}$$

    - ○ 19
    - ○ 32
    - ○ 33
    - ○ 34

6. Which of these numbers is greater than 329? (Lesson 2.10)

    - ○ 328
    - ○ 335
    - ○ 213
    - ○ 312

Lesson 7.3

Name _____

Record 3-Digit Addition: Regroup Tens

Write the sum.

1.
   1 8 7
 + 2 3 2

2.
   3 2 2
 + 3 5 6

3.
   2 8 5
 + 5 3 1

4.
   4 4 5
 +   3 4

5.
   6 2 0
 +   2 8

6.
   5 5 7
 + 1 8 0

7.
   6 7 1
 + 1 5 4

8.
   4 6 3
 + 4 8 1

9.
   7 4 6
 + 1 3 3

PROBLEM SOLVING

Solve. Write or draw to explain.

10. At the toy store there are 142 toy cars and 293 toy trucks. How many toy cars and trucks are at the store?

   _____ toy cars and trucks

Chapter 7 — one hundred forty-three P143

Lesson Check

1. What is the sum?

    472
    + 255

    ○ 627
    ○ 727
    ○ 728
    ○ 6,127

2. What is the sum?

    144
    + 284

    ○ 328
    ○ 418
    ○ 428
    ○ 518

Spiral Review

3. What is the sum? (Lesson 4.6)

    56
    + 38

    ○ 82
    ○ 84
    ○ 92
    ○ 94

4. Which is true? (Lesson 2.10)

    ○ 38 < 83
    ○ 29 > 32
    ○ 45 > 47
    ○ 65 < 56

5. Which number sentence is true? (Lesson 3.10)

    ○ 7 + 5 ≠ 6 + 6
    ○ 13 − 8 = 15 − 7
    ○ 18 − 9 ≠ 12 − 3
    ○ 3 + 5 = 6 + 2

6. Which number is 100 more than 437? (Lesson 2.7)

    ○ 337
    ○ 447
    ○ 537
    ○ 547

Name _____

Lesson 7.4

3-Digit Addition

Write the sum.

1.
```
   5 4 7
 + 4 3 5
 _____
```

2.
```
   3 6 7
 + 2 8 4
 _____
```

3.
```
   4 8 5
 + 4 5 6
 _____
```

4.
```
   1 8 7
 + 3 0 6
 _____
```

5.
```
   6 4 7
 + 1 2 8
 _____
```

6.
```
   5 2 3
 + 1 7 4
 _____
```

Rewrite the numbers. Then find the sum.

7. 255 + 231

   +_____

8. 294 + 176

   +_____

9. 375 + 364

   +_____

PROBLEM SOLVING

Solve. Write or draw to explain.

10. Saul and Luisa each scored 167 points on a computer game. How many points did they score in all?

    _____ points

Chapter 7   one hundred forty-five **P145**

Lesson Check

1. What is the sum?

    348
    + 272

    ○ 136
    ○ 510
    ○ 520
    ○ 620

2. What is the sum?

    123
    + 217

    ○ 314
    ○ 330
    ○ 340
    ○ 417

Spiral Review

3. Which number completes the number sentence? (Lesson 3.9)

    3 + 6 = ☐ + 5

    ○ 4   ○ 9
    ○ 5   ○ 14

4. What is the sum? (Lesson 4.11)

    32
    15
    + 46

    ○ 47   ○ 83
    ○ 78   ○ 93

5. Dana counted 34 peppers and 28 tomatoes. Which number sentence can be used to find how many items she counted in all? (Lesson 4.12)

    ○ 34 − 28 = 6
    ○ 34 − 6 = 28
    ○ 34 + 28 = 62
    ○ 34 + 82 = 116

6. Tom had 25 pretzels. He ate 12 pretzels. Which number sentence can be used to find how many pretzels are left? (Lesson 5.9)

    ○ 25 − 21 = 4
    ○ 25 − 12 = 13
    ○ 12 + 25 = 37
    ○ 25 + 21 = 46

Name _____

Lesson 7.5

Practice 3-Digit Addition

Write the sum.

1.
```
  532
+ 248
```

2.
```
  526
+ 558
```

3.
```
  323
+ 325
```

4.
```
  743
+ 869
```

5.
```
  743
+ 218
```

6.
```
  423
+ 156
```

7.
```
  737
+ 405
```

8.
```
  347
+ 324
```

9.
```
  481
+ 172
```

PROBLEM SOLVING  REAL WORLD

Solve.

10. Last week Paulo read 185 pages about space travel. This week he read 185 pages about animals. How many pages did he read in the two weeks?

_____ pages

Lesson Check

1. What is the sum?

    481
    + 357

    - ○ 736
    - ○ 738
    - ○ 838
    - ○ 938

2. What is the sum?

    529
    + 374

    - ○ 295
    - ○ 893
    - ○ 895
    - ○ 903

Spiral Review

3. What is the difference? (Lesson 5.6)

    78
    − 56

    - ○ 12
    - ○ 22
    - ○ 24
    - ○ 134

4. What is the sum? (Lesson 4.7)

    96
    + 59

    - ○ 37
    - ○ 145
    - ○ 155
    - ○ 157

5. What is the sum? (Lesson 4.2)

    47 + 26 = ?

    - ○ 73
    - ○ 72
    - ○ 63
    - ○ 61

6. Which is another way to write the number 87? (Lesson 1.3)

    - ○ 87 tens 0 ones
    - ○ 7 tens 8 ones
    - ○ 8 tens 7 ones
    - ○ 8 tens 0 ones

Name _____

Make a Model • 3-Digit Subtraction

**PROBLEM SOLVING
Lesson 7.6**

Make a model. Show how you solved the problem.

1. On Saturday, 770 people went to the snack shop. On Sunday, 628 people went. How many more people went to the snack shop on Saturday than on Sunday?

   _____ more people

2. There were 395 lemon ice cups at the snack shop. People bought 177 lemon ice cups. How many lemon ice cups are still at the snack shop?

   _____ cups

3. There were 576 bottles of water at the snack shop. People bought 469 bottles of water. How many bottles of water are at the shop now?

   _____ bottles

4. There were 279 bags of apple chips at the store. Then 134 bags of apple chips were bought. How many bags of apple chips are at the store now?

   _____ bags

Chapter 7   one hundred forty-nine **P149**

Lesson Check

1. There are 278 math and science books. 128 are math books. How many science books are there?
   - ○ 50
   - ○ 140
   - ○ 150
   - ○ 406

2. A book has 176 pages. Seth has read 119 pages. How many pages does he have left to read?
   - ○ 55
   - ○ 57
   - ○ 67
   - ○ 295

Spiral Review

3. What is the difference? (Lesson 5.5)

   $$\begin{array}{r} 92 \\ -66 \\ \hline \end{array}$$

   - ○ 16
   - ○ 26
   - ○ 36
   - ○ 158

4. What is the next number in this pattern? (Lesson 2.8)

   20, 25, 30, 35, ☐

   - ○ 45
   - ○ 44
   - ○ 40
   - ○ 36

5. There are 47 cars and 18 vans. Which number sentence could be used to find how many cars and vans there are in all? (Lesson 4.12)
   - ○ 47 + 18 = 65
   - ○ 47 − 8 = 39
   - ○ 74 + 18 = 92
   - ○ 47 − 18 = 29

6. What is the value of the underlined digit? (Lesson 2.4)

   <u>7</u>65

   - ○ 7
   - ○ 70
   - ○ 76
   - ○ 700

Name _____

Record 3-Digit Subtraction: Regroup Tens

Lesson 7.7

Solve. Write the difference.

1.
Hundreds	Tens	Ones
	☐	☐
7	7	4
− 2	3	6

2.
Hundreds	Tens	Ones
	☐	☐
5	5	1
− 1	1	3

3.
Hundreds	Tens	Ones
	☐	☐
4	8	9
− 2	7	3

4.
Hundreds	Tens	Ones
	☐	☐
7	7	2
− 2	5	4

PROBLEM SOLVING  REAL WORLD

Solve. Write or draw to explain.

5. There were 985 pencils at the store. 559 pencils were bought. How many pencils are left to sell?

_____ pencils

Chapter 7   one hundred fifty-one **P151**

Lesson Check

1. What is the difference?

    346
    − 127

    ○ 119
    ○ 219
    ○ 229
    ○ 473

2. What is the difference?

    568
    − 226

    ○ 342
    ○ 344
    ○ 742
    ○ 794

Spiral Review

3. What is the difference? (Lesson 5.1)

    45 − 7 = ___

    ○ 32
    ○ 36
    ○ 38
    ○ 42

4. Which is another way to write 647? (Lesson 1.3)

    ○ 6 tens 47 ones
    ○ 60 + 40 + 7
    ○ 6 hundreds 47 tens
    ○ 600 + 40 + 7

5. Look at the pictograph. How many children chose grapes? (Lesson 6.3)

    ○ 30
    ○ 15
    ○ 6
    ○ 3

Favorite Fruit					
Apples	☺	☺	☺	☺	
Oranges	☺	☺			
Grapes	☺	☺	☺		

Key: Each ☺ = 5 children.

Name _____

Record 3-Digit Subtraction: Regroup Hundreds

Lesson 7.8

Solve. Write the difference.

1. | Hundreds | Tens | Ones |
    |----------|------|------|
    | ☐ | ☐ | ☐ |
    | 7 | 2 | 7 |
    | − 2 | 5 | 6 |
    | | | |

2. | Hundreds | Tens | Ones |
    |----------|------|------|
    | ☐ | ☐ | ☐ |
    | 9 | 6 | 7 |
    | − 1 | 5 | 3 |
    | | | |

3. | Hundreds | Tens | Ones |
    |----------|------|------|
    | ☐ | ☐ | ☐ |
    | 6 | 3 | 9 |
    | − 4 | 7 | 2 |
    | | | |

4. | Hundreds | Tens | Ones |
    |----------|------|------|
    | ☐ | ☐ | ☐ |
    | 4 | 4 | 8 |
    | − 3 | 6 | 3 |
    | | | |

PROBLEM SOLVING 

Solve. Write or draw to explain.

5. There were 537 people in the parade. 254 of these people were playing an instrument. How many people were not playing an instrument?

   _____ people

Chapter 7 one hundred fifty-three **P153**

Lesson Check

1. What is the difference?

    538
    − 135

    ○ 403
    ○ 463
    ○ 663
    ○ 673

2. What is the difference?

    218
    − 126

    ○ 82
    ○ 92
    ○ 132
    ○ 192

Spiral Review

3. What is the difference? (Lesson 5.2)

    52 − 15 = _____

    ○ 63
    ○ 43
    ○ 37
    ○ 33

4. Which number sentence is true? (Lesson 3.10)

    ○ 5 + 6 = 3 + 7
    ○ 8 + 7 ≠ 9 + 6
    ○ 4 + 9 = 5 + 7
    ○ 6 + 7 ≠ 9 + 5

5. The graph shows eye colors of a group of children. How many children have blue eyes? (Lesson 6.5)

    ○ 2
    ○ 3
    ○ 6
    ○ 8

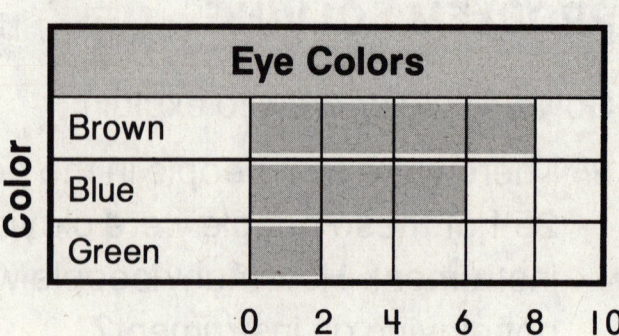

Name _____

Chapter 7 Extra Practice

Lesson 7.1 (pp. 293 – 296)
Break apart the addends. Find the total sum.

1. 121 ⟶ ____ + ____ + ____
  + 269 ⟶ ____ + ____ + ____

  ____ + ____ + ____ = ____

Lesson 7.2 (pp. 297 – 300)
Write the sum.

1.

Hundreds	Tens	Ones
	☐	
6	5	8
+ 2	1	6

2.

Hundreds	Tens	Ones
	☐	
4	0	3
+ 3	2	9

Lessons 7.3 – 7.5 (pp. 301 – 311)
Write the sum.

1. 2 9 3
  + 5 8 5

2. 3 6 8
  + 4 6 4

3. 4 5 3
  + 7 4 4

Chapter 7 one hundred fifty-five P155

Lesson 7.6 (pp. 313 – 316)
Make a model. Show how you solved the problem.

1. There are 485 books on the shelves and 114 books on the tables. How many more books are on the shelves than on the tables?

    _____ more books

Lesson 7.7 (pp. 317 – 320)
Solve. Write the difference.

1.
Hundreds	Tens	Ones
	☐	☐
6	8	1
− 3	1	2

2.
Hundreds	Tens	Ones
	☐	☐
7	3	4
− 5	2	6

Lesson 7.8 (pp. 321 – 324)
Solve. Write the difference.

1.
Hundreds	Tens	Ones
☐	☐	
6	1	3
− 2	8	3

2.
Hundreds	Tens	Ones
☐	☐	
8	7	5
− 2	8	3

Chapter 8
School-Home Letter

Dear Family,

My class started Chapter 8 this week. I will learn about number patterns and multiplication. I will use repeated addition, arrays, and number sentences for multiplication.

Love, _____

Vocabulary

multiplication sentence A number sentence that relates the number of equal groups, the number in each group, and the number in all

$3 \times 2 = 6$ is a multiplication sentence.

array An arrangement that shows objects in equal rows and columns

Home Activity

Write five multiplication sentences, such as $3 \times 4 = 12$ on individual index cards. Have your child use pennies to model each multiplication sentence.

$3 \times 4 = 12$

Literature

Reading math stories reinforces learning. Look for these books at the library.

Too Many Kangaroo Things to Do by Stuart J. Murphy. Harper Collins, 1996.

Amanda Bean's Amazing Dream by Cindy Neuschwander. Scholastic, 1998.

Capítulo 8

Carta para la casa

Querida familia:

Mi clase comenzó hoy el Capítulo 8. En este capítulo, aprenderé acerca de los patrones numéricos y la multiplicación. Usaré sumas repetidas, matrices y oraciones numéricas para la multiplicación.

Con cariño, _____

Vocabulario

oración de multiplicación Una oración numérica que relaciona el número de grupos iguales, el número en cada grupo y el número en todos

$3 \times 2 = 6$ es una oración de multiplicación.

matriz Un arreglo que muestra objetos en columnas e hileras iguales

Actividad para la casa

Escriba cinco oraciones de multiplicación del tipo $3 \times 4 = 12$ en tarjetas de fichero individuales. Pida a su hijo que use monedas de 1¢ para modelar cada oración de multiplicación.

$3 \times 4 = 12$

Literatura

Leer cuentos de matemáticas refuerza los conceptos. Busquen estos libros en la biblioteca.

Too Many Kangaroo Things to Do por Stuart J. Murphy. Harper Collins, 1996.

Amanda Bean's Amazing Dream por Cindy Neuschwander, Scholastic, 1998.

Name _____

Lesson **8.1**

Skip Count on a Hundred Chart

Skip count. Show the pattern on the hundred chart.

1. Count by fives. Circle the numbers.

2. Count by tens. Put an X on the numbers.

3. Start at 30. Count by threes. Write the numbers.

   30, ____, ____, ____, ____, ____, ____

1	2	3	4	5	6	7	8	9	10
11	12	13	14	15	16	17	18	19	20
21	22	23	24	25	26	27	28	29	30
31	32	33	34	35	36	37	38	39	40
41	42	43	44	45	46	47	48	49	50
51	52	53	54	55	56	57	58	59	60
61	62	63	64	65	66	67	68	69	70
71	72	73	74	75	76	77	78	79	80
81	82	83	84	85	86	87	88	89	90
91	92	93	94	95	96	97	98	99	100

PROBLEM SOLVING REAL WORLD

4. Felix skip counts by twos. He starts on 2. Which of the following numbers will he say? Circle them.

   22   31   50   23   28   42   47

Chapter 8   one hundred fifty-nine **P159**

Lesson Check

1. What number is next in the skip-counting pattern?
   6, 8, 10, 12, _____

   - ○ 14
   - ○ 13
   - ○ 11
   - ○ 10

1	2	3	4	5	6	7	8	9	10
11	12	13	14	15	16	17	18	19	20
21	22	23	24	25	26	27	28	29	30
31	32	33	34	35	36	37	38	39	40
41	42	43	44	45	46	47	48	49	50

Spiral Review

2. What is the sum? (Lesson 4.11)

   ```
     12
     22
   + 18
   ```

   - ○ 52
   - ○ 50
   - ○ 42
   - ○ 35

3. There are 175 girls and 160 boys in a school. How many students are there in all? (Lesson 7.5)

   - ○ 315
   - ○ 335
   - ○ 340
   - ○ 345

4. Which shows the numbers in order from greatest to least? (Lesson 2.11)

   - ○ 345, 140, 410
   - ○ 140, 410, 345
   - ○ 410, 140, 345
   - ○ 410, 345, 140

5. What is the difference?
   8 − 4 = _____ (Lesson 3.6)

   - ○ 1
   - ○ 3
   - ○ 4
   - ○ 12

Name _____

Act It Out • Patterns

**PROBLEM SOLVING
Lesson 8.2**

Act out the problem. Draw to show what you did.

1. Mr. Anderson has 4 plates of cookies. There are 5 cookies on each plate. How many cookies are there in all?

   _____ cookies

2. Ms. Trane put 2 stickers on each page. How many stickers did she put on 6 pages?

   _____ stickers

3. There are 10 books in each box. How many books are in 5 boxes?

   _____ books

Chapter 8

one hundred sixty-one **P161**

Lesson Check

1. Jaime puts 3 oranges on each tray. How many oranges are on 5 trays?
   - ○ 8
   - ○ 15
   - ○ 35
   - ○ 53

2. Maurice has 3 rows of toys with 6 toys in each row. How many toys does he have in all?
   - ○ 3
   - ○ 9
   - ○ 18
   - ○ 36

Spiral Review

3. A book has 256 pages. Margo read 132 pages. How many pages does she have left to read? (Lesson 7.7)
   - ○ 114
   - ○ 124
   - ○ 387
   - ○ 397

4. Pedro has 37 baseball cards. He has 45 basketball cards. How many cards does he have in all? (Lesson 4.2)
   - ○ 93
   - ○ 83
   - ○ 82
   - ○ 72

5. Which of these is an even number? (Lesson 1.6)
   - ○ 1
   - ○ 3
   - ○ 5
   - ○ 8

6. What is the sum? (Lesson 3.1)

   $7 + 9 = \underline{}$
   - ○ 16
   - ○ 17
   - ○ 18
   - ○ 19

Lesson 8.3

Name _____

Algebra: Extend Patterns

Complete each table to solve.

1. There are 5 computers in each row.

   How many computers are in 5 rows?

number of rows	1	2	3	4	5
number of computers	5				

   _____ computers

2. There are 10 pencils in each cup.

   How many pencils are in 5 cups?

number of cups	1	2			
number of pencils					

   _____ pencils

3. There are 3 books on each desk.

   How many books are on 6 desks?

number of desks	1					
number of books						

   _____ books

Lesson Check

1. There are 5 fish in each tank. How many fish are in 6 tanks?

number of tanks	1	2	3	4	5	6
number of fish	5	10				

   ○ 5
   ○ 15
   ○ 30
   ○ 50

Spiral Review

2. Which is another way to show the number 47? (Lesson 1.2)

   ○ 4 + 7
   ○ 4 + 70
   ○ 40 + 70
   ○ 40 + 7

3. Which is another way to show the number 42? (Lesson 1.4)

   ○ 3 tens 12 ones
   ○ 4 tens 12 ones
   ○ 5 tens 12 ones
   ○ 2 tens 12 ones

4. There are 4 boys playing baseball and 5 more boys join them. How many boys are playing baseball altogether? (Lesson 3.1)

   ○ 1
   ○ 6
   ○ 9
   ○ 10

5. Greg's book has 372 pages. Judy's book has 266 pages. How many more pages does Greg's book have than Judy's book? (Lesson 7.7)

   ○ 104
   ○ 106
   ○ 114
   ○ 116

P164   one hundred sixty-four

Name _____

Lesson 8.4

Connect Addition and Multiplication

Show the addition.
Then write the multiplication sentence.

1. 3 groups of 2

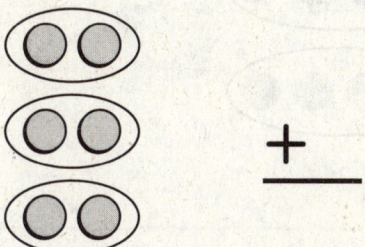 ____ + ____

_____

2. 2 groups of 5

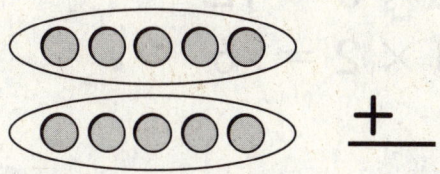 ____ + ____

_____

3. 2 groups of 6

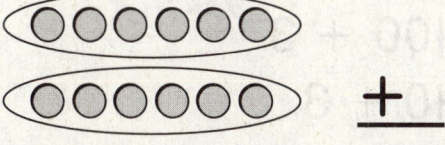 ____ + ____

_____

4. 3 groups of 3

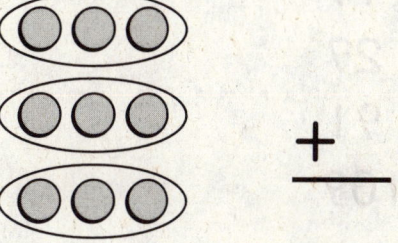 ____ + ____

_____

PROBLEM SOLVING · REAL WORLD

Solve. Draw or write to explain.

5. Sam has 5 pages in his album.
   He puts 4 stickers on each page.
   How many stickers does he use?

    stickers

Chapter 8   one hundred sixty-five **P165**

Lesson Check

1. Which multiplication sentence do these counters show?

   ○ 3 × 3 = 9
   ○ 3 × 4 = 12
   ○ 2 × 6 = 12
   ○ 3 × 2 = 6

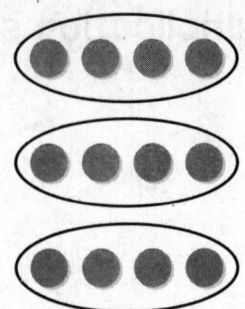

Spiral Review

2. Which is another way to write 10 + 9? (Lesson 1.3)

   ○ 19
   ○ 29
   ○ 91
   ○ 109

3. Which is another way to write the number 403? (Lesson 2.5)

   ○ 400 + 30
   ○ 400 + 3
   ○ 40 + 3
   ○ 40 + 30

4. Which number will make this sentence true? (Lesson 3.9)

   5 + 4 = 2 + ___

   ○ 3
   ○ 5
   ○ 7
   ○ 9

5. Which number is greater than 827? (Lesson 2.10)

   ○ 799
   ○ 819
   ○ 800
   ○ 912

Name _____

Model Multiplication

**HANDS ON
Lesson 8.5**

Make an array with ◯.
Then shade squares and write the multiplication sentence.

1. 2 rows of 3

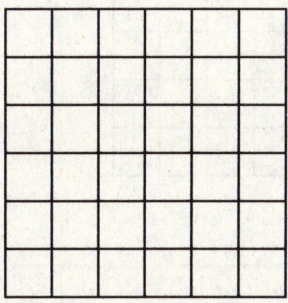

_____

2. 5 rows of 5

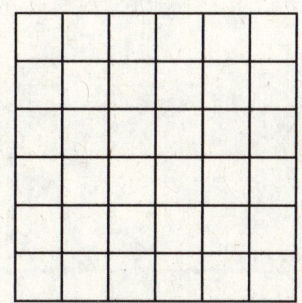

_____

3. 4 rows of 6

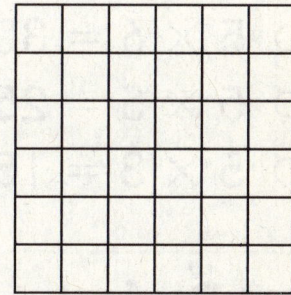

_____

4. 3 rows of 5

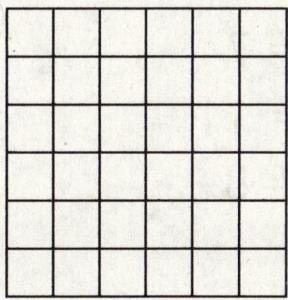

_____

5. 6 rows of 1

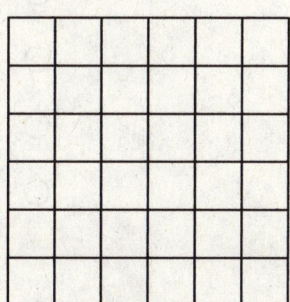

_____

6. 3 rows of 6

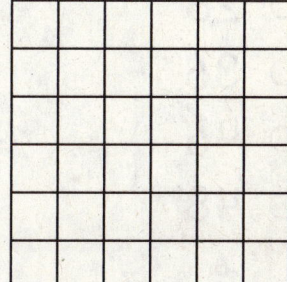

_____

PROBLEM SOLVING

Solve. Write or draw to explain.

7. The room has 5 rows of chairs.
There are 4 chairs in each row.
How many chairs are in the room?

_____ chairs

Chapter 8

one hundred sixty-seven **P167**

Lesson Check

1. Which multiplication sentence does this model show?

    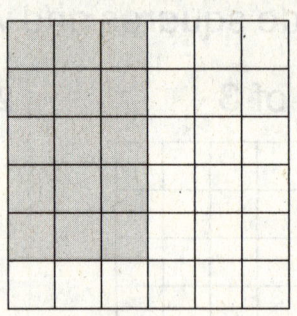

    ○ 3 × 3 = 9
    ○ 5 × 6 = 30
    ○ 5 × 5 = 25
    ○ 5 × 3 = 15

Spiral Review

2. What is the sum? (Lesson 4.1)

    37 + 9

    ○ 28
    ○ 36
    ○ 46
    ○ 48

3. Which number sentence is true? (Lesson 3.10)

    ○ 8 + 8 ≠ 17
    ○ 3 + 4 ≠ 7
    ○ 2 + 9 ≠ 11
    ○ 4 + 4 ≠ 8

4. How many books were read in Week 2? (Lesson 6.3)

    ○ 4
    ○ 5
    ○ 10
    ○ 14

Name _____

Lesson 8.6

Multiply with 2

Skip count by twos. Write the multiplication sentence.

1.

   _____

2.

   _____

3.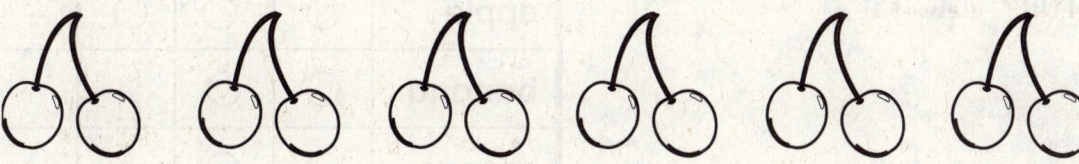

   _____

PROBLEM SOLVING REAL WORLD

Solve. Write or draw to explain.

4. There are 8 benches at the park.
   2 people are sitting on each bench.
   How many people are sitting on the benches in all?

   _____ people

Chapter 8   one hundred sixty-nine **P169**

Lesson Check

1. The pens are in groups of 2. Which multiplication sentence shows how many pens there are in all?

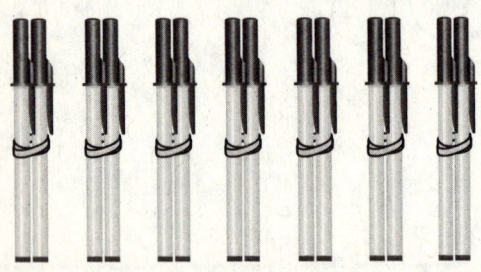

○ 7 × 7 = 49   ○ 7 × 2 = 14
○ 10 × 2 = 20   ○ 2 × 2 = 4

Spiral Review

2. Look at the graph. How many children chose apple as their favorite fruit? (Lesson 6.3)

   ○ 3
   ○ 4
   ○ 5
   ○ 6

Favorite Fruit			
apple	○	○	○
banana	○	○	
orange	○	○	

Key: Each ○ stands for 2 children.

3. What is the value of the underlined digit? (Lesson 2.4)

   31<u>7</u>

   ○ 7
   ○ 70
   ○ 300
   ○ 700

4. What is the next number in the pattern? (Lesson 2.8)

   451, 551, 651, 751, ____

   ○ 761
   ○ 851
   ○ 861
   ○ 862

Name _____

Lesson 8.7

Multiply with 5

Skip count by fives. Write the multiplication sentence.

1.

   _____

2.

   _____

3.

   _____

PROBLEM SOLVING REAL WORLD

Solve. Write or draw to explain.

4. Mara made 9 stacks of counters.
   She put 5 counters in each stack.
   How many counters in all did Mara put in stacks?

   _____ counters

Chapter 8   one hundred seventy-one   P171

Lesson Check

1. The bananas are in groups of 5. Which multiplication sentence shows how many bananas there are in all?

- ○ 7 × 7 = 49
- ○ 10 × 5 = 50
- ○ 7 × 5 = 35
- ○ 5 × 4 = 20

Spiral Review

2. What is the value of the underlined digit? (Lesson 2.4)

    4_1_9

    - ○ 1
    - ○ 10
    - ○ 100
    - ○ 1,000

3. What is another way to write 200 + 3? (Lesson 2.5)

    - ○ 203
    - ○ 230
    - ○ 320
    - ○ 500

4. Keesha read 34 pages on Monday and 25 pages on Tuesday. Which number sentence shows how many pages she read in all? (Lesson 4.12)

    - ○ 34 − 25 = 9
    - ○ 34 + 52 = 86
    - ○ 34 + 25 = 59
    - ○ 59 + 34 = 93

5. Justin has 347 stickers in his album. Ella has the same number in her album. How many stickers do they have in all? (Lesson 7.5)

    - ○ 469
    - ○ 584
    - ○ 684
    - ○ 694

Name _____

Chapter 8 Extra Practice

Lesson 8.1 (pp. 333 – 336)
Skip count. Show the pattern on the hundred chart.

1	2	3	4	5	6	7	8	9	10
11	12	13	14	15	16	17	18	19	20
21	22	23	24	25	26	27	28	29	30
31	32	33	34	35	36	37	38	39	40
41	42	43	44	45	46	47	48	49	50
51	52	53	54	55	56	57	58	59	60
61	62	63	64	65	66	67	68	69	70
71	72	73	74	75	76	77	78	79	80
81	82	83	84	85	86	87	88	89	90
91	92	93	94	95	96	97	98	99	100

1. Count by fours. Place an **X** on the numbers.

2. Count by fives. Circle the numbers.

Lesson 8.2 (pp. 337 – 340)
Solve. Write or draw to explain.

1. Michael has 4 rows of blocks. Each row has 6 blocks. How many blocks does he have in all?

   ____ blocks

2. There are 5 stacks of crackers. There are 7 crackers in each stack. How many crackers are there in all?

   ____ crackers

Chapter 8   one hundred seventy-three   **P173**

Lesson 8.3 (pp. 341–343)

Complete the table to solve.

1. There are 4 pennies in each pocket.
   How many pennies are in 6 pockets?

number of pockets	1	2	3	4	5	6
number of pennies	4					

   There are _____ pennies in 6 pockets.

Lesson 8.4 (pp. 345–348)

Show the addition.
Then write the multiplication sentence.

1. 2 groups of 5

2. 4 groups of 3

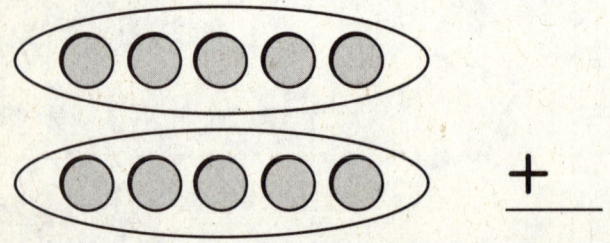

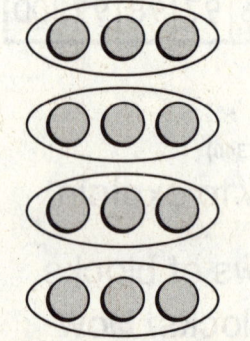

Lesson 8.6 – 8.7 (pp. 353–360)

Skip count. Write a multiplication sentence to show how many flowers in all.

1. _____

2. _____

P174 one hundred seventy-four

Chapter 9

School-Home Letter

Dear Family,

My class started Chapter 9 this week. In this chapter, I will learn how to measure using string and rulers. I will also learn about inches, feet, yards, centimeters, and meters.

Love, _____

Vocabulary

inch Unit of length

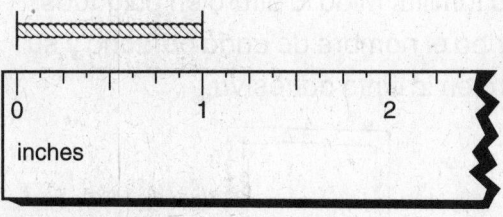

foot 12 inches

yard 3 feet

Home Activity

Record each family member's height with masking tape in a doorway of your house. Measure the height in inches. Write each person's name and height on the tape.

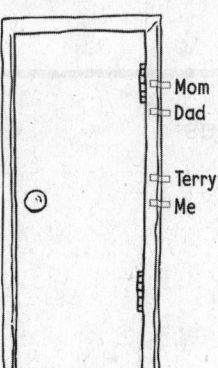

Literature

Reading math stories reinforces ideas. Look for these books at the library.

Measuring Penny by Loreen Leedy. Henry Holt and Company, 1998.

Length by Henry Arthur Pluckrose. Children's Press, 1995.

Capítulo 9
Carta para la casa

Querida familia:

Mi clase comenzó esta semana el Capítulo 9. En este capítulo, aprenderé a medir usando reglas y cuerdas. También aprenderé acerca de pulgadas, pies, yardas, centímetros y metros.

Con cariño, _____

Vocabulario

pulgada unidad de longitud

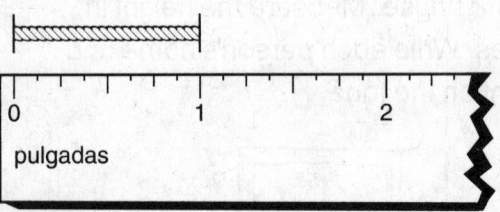

pie 12 pulgadas

yarda 3 pies

Actividad para la casa

En el marco de una puerta, marque con cinta adhesiva la altura de cada miembro de la familia. Mida la altura en pulgadas. Escriba el nombre de cada persona y su altura en la cinta adhesiva.

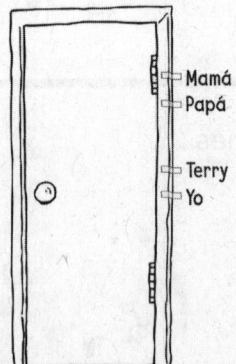

Literatura

Leer cuentos de matemáticas refuerza los conceptos. Busquen estos libros en la biblioteca.

Measuring Penny por Loreen Leedy. Henry Holt and Company, 1998.

Length por Henry Arthur Pluckrose. Children's Press, 1995.

Name _____

Indirect Measurement

**HANDS ON
Lesson 9.1**

Find the real objects. Use string and scissors.
Circle the picture that answers the question.

1. Which is longer?

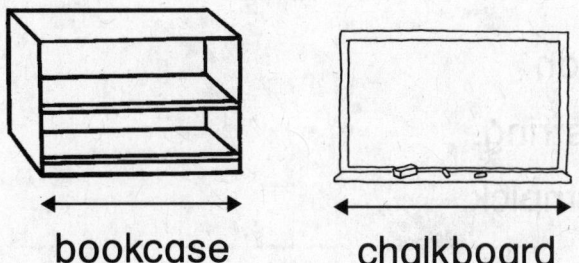

bookcase   chalkboard

2. Which is shorter?

bulletin board   your desk

3. Which is wider?

door   poster

4. Which is longer?

chalkboard   teacher's desk

PROBLEM SOLVING  REAL WORLD

5. Think of an object that is shorter than your pencil. Draw a picture of the object and label it.

Chapter 9   one hundred seventy-seven **P177**

Lesson Check

1. Compare the lengths of the ribbon, the toothpick, and the string. Which statement is true?
    - ○ The toothpick is longer than the ribbon.
    - ○ The string is shorter than the ribbon.
    - ○ The toothpick is shorter than the string.
    - ○ The ribbon is shorter than the toothpick.

Spiral Review

2. What is the sum? (Lesson 4.7)

    $$\begin{array}{r} 68 \\ + 26 \\ \hline \end{array}$$

    - ○ 42
    - ○ 84
    - ○ 94
    - ○ 96

3. One box has 157 books. The other box has 206 books. How many books are there in both boxes altogether? (Lesson 7.5)
    - ○ 363
    - ○ 361
    - ○ 353
    - ○ 349

4. What is the difference? (Lesson 7.8)

    $$\begin{array}{r} 458 \\ - 231 \\ \hline \end{array}$$

    - ○ 689
    - ○ 287
    - ○ 237
    - ○ 227

5. There are 5 markers in each pack. How many markers in all are in 4 packs? (Lesson 8.7)
    - ○ 9
    - ○ 15
    - ○ 20
    - ○ 25

Name _____

Lesson 9.2

Compare Lengths

Write shorter than or longer than.

1. Mike's skateboard is longer than Kevin's skateboard. Kevin's skateboard is longer than Norm's skateboard.

   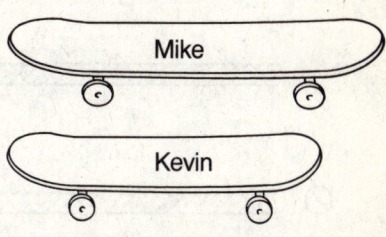

   Mike's skateboard is _____ Norm's skateboard.

2. Maria's ribbon is shorter than Amy's ribbon. Amy's ribbon is shorter than Nicole's ribbon.

   Maria's ribbon is _____ Nicole's ribbon.

3. Lady's leash is longer than Bingo's leash. Bingo's leash is longer than Muffin's leash.

   Lady's leash is _____ Muffin's leash.

PROBLEM SOLVING REAL WORLD

4. Trace the length of your pencil with a crayon. Draw a pencil that is longer than your pencil. Then draw a pencil that is shorter than your pencil.

Chapter 9 one hundred seventy-nine **P179**

Lesson Check

1. Which string is shorter than this string?

   - ○ (string)
   - ○ (string)
   - ○ (string)
   - ○ (string)

Spiral Review

2. Sal has 7 markers. His sister has 10 more markers than Sal. How many markers does Sal's sister have? (Lesson 3.2)
   - ○ 7
   - ○ 10
   - ○ 17
   - ○ 27

3. What is the sum? (Lesson 4.11)

   $$\begin{array}{r} 12 \\ 23 \\ +\ 18 \\ \hline \end{array}$$

   - ○ 153
   - ○ 53
   - ○ 43
   - ○ 41

4. What is the difference? (Lesson 5.6)

   $$\begin{array}{r} 54 \\ -\ 28 \\ \hline \end{array}$$

   - ○ 82
   - ○ 45
   - ○ 36
   - ○ 26

5. There are 319 students in King Street School. If 128 students are girls, how many are boys? (Lesson 7.8)
   - ○ 191
   - ○ 201
   - ○ 291
   - ○ 447

Name _____

Measure with Inch Models

**HANDS ON
Lesson 9.3**

Use color tiles. Measure the length of the object in inches.

1.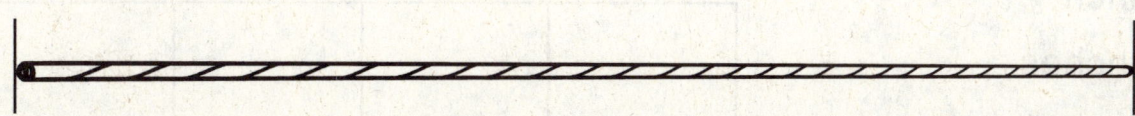

   _____ inches

2.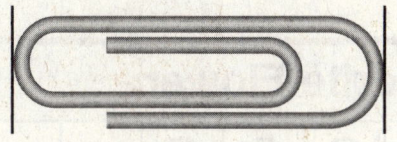

   _____ inches

3.

   _____ inches

4.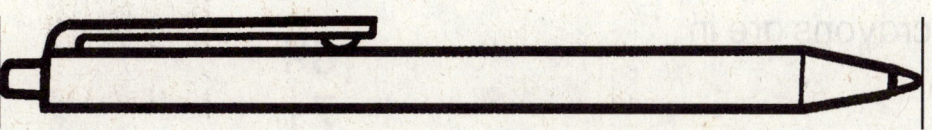

   _____ inches

PROBLEM SOLVING

5. Look around your classroom.
   Find an object that is about 4 inches long.
   Draw and label the object.

Chapter 9   one hundred eighty-one   P181

Lesson Check

1. Jessie used color tiles to measure the rope. How long is the rope?

   ○ 1 inch
   ○ 2 inches
   ○ 3 inches
   ○ 4 inches

Spiral Review

2. Look at the pictograph. How many children chose daisies? (Lesson 6.3)

   ○ 10
   ○ 5
   ○ 4
   ○ 3

   Favorite Flower

Roses	☺	☺	☺	☺		
Tulips	☺	☺	☺			
Daisies	☺	☺	☺	☺	☺	

   Key: Each ☺ stands for 2 children.

3. There are 10 crayons in each box. How many crayons are in 3 boxes? (Lesson 8.3)

Boxes	1	2	3
Crayons	10		

   ○ 13
   ○ 15
   ○ 20
   ○ 30

4. What is the sum? (Lesson 4.7)

   $$\begin{array}{r} 84 \\ + 71 \\ \hline \end{array}$$

   ○ 165
   ○ 155
   ○ 53
   ○ 13

Name _____

Make and Use a Ruler

**HANDS ON
Lesson 9.4**

Measure the length with your ruler.
Count how many inches.

1.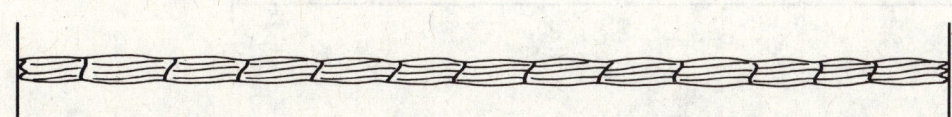

   _____ inches

2.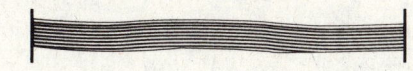

   _____ inches

3.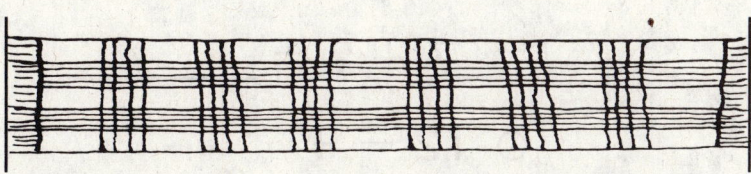

   _____ inches

4.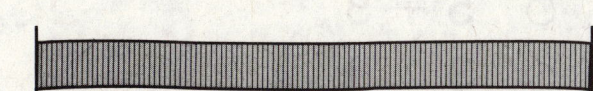

   _____ inches

PROBLEM SOLVING

5. Use your ruler. Measure the width of this page in inches.

   _____ inches

Lesson Check

1. Use your ruler. What is the length of this ribbon?

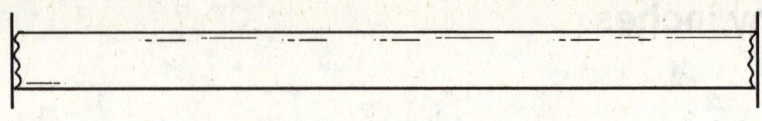

- ○ 2 inches
- ○ 3 inches
- ○ 4 inches
- ○ 5 inches

Spiral Review

2. Which is an even number? (Lesson 1.6)
   - ○ 11
   - ○ 28
   - ○ 33
   - ○ 45

3. Which makes the number sentence true? (Lesson 3.10)

   $7 + 2 = $ _____
   - ○ 12 − 4
   - ○ 11 − 2
   - ○ 5 + 3
   - ○ 3 + 4

4. The first group collected 238 cans. The second group collected 345 cans. How many cans did the groups collect in all? (Lesson 7.4)
   - ○ 107
   - ○ 573
   - ○ 583
   - ○ 585

5. There are 2 children in each row. How many children are in 6 rows? (Lesson 8.6)
   - ○ 4
   - ○ 8
   - ○ 10
   - ○ 12

Name _____

Lesson 9.5

Estimate Lengths

The bead is 1 inch long.
Circle the best estimate for the length
of the string.

1.

          1 inch   4 inches   7 inches

2.

          3 inches   6 inches   9 inches

3.

          2 inches   3 inches   6 inches

4.

          2 inches   5 inches   8 inches

PROBLEM SOLVING

Solve. Write or draw to explain.

5. Ashley has some beads. Each bead is 2 inches long. How many beads will fit on a string that is 8 inches long?

                     _____ beads

Lesson Check

1. The bead is 1 inch long. Which is the best estimate of the length of the string?

- ○ 1 inch
- ○ 3 inches
- ○ 5 inches
- ○ 7 inches

Spiral Review

2. What is the value of the underlined digit? (Lesson 2.4)

   9<u>8</u>2

   - ○ 8
   - ○ 80
   - ○ 82
   - ○ 800

3. What is the sum? (Lesson 4.2)

   38 + 24 = ___

   - ○ 54
   - ○ 60
   - ○ 62
   - ○ 66

4. Ella read 16 pages of her book on Monday and 26 pages on Tuesday. There are 64 pages in the book. How many more pages are left for Ella to read? (Lesson 5.10)

   - ○ 106
   - ○ 32
   - ○ 34
   - ○ 22

5. Which multiplication sentence describes this model? (Lesson 8.5)

   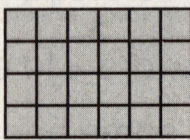

   - ○ 6 × 6 = 36
   - ○ 4 × 6 = 24
   - ○ 4 × 4 = 16
   - ○ 4 × 3 = 12

Name _____

Measure with an Inch Ruler

**HANDS ON
Lesson 9.6**

Measure the length to the nearest inch.

1.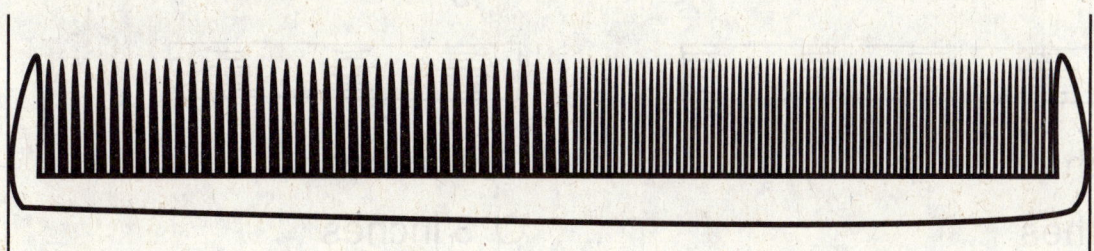

_____ inches

2.

_____ inches

3.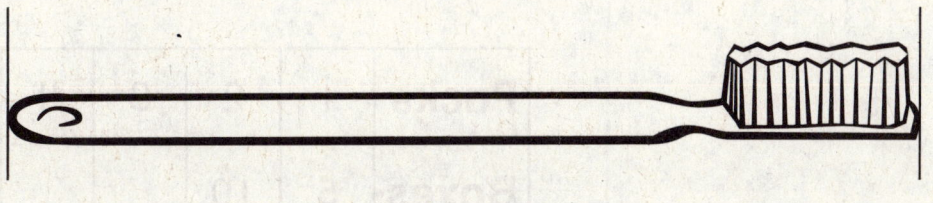

_____ inches

4.

_____ inches

PROBLEM SOLVING REAL WORLD

5. Measure the string. What is its total length?

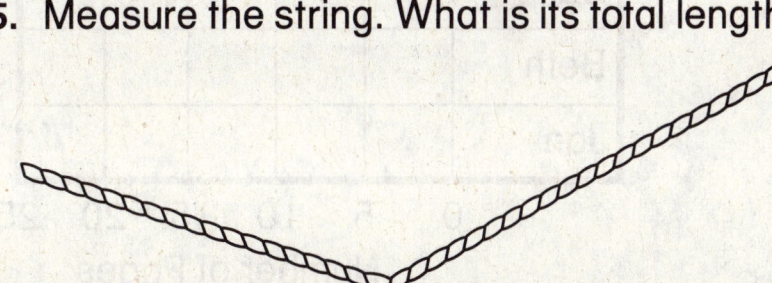

_____ inches

Chapter 9

Lesson Check

1. Use an inch ruler. What is the length to the nearest inch?

   ○ 1 inch
   ○ 2 inches
   ○ 3 inches
   ○ 4 inches

2. Use an inch ruler. What is the length to the nearest inch?

   ○ 2 inches
   ○ 3 inches
   ○ 4 inches
   ○ 5 inches

Spiral Review

3. Which is another way to write 74? (Lesson 1.2)

   ○ 7 + 4
   ○ 40 + 7
   ○ 70 + 4
   ○ 70 + 40

4. There are 5 juice boxes in each pack. How many boxes are in 4 packs? (Lesson 8.3)

Packs	1	2	3	4
Boxes	5	10		

   ○ 5   ○ 20
   ○ 15   ○ 40

5. Use the bar graph. How many pages did Beth color? (Lesson 6.5)

   ○ 5
   ○ 15
   ○ 10
   ○ 20

   Pages Colored

Name _____

Lesson 9.7

Estimate and Measure Length

Estimate the length of each object in inches. Use the 1-inch mark as a guide. Then measure the length to the nearest inch.

1. |— 1 inch —|

                           estimated length: _____ inches

                           actual length: _____ inches

2. |— 1 inch —|

                           estimated length: _____ inches

                           actual length: _____ inches

3. |— 1 inch —|

                           estimated length: _____ inches

                           actual length: _____ inches

PROBLEM SOLVING · REAL WORLD

4. Draw a 4-inch crayon using the 1-inch mark as a guide.

Chapter 9

Lesson Check

1. Which is the best estimate for the length of the toothbrush?

   ○ 1 inch
   ○ 2 inches
   ○ 5 inches
   ○ 10 inches

Spiral Review

2. Which makes the number sentence true? (Lesson 3.6)

   ___ = 12 − 8

   ○ 4
   ○ 5
   ○ 8
   ○ 20

3. What is the difference? (Lesson 5.5)

   35
   -19

   ○ 6
   ○ 16
   ○ 26
   ○ 54

4. Russell has 235 stickers. 128 of the stickers are cars. The other stickers are trucks. How many stickers are trucks? (Lesson 7.8)

   ○ 363
   ○ 353
   ○ 117
   ○ 107

5. Which multiplication sentence could be used to find the total for 3 groups of 5? (Lesson 8.4)

   5
   5
   $+5$

   ○ 4 × 4 = 16
   ○ 3 × 3 = 9
   ○ 3 × 5 = 15
   ○ 4 × 3 = 12

Name _____

Measure in Inches and Feet

**HANDS ON
Lesson 9.8**

**Measure to the nearest inch.
Then measure to the nearest foot.**

Find the real object.	Measure.
1. bookcase	_____ inches _____ feet
2. window	_____ inches _____ feet
3. chair	_____ inches _____ feet

PROBLEM SOLVING REAL WORLD

4. Jake has a piece of yarn that is 4 feet long.
   Blair has a piece of yarn that is 4 inches long.
   Who has the longer piece of yarn? Explain.

_____

Chapter 9   one hundred ninety-one **P191**

Lesson Check

1. Larry is telling his sister about using a ruler to measure length. Which sentence is true?
   - ○ 1 foot is shorter than 1 inch.
   - ○ 1 foot is longer than 1 inch.
   - ○ 1 inch is longer than 1 foot.
   - ○ 1 foot is the same length as 1 inch.

Spiral Review

2. Each child has 2 notebooks. How many notebooks do 8 children have? (Lesson 8.6)
   - ○ 6
   - ○ 10
   - ○ 14
   - ○ 16

3. What is the sum? (Lesson 7.2)

   548
   + 436

   - ○ 112
   - ○ 912
   - ○ 974
   - ○ 984

4. Which multiplication sentence describes this model? (Lesson 8.5)

   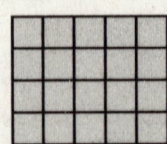

   - ○ 4 × 7 = 28
   - ○ 4 × 5 = 20
   - ○ 4 × 6 = 24
   - ○ 5 × 5 = 25

5. Ali had 38 game cards. His friend gave him 15 more game cards. How many game cards does Ali have now? (Lesson 4.7)
   - ○ 53
   - ○ 48
   - ○ 43
   - ○ 23

Name _____

**HANDS ON
Lesson 9.9**

Measure in Feet and Yards

**Measure to the nearest foot.
Then measure to the nearest yard.**

Find the real object.	Measure.
1. bookcase	_____ feet _____ yards
2. chalkboard	_____ feet _____ yards
3. table	_____ feet _____ yards

PROBLEM SOLVING

4. Shasha wants to measure the length of the bulletin board. Will there be more feet or more yards in the length? Explain how you know.

_____

_____

Chapter 9   one hundred ninety-three **P193**

Lesson Check

1. Mr. Nelson measured a classroom wall in yards. Then he measured the wall in feet. Which statement about the measurements is true?

   ○ The number of yards and the number of feet are the same.
   ○ The number of yards is more than the number of feet.
   ○ The number of feet is fewer than the number of yards.
   ○ The number of yards is fewer than the number of feet.

Spiral Review

2. Which shows the number 402 another way? (Lesson 2.5)

   ○ 40 + 2
   ○ 40 + 20
   ○ 400 + 2
   ○ 4,002

3. What is the sum? (Lesson 4.1)

   $65 + 9 =$ _____

   ○ 56
   ○ 74
   ○ 79
   ○ 84

4. There are 24 flowers in the vase. 18 of the flowers are yellow. How many flowers are not yellow? (Lesson 5.5)

   ○ 6
   ○ 14
   ○ 16
   ○ 42

5. Becky has 236 bird stickers and 173 fish stickers. How many stickers does Becky have in all? (Lesson 7.4)

   ○ 63
   ○ 309
   ○ 409
   ○ 419

Name _____

Measure with a Centimeter Model

**HANDS ON
Lesson 9.10**

Use a unit cube. Measure the length in centimeters.

1.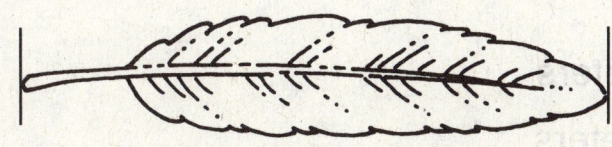

   _____ centimeters

2.

   _____ centimeters

3.

   _____ centimeters

4.

   _____ centimeters

PROBLEM SOLVING REAL WORLD

5. Susan has a pencil that is 3 centimeters shorter than this string. How long is the pencil?

   _____ centimeters

Chapter 9 — one hundred ninety-five P195

Lesson Check

1. Sarah used unit cubes to measure the ribbon. How long is the ribbon?

   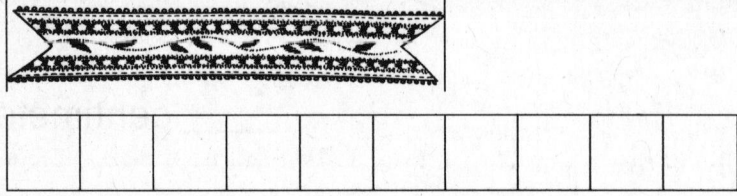

   ○ 1 centimeter   ○ 6 centimeters
   ○ 4 centimeters ○ 10 centimeters

Spiral Review

2. Use the tally chart. How many more children chose art than reading? (Lesson 6.1)

   ○ 10
   ○ 8
   ○ 3
   ○ 2

Favorite Subject	
Reading	||||| |||
Math	||||| ||||
Science	|||||
Art	||||| |||||

3. What is the sum? (Lesson 7.3)

   $$568 + 213$$

   ○ 781
   ○ 771
   ○ 355
   ○ 345

4. Five people can sit in 1 car. How many people can sit in 3 cars? (Lesson 8.7)

   ○ 8
   ○ 9
   ○ 15
   ○ 20

Name _____

Measure with a Centimeter Ruler

HANDS ON
Lesson 9.11

Measure the length to the nearest centimeter.

1.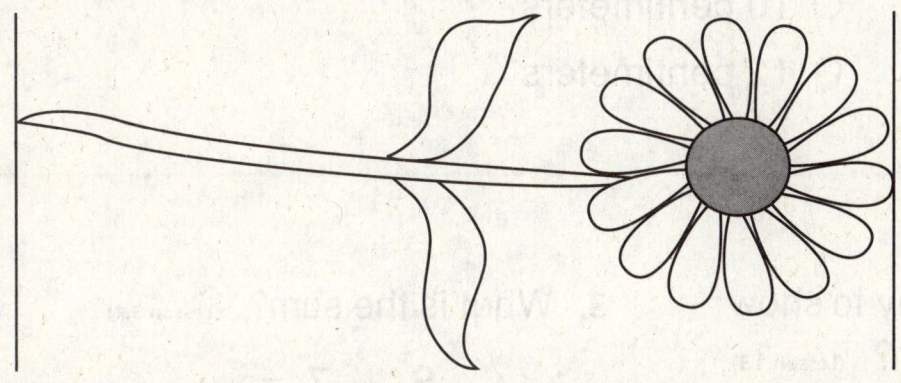

   _____ centimeters

2.

   _____ centimeters

3.

   _____ centimeters

PROBLEM SOLVING

4. Draw a string that is about 8 centimeters long. Then use a centimeter ruler to check the length.

Chapter 9   one hundred ninety-seven   P197

Lesson Check

1. Use a centimeter ruler. What is the length of the pencil to the nearest centimeter?

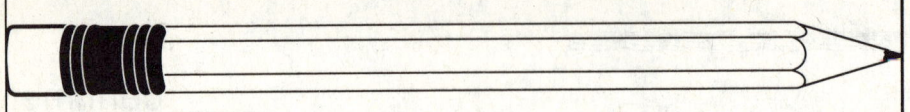

- ○ 5 centimeters
- ○ 6 centimeters
- ○ 10 centimeters
- ○ 12 centimeters

Spiral Review

2. Which is another way to show the number nineteen? (Lesson 1.3)

   - ○ 10 + 9
   - ○ 90 + 1
   - ○ 90
   - ○ 91

3. What is the sum? (Lesson 3.1)

   8 + 7 = ___

   - ○ 17
   - ○ 16
   - ○ 15
   - ○ 13

4. There are 308 birds roosting and 275 birds flying. How many birds are there in all? (Lesson 7.5)

   - ○ 683
   - ○ 583
   - ○ 573
   - ○ 533

5. There are 3 wheels on a tricycle. How many wheels are on 4 tricycles? (Lesson 8.3)

Tricycles	1	2	3	4
Wheels	3	6		

   - ○ 7
   - ○ 9
   - ○ 10
   - ○ 12

Name _____

Make Reasonable Estimates

Lesson 9.12

Estimate.

1. The toothpick is about 6 centimeters long. Circle the best estimate for the length of the straw.

   6 centimeters

   9 centimeters

   12 centimeters

2. The pen is about 11 centimeters long. Circle the best estimate for the length of the eraser.

   4 centimeters

   10 centimeters

   14 centimeters

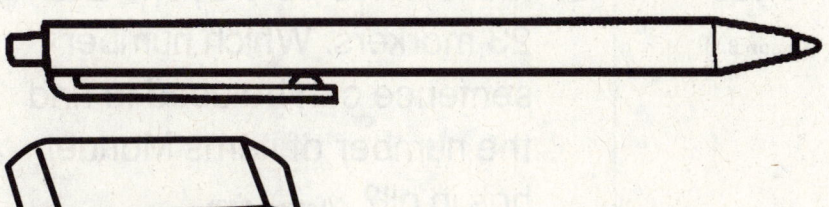

3. The string is about 6 centimeters long. Circle the best estimate for the length of the crayon.

   7 centimeters

   9 centimeters

   14 centimeters

PROBLEM SOLVING · REAL WORLD

4. The string is 6 centimeters long. Draw a pencil that is about 12 centimeters long.

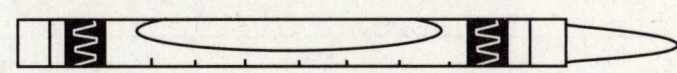

Chapter 9 one hundred ninety-nine **P199**

Lesson Check

1. The length of the pencil is about 12 centimeters. Which is the best estimate for the length of the yarn?

- ○ 5 centimeters
- ○ 10 centimeters
- ○ 12 centimeters
- ○ 24 centimeters

Spiral Review

2. Which multiplication sentence describes this model? (Lesson 8.5)

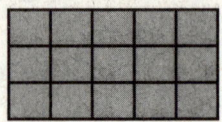

- ○ 5 × 5 = 25
- ○ 3 × 6 = 18
- ○ 3 × 5 = 15
- ○ 3 × 3 = 9

3. Manuel has 18 crayons and 23 markers. Which number sentence can be used to find the number of items Manuel has in all? (Lesson 4.12)

- ○ 23 − 18 = 5
- ○ 23 + 18 = 41
- ○ 13 − 8 = 5
- ○ 32 − 18 = 14

4. What is the difference? (Lesson 5.6)

$$62 - 34$$

- ○ 96
- ○ 38
- ○ 32
- ○ 28

5. What is the next number in this pattern? (Lesson 2.8)

48, 58, 68, 78, ☐

- ○ 79
- ○ 80
- ○ 87
- ○ 88

Name _____

**HANDS ON
Lesson 9.13**

Centimeters and Meters

Measure to the nearest centimeter.
Then measure to the nearest meter.

Find the real object.	Measure.
1. bookcase	_____ centimeters _____ meters
2. window	_____ centimeters _____ meters
3. map	_____ centimeters _____ meters

PROBLEM SOLVING

4. Maxine will measure the length of a wall in centimeters and meters. Will there be fewer centimeters or fewer meters? Explain.

_____

_____

Chapter 9   two hundred one **P201**

Lesson Check

1. Use a centimeter ruler. Which is the best choice for the length of the toothbrush?

   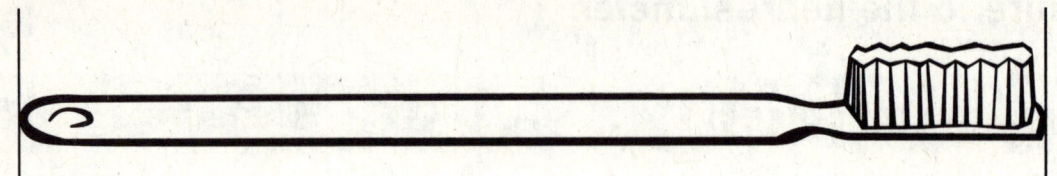

   - ○ 4 centimeters
   - ○ 14 centimeters
   - ○ 20 centimeters
   - ○ 25 centimeters

Spiral Review

2. How many more books did Tyrone read than Mara? (Lesson 6.3)

   - ○ 3
   - ○ 6
   - ○ 8
   - ○ 12

   Books Read

Steve	■	■				
Mara	■	■	■			
Tyrone	■	■	■	■	■	■

   Key: Each ■ stands for 2 books.

3. Which is another way to show the number 57? (Lesson 1.4)

   - ○ 7 tens 5 ones
   - ○ 5 ones 7 tens
   - ○ 7 tens 12 ones
   - ○ 5 tens 7 ones

4. Mrs. Ruiz gives 2 carrots to each child. How many carrots does she give to 4 children? (Lesson 8.6)

   - ○ 8
   - ○ 6
   - ○ 4
   - ○ 2

Name _____

Act It Out • Length

PROBLEM SOLVING
Lesson 9.14

Choose the best tool for measuring.

centimeter ruler   string

yardstick   inch ruler

1. Christy plays hockey. Which tool should be used to measure the length of the gym floor?

   _____

2. Which tool should Gina use to measure the distance across the top of the hockey puck?

   _____

3. Which tools should Chris use to measure the distance around the edge of the hockey puck?

   _____

4. Which tool should Shane use to measure the width of the hockey goal?

   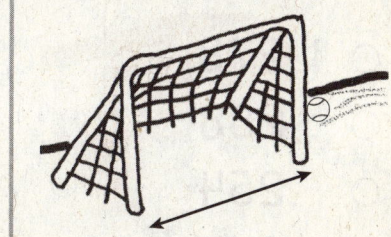

   _____

Chapter 9   two hundred three **P203**

Lesson Check

1. Carl wants to measure the length of his thumb. Which is the best tool to use?
   - ○ meterstick
   - ○ yardstick
   - ○ centimeter ruler
   - ○ string

2. Gina wants to measure the length of a wall in the gym. Which is the best tool to use?
   - ○ yardstick
   - ○ centimeter ruler
   - ○ color tile
   - ○ inch ruler

Spiral Review

3. During the game, Donnie scored 14 points and Jim scored 8 points. How many more points did Donnie score than Jim? (Lesson 3.4)
   - ○ 4
   - ○ 6
   - ○ 8
   - ○ 22

4. Tom has 24 red marbles and 28 blue marbles. Hector has 12 fewer marbles than Tom. How many marbles does Hector have? (Lesson 5.10)
   - ○ 12
   - ○ 36
   - ○ 40
   - ○ 52

5. What is the difference? (Lesson 7.8)

   $$\begin{array}{r} 766 \\ -512 \\ \hline \end{array}$$

   - ○ 1,278
   - ○ 258
   - ○ 254
   - ○ 244

6. Each album page has 5 photos on it. How many photos are on 6 album pages? (Lesson 8.7)
   - ○ 11
   - ○ 20
   - ○ 25
   - ○ 30

Name _____

Lesson 9.14A Dig Deeper

Graph Measurements

Essential Question How can you graph data on a dot plot?

Activity • A **dot plot** shows data on a number line.

Some children measured their hand spans to the nearest centimeter.

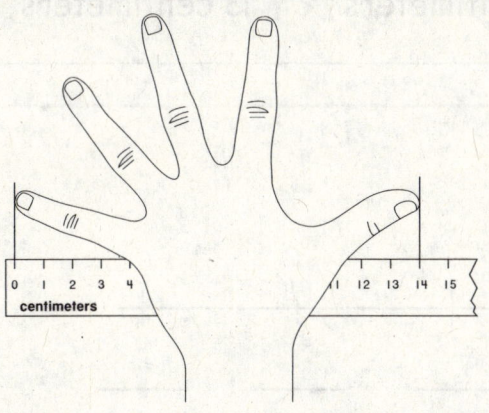

They recorded the data.

Lengths of Hand Spans in Centimeters

16 centimeters	16 centimeters
15 centimeters	17 centimeters
14 centimeters	17 centimeters
13 centimeters	15 centimeters
16 centimeters	18 centimeters
15 centimeters	16 centimeters

Then they made a dot plot to show the data.

4 children have hand spans that are 16 centimeters.

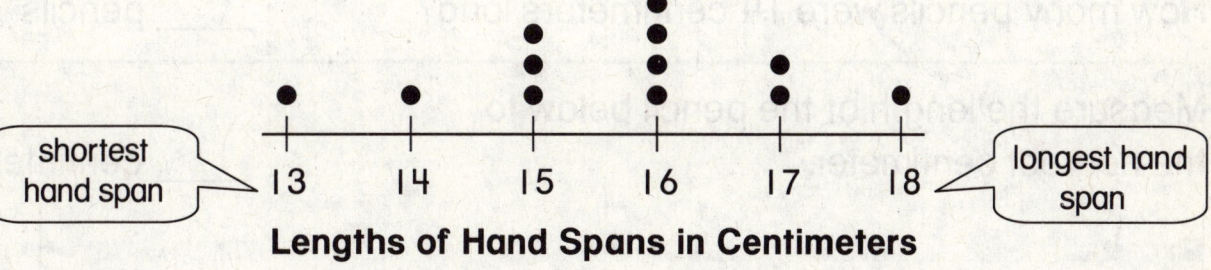

shortest hand span — longest hand span

Lengths of Hand Spans in Centimeters

Practice

1. Which length has the most dots? _____ centimeters

2. What is your hand span to the nearest centimeter? _____ centimeters

3. Put a • in the dot plot for your hand span.

Chapter 9 — two hundred four **P204a**

Eric measured the lengths of some pencils. He recorded the data in a list.

Lengths of Pencils in Centimeters	
14 centimeters	15 centimeters
17 centimeters	18 centimeters
17 centimeters	13 centimeters
15 centimeters	17 centimeters
14 centimeters	17 centimeters
16 centimeters	15 centimeters
12 centimeters	13 centimeters

4. Complete the dot plot.
   - Write the title under the dot plot.
   - Write the numbers.
   - Draw the dots.

5. How long was the longest pencil? _____ centimeters

6. How many pencils were 14 centimeters long? _____ pencils

7. Measure the length of the pencil below to the nearest centimeter. _____ centimeters

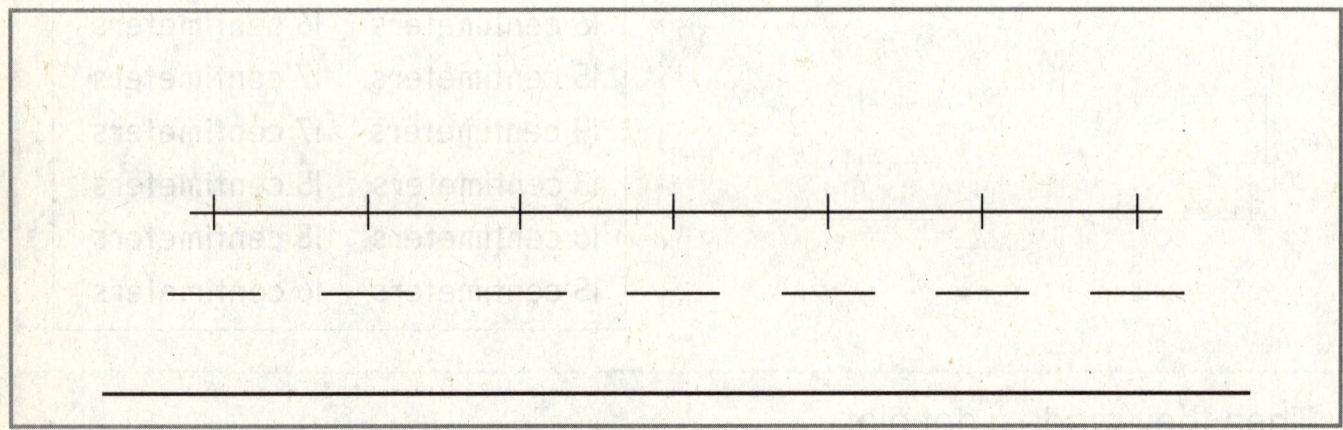

8. Put a ● in the dot plot for this pencil.

Math Talk
Explain how you knew what numbers to write on the number line.

P204b two hundred four

Name _____

Chapter 9 Extra Practice

Lesson 9.2 (pp. 381–384)
Write **shorter than** or **longer than**.

1. Mike

   Tom

   Mike's board is longer than Tom's board.
   Tom's board is longer than Jim's board.

   Mike's board is _____ Jim's board.

Lesson 9.3 (pp. 385–388)
Use color tiles. Measure the length of the object in inches.

1.

   ____ inches

Lesson 9.5 (pp. 393–396)
The bead is 1 inch long. Circle the best estimate for the length of the string.

1.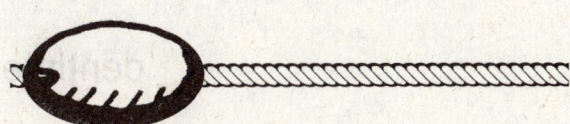

   3 inches   5 inches   7 inches

Lesson 9.6 (pp. 397–400)
Measure the length to the nearest inch.

1.

   ____ inches

Chapter 9 — two hundred five P205

Lesson 9.8 (pp. 405–408)

Measure to the nearest inch.
Then measure to the nearest foot.

Find the real object.	Measure.
1. chair 	_____ inches _____ feet

Lesson 9.11 (pp. 417–420)

Measure the length to the nearest centimeter.

1.

_____ centimeters

2.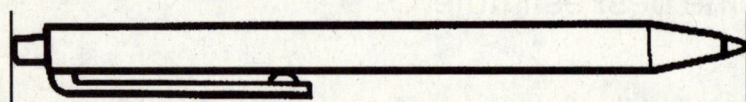

_____ centimeters

Lesson 9.12 (pp. 421–424)

1. The leaf is about 6 centimeters long. Circle the best estimate for the length of the string.

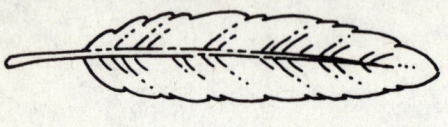
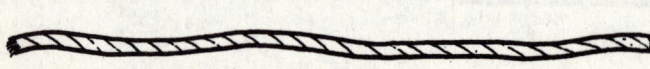

6 centimeters

9 centimeters

12 centimeters

P206 two hundred six

Chapter 10
School-Home Letter

Dear Family,

My class started Chapter 10 this week. In this chapter, I will learn about customary and metric units, and how to measure weight, mass, and capacity.

Love, _____

Vocabulary

capacity The amount a container can hold; cup, quart, milliliter, and liter are units of capacity.

mass How much matter an object has; gram and kilogram are units of mass.

weight How heavy an object is; ounce and pound are units of weight.

Home Activity

Show your child a food item that weighs 1 pound. Let your child hold the object to get an idea of how that amount of weight feels. Then have your child choose 3 or 4 more food items and estimate each weight as more than 1 pound or less than 1 pound. Use the weights on the packages to check your child's estimates.

Literature

Reading math stories reinforces learning. Look for these books at the library.

Everybody Cooks Rice by Norah Dooley. Lerner Publications, 1991.

Measuring Penny by Loreen Leedy. Henry Holt, 1997.

Capítulo 10
Carta para la casa

Querida familia:
Mi clase comenzó hoy el Capítulo 10. En este capítulo, aprenderé acerca de las unidades del sistema usual de medición y del sistema métrico. También aprenderé a medir peso, masa y capacidad.

Con cariño, _____

Vocabulario

capacidad la cantidad que contiene un recipiente; taza, cuarto, mililitro y litro son unidades de capacidad

masa la cantidad de materia que tiene un objeto; gramo y kilogramo son unidades de masa

peso lo pesado o ligero que es un objeto; onza y libra son unidades de peso

Actividad para la casa

Muéstrele a su hijo un artículo de comida que pese 1 libra. Pídale que lo sostenga con sus manos para que tenga una idea del peso. Luego, pídale que elija 3 o 4 objetos más y que estime el peso de cada uno como "más de 1 libra" o "menos de 1 libra". Compruebe las estimaciones de su hijo con el peso real que aparece en los artículos.

Literatura

Leer cuentos de matemáticas refuerza el aprendizaje. Busquen estos libros en la biblioteca.

Everybody Cooks Rice
por Norah Dooley.
Lerner Publications, 1991.

Measuring Penny
por Loreen Leedy.
Henry Holt, 1997.

Name _____

Lesson 10.1

Ounces and Pounds

Find the object.	Choose the unit.	Measure.
1. marker	ounce pound	about _____
2. shoe	ounce pound	about _____
3. crayon box	ounce pound	about _____
4. glue stick	ounce pound	about _____

PROBLEM SOLVING  REAL WORLD

Solve. Write or draw to explain.

5. Morgan has 3 books. Each book weighs 4 pounds. How many pounds do the books weigh altogether?

_____ pounds

Chapter 10 — two hundred nine P209

Lesson Check

1. Ben wants to weigh a shell. Which unit of measure should he use?

   ○ ounce
   ○ meter
   ○ inch
   ○ yard

2. Sara wants to weigh a watermelon. Which unit of measure should she use?

   ○ centimeter
   ○ foot
   ○ meter
   ○ pound

Spiral Review

3. There are 324 green beads and 435 blue beads. How many beads are there in all? (Lesson 7.5)

   ○ 758
   ○ 759
   ○ 769
   ○ 859

4. Which is another way to write 2 hundreds 3 tens 9 ones? (Lesson 2.5)

   ○ 200 + 3 + 9
   ○ 200 + 90 + 3
   ○ 200 + 30 + 9
   ○ 20 + 30 + 9

5. What is the sum? (Lesson 4.6)

   $$\begin{array}{r} 64 \\ + 17 \\ \hline \end{array}$$

   ○ 47   ○ 72
   ○ 71   ○ 81

6. Which number completes the number sentence? (Lesson 3.9)

   5 + 7 = ___ + 8

   ○ 20   ○ 4
   ○ 12   ○ 3

Name _____

Grams and Kilograms

Lesson 10.2

Find the object.	Choose the unit.	Measure.
1. ruler	gram kilogram	about _____
2. pencil case	gram kilogram	about _____
3. backpack	gram kilogram	about _____
4. eraser	gram kilogram	about _____

PROBLEM SOLVING

Solve. Write or draw to explain.

5. The book has a mass of 2 kilograms. What is the mass of 3 of these books?

_____ kilograms

Chapter 10   two hundred eleven   P211

Lesson Check

1. Which is most likely the mass of a brick?
   - ○ 2 grams
   - ○ 20 grams
   - ○ 2 kilograms
   - ○ 20 kilograms

2. Which is most likely the mass of a marker?
   - ○ 30 kilograms
   - ○ 30 grams
   - ○ 300 kilograms
   - ○ 3,000 grams

Spiral Review

3. Use an inch ruler. What is the length of the string to the nearest inch? (Lesson 9.6)

   - ○ 2 inches
   - ○ 3 inches
   - ○ 5 inches
   - ○ 8 inches

4. There are 175 girls and 218 boys at a game. How many children are there in all? (Lesson 7.4)
   - ○ 393
   - ○ 392
   - ○ 383
   - ○ 382

5. What is the sum? (Lesson 3.2)

   $9 + 9 =$ _____
   - ○ 14
   - ○ 16
   - ○ 17
   - ○ 18

Name _____

Lesson 10.3

Cups and Quarts

Find the container.	Choose the unit.	Measure.
1. teapot	cup quart	about _____
2. mug	cup quart	about _____
3. milk jug	cup quart	about _____
4. soup bowl	cup quart	about _____

PROBLEM SOLVING

Solve. Write or draw to explain.

5. Mr. Mann bought 3 quarts of apple juice. Miss Jones bought two times as much juice as Mr. Mann. How many quarts of juice did they buy in all?

_____ quarts

Chapter 10 two hundred thirteen **P213**

Lesson Check

1. Which is most likely the capacity of this juice carton?

   - ○ 4 cups
   - ○ 16 cups
   - ○ 4 quarts
   - ○ 16 quarts

2. Which is most likely the capacity of this milk jug?

   - ○ 1 cup
   - ○ 4 quarts
   - ○ 10 quarts
   - ○ 20 quarts

Spiral Review

3. Which is the best estimate for the mass of a paper clip? (Lesson 10.2)

   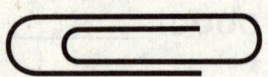

   - ○ 1 gram
   - ○ 50 grams
   - ○ 1 kilogram
   - ○ 50 kilograms

4. What is the sum? (Lesson 4.7)

   $$\begin{array}{r} 21 \\ + 17 \\ \hline \end{array}$$

   - ○ 3
   - ○ 13
   - ○ 28
   - ○ 38

5. What is the difference? (Lesson 8.1)

   $$\begin{array}{r} 656 \\ - 245 \\ \hline \end{array}$$

   - ○ 901
   - ○ 411
   - ○ 401
   - ○ 311

6. What is the sum? (Lesson 3.3)

   2 + 6 + 4 = _____

   - ○ 8
   - ○ 10
   - ○ 11
   - ○ 12

Name _____

Milliliters and Liters

Lesson 10.4

Find the container.	Choose the unit.	Measure.
1. juice carton	milliliter liter	about _____
2. juice jug	milliliter liter	about _____
3. soup can	milliliter liter	about _____
4. watering can	milliliter liter	about _____

PROBLEM SOLVING REAL WORLD

Solve. Draw or write to explain.

5. Jenny used 350 milliliters of orange juice, 225 milliliters of pineapple juice, and 400 milliliters of apple juice to make punch. How many milliliters of juice did Jenny use to make punch?

_____ milliliters

Chapter 10 two hundred fifteen P215

Lesson Check

1. Which is the best estimate for the capacity of a juice box?

   - ○ 25 liters
   - ○ 2 liters
   - ○ 250 milliliters
   - ○ 2 milliliters

2. Which is the best estimate for the capacity of this milk jug?

   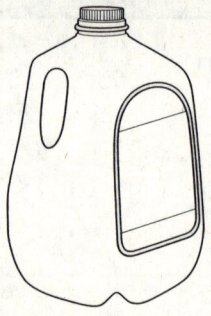

   - ○ 20 liters
   - ○ 4 liters
   - ○ 20 milliliters
   - ○ 4 milliliters

Spiral Review

3. Which is the best estimate for the capacity of a soup can? (Lesson 10.3)

   - ○ 1 cup
   - ○ 5 cups
   - ○ 5 quarts
   - ○ 10 quarts

4. What is the sum? (Lesson 4.11)

   ```
     32
     48
   +  5
   ```

   - ○ 85
   - ○ 84
   - ○ 75
   - ○ 74

5. Mr. Smith has 28 blue crayons and 16 yellow crayons. How many crayons does he have in all? (Lesson 4.11)

   - ○ 32
   - ○ 34
   - ○ 42
   - ○ 44

6. There are 5 oranges in each bag. How many oranges are in 4 bags? (Lesson 8.3)

bags	1	2	3	4
oranges	5			

   - ○ 9
   - ○ 10
   - ○ 15
   - ○ 20

Name _____

Lesson 10.5

Choose the Unit

Circle the better unit of measure for the weight or the mass of the object.

1. **phone**

   ounce   pound

2. **dog**

   gram   kilogram

3. **book**

   ounce   pound

4. **banana**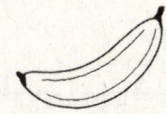

   gram   kilogram

Circle the better unit of measure for the capacity of the container.

5. **mug**

   cup   quart

6. **watering can**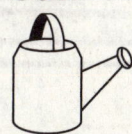

   milliliter   liter

7. **sink**

   cup   quart

8. **spoon**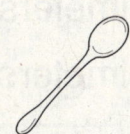

   milliliter   liter

PROBLEM SOLVING

9. Jason is using a 1-quart container to fill a punch bowl. He puts 4 quarts of punch in the bowl and the bowl is half full. About how much will the punch bowl hold?

   _____ quarts

Chapter 10   two hundred seventeen   **P217**

Lesson Check

1. Which is the best unit for measuring the weight of a strawberry?
   - ○ milliliter
   - ○ liter
   - ○ ounce
   - ○ pound

2. Which is the best unit for measuring the capacity of a sink?
   - ○ ounce
   - ○ pound
   - ○ milliliter
   - ○ liter

Spiral Review

3. Use a centimeter ruler. Which is the best choice for the length of this pencil? (Lesson 9.11)

   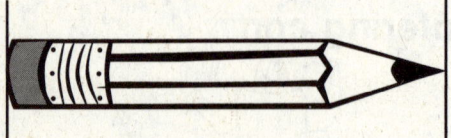

   - ○ 1 centimeter
   - ○ 6 centimeters
   - ○ 9 centimeters
   - ○ 12 centimeters

4. Use an inch ruler. Which is the best choice for the length of this paper clip? (Lesson 9.6)

   - ○ 1 inch
   - ○ 2 inches
   - ○ 3 inches
   - ○ 4 inches

5. This bar graph shows how many bowls were sold at the fair. How many yellow bowls were sold? (Lesson 6.5)

   - ○ 1
   - ○ 4
   - ○ 8
   - ○ 10

   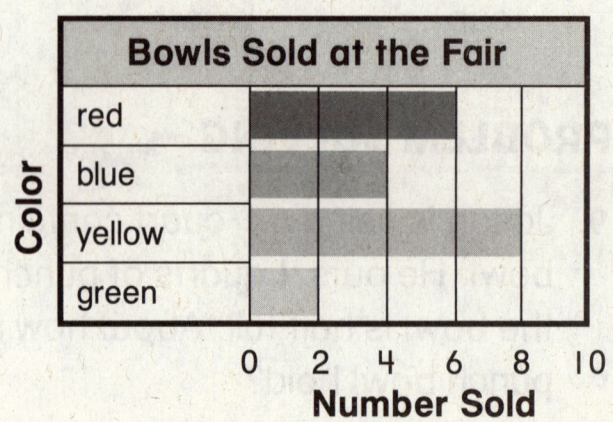

P218 two hundred eighteen

Name _____

Act It Out • Measurement

PROBLEM SOLVING
Lesson 10.6

Choose the best tool to measure.

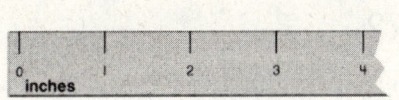 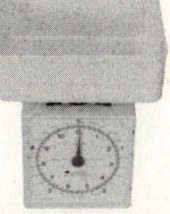 

ruler   scale   liter container

1. Kelsey wants to know how long a ribbon is. Which tool should she use?

   _____

2. Tara wants to know how much milk is in a jug. Which tool should she use?

   _____

3. David wants to know how much a rock weighs. Which tool should he use?

   _____

4. Megan wants to know how heavy an apple is. Which tool should she use?

   _____

5. Alex wants to know how much juice is in the pitcher. Which tool should he use?

   _____

6. Bailey wants to know how wide her math book is. Which tool should she use?

   _____

Chapter 10   two hundred nineteen   P219

Lesson Check

1. Which is the best tool for measuring the length of a marker?

    ○ ruler
    ○ scale
    ○ liter container
    ○ thermometer

2. Which is the best tool for measuring the weight of a book?

    ○ ruler
    ○ scale
    ○ liter container
    ○ thermometer

Spiral Review

3. Use a centimeter ruler. What is the length of the spoon to the nearest centimeter? (Lesson 9.11)

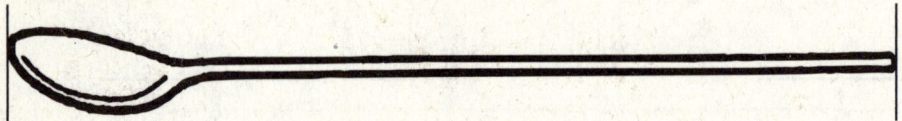

    ○ 5 centimeters
    ○ 8 centimeters
    ○ 12 centimeters
    ○ 17 centimeters

4. What is the sum? (Lesson 4.7)

    53
    + 62

    ○ 95
    ○ 105
    ○ 115
    ○ 125

5. Which will make this number sentence true? (Lesson 3.9)

    3 + 4 = ☐ + 6

    ○ 1
    ○ 2
    ○ 7
    ○ 13

Name _____

Chapter 10 Extra Practice

Lessons 10.1 – 10.2 (pp. 441–448)

Find the object.	Choose the unit.	Measure.
1. pencil case	ounce pound	about _____
2. jump rope	ounce pound	about _____
3. crayon	ounce pound	about _____
4. baseball	gram kilogram	about _____
5. dictionary	gram kilogram	about _____

Chapter 10   two hundred twenty-one   P221

Lessons 10.3 – 10.4 (pp. 449–455)

Find the container.	Choose the unit.	Measure.
1. milk jug	cup quart	about _____
2. bottle	cup quart	about _____
3. juice box	milliliter liter	about _____

Lesson 10.6 (pp. 461–464)

Choose the best tool to measure.

ruler	scale	liter container
1. Suzy wants to know how long the pen is. Which tool should she use? _____		2. Jeff wants to know how much a hammer weighs. Which tool should he use? _____

P222 two hundred twenty-two

Chapter 11
School-Home Letter

Dear Family,

My class started Chapter 11 this week. In this chapter, I will learn about the values of coins and how to find the total value for a group of coins. I will also learn how to tell time on analog clocks and digital clocks.

Love, _____

Vocabulary

penny a coin with a value of 1 cent

nickel a coin with a value of 5 cents

dime a coin with a value of 10 cents

quarter a coin with a value of 25 cents

half dollar a coin with a value of 50 cents

dollar an amount equal to 100 cents

Home Activity

With your child, set up a play store together. Use objects such as food items or small toys. Put price tags on each object, using amounts less than one dollar. On a sheet of paper, have your child write the price of an object and then draw a group of coins that has that as its total value. Take turns doing this for several objects.

Literature

Reading math stories reinforces ideas. Look for these books at the library.

A Dollar for Penny by Julie Glass. Random House Books for Young Readers, 2000.

What Time Is It, Mr. Crocodile? by Judy Sierra. Gulliver Books, 2004.

Capítulo 11
Carta para la casa

Querida familia:

Mi clase comenzó esta semana el Capítulo 11. En este capítulo, aprenderé acerca del valor de las monedas y cómo hallar el valor total de un grupo de monedas. También aprenderé cómo leer la hora en relojes analógicos y en relojes digitales.

Con cariño, _____

Vocabulario

moneda de 1¢

moneda de 25¢

moneda de 5¢

moneda de 50¢

moneda de 10¢

Actividad para la casa

Juntos, jueguen a que están en una tienda. Use objetos tales como artículos de comida o juguetes pequeños. Coloque etiquetas en cada artículo con un precio menor de un dólar. En una hoja de papel, pida a su hijo que escriba el precio de un "artículo de la tienda" y que dibuje un grupo de monedas que sumen ese precio. Túrnense para repetir la actividad con diferentes objetos.

Literatura

Leer cuentos de matemáticas refuerza los conceptos. Busquen estos libros en la biblioteca.

A Dollar for Penny por Julie Glass. Random House Books for Young Readers, 2000.

What Time Is It, Mr. Crocodile? por Judy Sierra. Gulliver Books, 2004.

Name _____

Lesson 11.1

Dimes, Nickels, and Pennies

Count on to find the total value.

1.

   _____

   ☐ total value

2.

   _____

   ☐ total value

3.

   ☐ total value

4.

   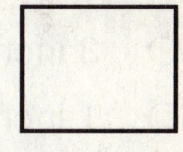 total value

PROBLEM SOLVING

Solve.

5. Aaron has 5 dimes and 2 nickels in his pocket. What is the total value of the coins Aaron has?

   ☐ total value

Chapter 11   two hundred twenty-five **P225**

Lesson Check

1. What is the total value of this group of coins?

   ○ 21¢   ○ 26¢   ○ 31¢   ○ 36¢

Spiral Review

2. The bead is 1 inch long. Which is the best estimate for the length of the string? (Lesson 9.5)

   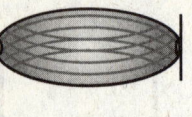

   ○ 10 inches
   ○ 7 inches
   ○ 3 inches
   ○ 1 inch

3. What is the sum? (Lesson 4.7)

   $$58 + 37$$

   ○ 21
   ○ 81
   ○ 85
   ○ 95

4. Use an inch ruler. What is the length to the nearest inch? (Lesson 9.6)

   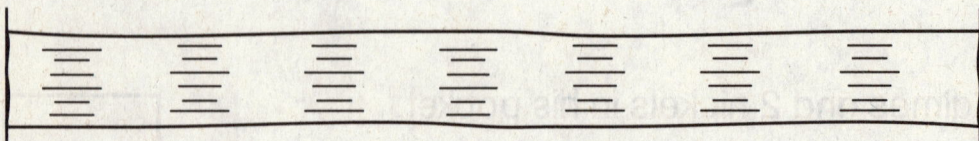

   ○ 8 inches
   ○ 5 inches
   ○ 3 inches
   ○ 2 inches

Name _____

Half Dollars and Quarters

Lesson 11.2

Count on to find the total value.

1.

   _____ ☐ total value

2.

   _____ ☐ total value

3.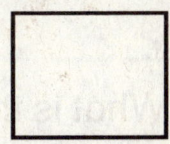

    ☐ total value

PROBLEM SOLVING — REAL WORLD

Solve.

4. Claire has 2 quarters and 3 dimes in her hand. What is the total value of the coins Claire has?

   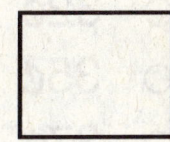 total value

Chapter 11 — two hundred twenty-seven P227

Lesson Check

1. What is the total value of this group of coins?

   ○ 85¢   ○ 87¢   ○ 90¢   ○ 95¢

Spiral Review

2. Which is the best unit for measuring how much soup is in a spoonful? (Lesson 10.5)

   ○ pound
   ○ liter
   ○ kilogram
   ○ milliliter

3. Which is the best unit for measuring the weight of a dog? (Lesson 10.5)

   ○ cup
   ○ liter
   ○ pound
   ○ milliliter

4. What is the total value of this group of coins? (Lesson 11.1)

   ○ 22¢
   ○ 32¢
   ○ 35¢
   ○ 37¢

P228 two hundred twenty-eight

Name _____

Count Collections

Lesson **11.3**

Draw and label the coins from greatest to least value. Find the total value.

1.

_____

2.

_____

3.

_____

PROBLEM SOLVING  REAL WORLD

4. Rebecca had these coins.
   She spent 1 quarter at the store.
   How much money does she have left?

   _____

Chapter 11 two hundred twenty-nine P229

Lesson Check

1. What is the total value of this group of coins?

  ○ 37¢   ○ 47¢   ○ 62¢   ○ 72¢

Spiral Review

2. Use a centimeter ruler. What is the length to the nearest centimeter? **(Lesson 9.11)**

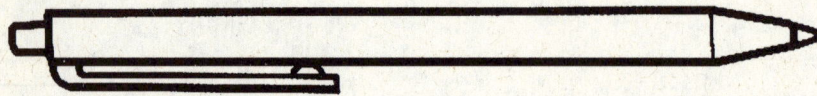

  ○ 15 centimeters
  ○ 11 centimeters
  ○ 8 centimeters
  ○ 5 centimeters

3. What is the difference? **(Lesson 5.6)**

$$\begin{array}{r} 83 \\ -37 \\ \hline \end{array}$$

  ○ 46
  ○ 54
  ○ 64
  ○ 73

4. Vanessa puts 4 pretzels on each plate. How many pretzels are on 5 plates? **(Lesson 8.2)**

  ○ 9
  ○ 16
  ○ 20
  ○ 45

PROBLEM SOLVING
Lesson 11.4

Name _____

Find a Pattern • Money

Find a pattern. Complete the table.

1. Pablo has 5 dimes. He wants to trade them for nickels. How many nickels should he get?

dimes	1	2	3	4	5
nickels					

Pablo should get _____ nickels.

2. Stacy has 5 quarters. She wants to trade them for nickels. How many nickels should she get?

quarters	1	2	3	4	5
nickels					

Stacy should get _____ nickels.

3. Gabby has 5 dimes. She wants to trade them for pennies. How many pennies should she get?

dimes	1	2	3	4	5
pennies					

Gabby should get _____ pennies.

4. Omar has 4 quarters. He wants to trade them for pennies. How many pennies should he get?

quarters	1	2	3	4
pennies				

Omar should get _____ pennies.

Lesson Check

1. Ben has 4 half dollars. He wants to trade them for dimes. How many dimes should he get?

half dollars	1	2	3	4
dimes				

○ 20   ○ 40   ○ 100   ○ 200

Spiral Review

2. Mr. Velez has a full bottle of water. Which is most likely to be the capacity of the bottle? (Lesson 10.4)

   ○ 1 milliliter
   ○ 10 cups
   ○ 1 liter
   ○ 3 quarts

3. Which is the best unit of measure to use for measuring the weight of a phone? (Lesson 10.5)

   ○ cup
   ○ meter
   ○ yard
   ○ ounce

4. Use a centimeter ruler. What is the length to the nearest centimeter? (Lesson 10.4)

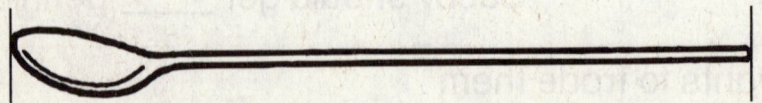

   ○ 4 centimeters
   ○ 10 centimeters
   ○ 14 centimeters
   ○ 18 centimeters

Name _____

Lesson 11.5

One Dollar

Circle coins to make $1.00.
Cross out the coins you do not use.

1.

2.

3.

PROBLEM SOLVING

Solve.

4. Amanda has 10 coins. The total value of the coins is $1.00. They are all the same kind of coin. What coins does Amanda have?

_____

Chapter 11 two hundred thirty-three **P233**

Lesson Check

1. Which group of coins has a value of $1.00?

○ ○ ○

Spiral Review

2. What is the difference? (Lesson 7.7)

    543
  − 218
  ─────

   ○ 225
   ○ 325
   ○ 335
   ○ 761

3. Each child has 2 books. How many books do 7 children have?

   (Lesson 8.6)

   ○ 5
   ○ 9
   ○ 14
   ○ 21

4. The bead is 1 inch long. Which is the best estimate of the length of the string? (Lesson 9.5)

○ 5 inches   ○ 11 inches
○ 8 inches   ○ 15 inches

P234 two hundred thirty-four

Name _____

Problem Solving with Money

Lesson 11.5A Connect

Essential Question How does counting coins and bills help you solve problems about money?

Real World • You can count coins to help you solve problems about money.

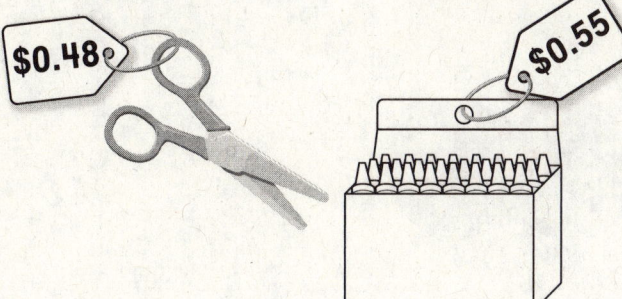

Teri has these coins.

She buys a box of crayons. How much money does she have left?

$0.60
−$0.55

$0.05

$0.05

Practice

Solve. Show your work.

1. Taylor has these coins.

She buys scissors. How much money does she have left?

Chapter 11   two hundred thirty-four **P234a**

Solve. Show your work.

2. Danny has these coins.

   He buys a kite. How much money
   does he have left? _____

3. Shannon buys a bear and a book.
   How much money does she spend?

   _____

4. Riley has three $1 bills. Her sister
   has twice as many dollar bills as
   Riley has. How many dollars do
   they have in all?

   _____

Math Talk

Explain how you solved Exercise 2.

Name _____

Lesson 11.6

Telling Time

Look at where the hour hand points. Write the time.

1.

_____

2.

_____

3.

_____

4.

_____

5.

_____

6.

_____

7.

_____

8.

_____

9.

_____

PROBLEM SOLVING

10. It is half past 1:00. Draw the hour hand to show this time.

Chapter 11   two hundred thirty-five **P235**

Lesson Check

1. What time is shown?

- ○ 3:00
- ○ half past 3:00
- ○ 4:00
- ○ half past 4:00

2. What time is shown?

- ○ 9:00
- ○ half past 9:00
- ○ 10:00
- ○ half past 10:00

Spiral Review

3. What is the sum? (Lesson 4.1)

    27 + 8 = _____

    - ○ 17
    - ○ 19
    - ○ 31
    - ○ 35

4. What is the difference? (Lesson 5.1)

    83 − 8 = _____

    - ○ 75
    - ○ 81
    - ○ 85
    - ○ 91

5. What is the total value of this group of coins? (Lesson 11.2)

- ○ 72¢
- ○ 62¢
- ○ 47¢
- ○ 37¢

Name _____

Lesson 11.7

Time to the Hour and Half Hour

Look at the clock hands.
Write the time.

1.

2.

3.

4.

5.

6.

PROBLEM SOLVING

7. Amy's music lesson begins at 2:30. Draw hands on the clock to show this time.

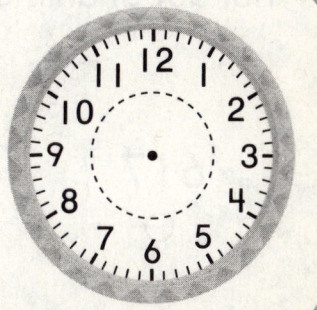

Chapter 11   two hundred thirty-seven **P237**

Lesson Check

1. What time is shown on this clock?

   - ○ 3:00
   - ○ 3:30
   - ○ 4:00
   - ○ 4:30

2. What time is shown on this clock?

   - ○ 12:00
   - ○ 12:30
   - ○ 6:00
   - ○ 6:30

Spiral Review

3. What is the sum? (Lesson 4.11)

   ```
     42
     13
   + 34
   ```

   - ○ 99
   - ○ 89
   - ○ 76
   - ○ 55

4. What is the difference? (Lesson 5.6)

   ```
     62
   - 24
   ```

   - ○ 86
   - ○ 48
   - ○ 42
   - ○ 38

5. There are 726 books in the library. 109 of the books are about animals. How many of the books are not about animals? (Lesson 7.7)

   617   623   627   717
    ○   ○   ○   ○

Name _____

Lesson 11.7A Connect

Hour Before and Hour After

Essential Question How do you tell the time 1 hour before and 1 hour after a given time?

Real World • You can look at the hour hand on a clock to help you tell the time 1 hour before or 1 hour after the time shown.

The hour hand is halfway between 5 and 6.

The time is __5:30__.

1 hour before 5:30

One hour before, the hour hand is halfway between 4 and 5.

The time is __4:30__.

1 hour after 5:30

One hour after, the hour hand is halfway between 6 and 7.

The time is __6:30__.

Practice

Write the time shown on the clock. Then write the time 1 hour before and the time 1 hour after.

1.

__9:00__

1 hour before is __8:00__.

1 hour after is _____ : _____.

Chapter 11 two hundred thirty-eight P238a

Write the time shown on the clock. Then write the time 1 hour before and the time 1 hour after.

2.

___ : ___

1 hour before is ___ : ___.

1 hour after is ___ : ___.

3.

___ : ___

1 hour before is ___ : ___.

1 hour after is ___ : ___.

4.

___ : ___

1 hour before is ___ : ___.

1 hour after is ___ : ___.

5.

___ : ___

1 hour before is ___ : ___.

1 hour after is ___ : ___.

Math Talk

Explain how to find the time 1 hour before and 1 hour after 2:30.

Name _____

Elapsed Time in Hours

Essential Question How do you use subtraction to find the amount of time between two times?

Lesson 11.7B Connect

Real World • You can subtract to find the time that has passed.

Soccer practice starts at 1:00. It ends at 4:00. How long does soccer practice last?

You can subtract to find the time that has passed.

4 − 1 = 3

So, soccer practice lasts 3 hours.

Starts   Ends

Practice

Subtract to solve the problem. Show your work.

1. Reading starts at 9:00. It ends at 11:00. How long does Reading last?

   11 − 9 = 2

   __2__ hours

2. The movie starts at 2:00. It ends at 5:00. How long is the movie?

   5 − 2 = 3

   ____ hours

3. The train leaves at 5:00. It arrives at 11:00. How long is the train trip?

   ____ hours

4. Tyler starts raking leaves at 4:30. He stops raking at 6:30. How long does he rake leaves?

   ____ hours

Chapter 11   two hundred thirty-eight **P238c**

Solve. Show your work.

5. The science fair starts at 2:00. It is over at 8:00. How long is the science fair?

_____ hours

6. Hailey puts a cake in the oven at 10:00. She takes it out of the oven at 11:00. How long is the cake in the oven?

_____ hour

7. The plane takes off at 4:00. It lands at 7:00. How long is the flight?

_____ hours

8. Mr. West finished painting his house at 7:00. He started painting at 2:00. How long did Mr. West paint?

_____ hours

9. Mike starts a hike at 8:00. He finishes the hike at 10:00. How long does Mike hike?

_____ hours

10. Emily goes to sleep at 2:00. She wakes up at 5:00. How long does Emily sleep?

_____ hours

11. Angie stopped reading her book at 6:30. She began reading at 4:30. How long did Angie read?

_____ hours

12. Nick leaves his house at 1:30. He returns home at 5:30. How long is he gone?

_____ hours

Math Talk
Explain how you find the time that passes between 6:30 and 9:30.

Name _____

Lesson 11.8

Time to 5 Minutes

Look at the clock hands.
Write the time.

1.

    ☐☐ : ☐☐

2.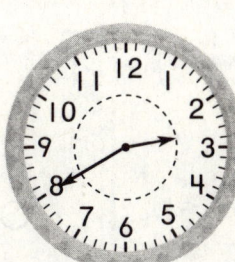

    ☐☐ : ☐☐

3.

    ☐☐ : ☐☐

4.

    ☐☐ : ☐☐

5.

    ☐☐ : ☐☐

6.

    ☐☐ : ☐☐

PROBLEM SOLVING

7. Christopher walked his dog at 4:45. Draw hands on the clock to show this time.

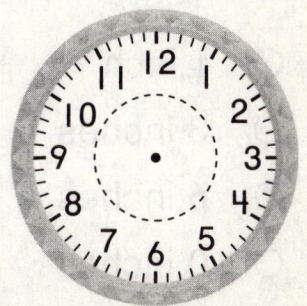

Chapter 11

two hundred thirty-nine **P239**

Lesson Check

1. What time is shown on this clock?

- ○ 8:05
- ○ 8:01
- ○ 1:40
- ○ 1:08

2. What time is shown on this clock?

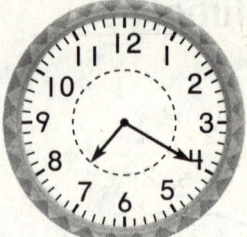

- ○ 4:07
- ○ 4:35
- ○ 7:20
- ○ 7:30

Spiral Review

3. What is the total value of this group of coins? (Lesson 11.1)

- ○ 19¢
- ○ 23¢
- ○ 35¢
- ○ 38¢

4. The bead is 1 inch long. Which is the best estimate for the length of the string? (Lesson 9.5)

- ○ 1 inch
- ○ 3 inches
- ○ 6 inches
- ○ 10 inches

Name _____

Lesson 11.9

Time to the Minute

Look at the clock hands.
Write the time.

1.

2.

   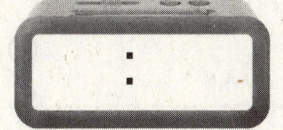

3.

4.

   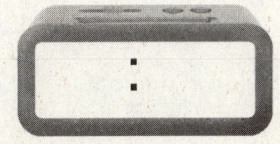

5.

   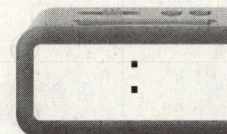

6.

   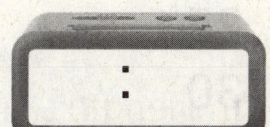

PROBLEM SOLVING

7. Jessie's bus gets to the bus stop at 3:37.
   Draw the minute hand to show this time.

Chapter 11 • two hundred forty-one P241

Lesson Check

1. What time is shown on this clock?

- ○ 6:11
- ○ 6:57
- ○ 11:30
- ○ 11:32

2. What time is shown on this clock?

- ○ 1:03
- ○ 1:14
- ○ 2:05
- ○ 3:05

Spiral Review

3. Each vase has 5 flowers in it. How many flowers are in 6 vases? (Lesson 8.7)

- ○ 11
- ○ 24
- ○ 25
- ○ 30

4. What is the sum? (Lesson 7.5)

842
+ 319

- ○ 1,161
- ○ 1,151
- ○ 537
- ○ 523

5. The length of the string is about 4 centimeters. Which is the best estimate for the length of the stick? (Lesson 9.12)

- ○ 4 centimeters
- ○ 8 centimeters
- ○ 12 centimeters
- ○ 16 centimeters

Lesson 11.10

Name _____

Units of Time

Write **more than**, **less than**, or **the same as** to complete the sentence.

Time Relationships
There are 60 minutes in 1 hour.
There are 24 hours in 1 day.
There are 7 days in 1 week.
There are about 4 weeks in 1 month.
There are 12 months in 1 year.

1. Jill was at camp for 5 days.

   This is _____ 1 week.

2. Daniel read a book for 40 minutes.

   This is _____ 1 hour.

3. Anthony's family stayed at the campground for 10 days.

   This is _____ 1 week.

4. Sue kept her library book for 18 days.

   This is _____ 1 month.

5. The swimming pool was closed for 6 weeks.

   This is _____ 1 month.

6. Tom played soccer for 60 minutes.

   This is _____ 1 hour.

Chapter 11

Lesson Check

1. Ally went to camp for 1 week. Which is the same amount of time as 1 week?
   ○ 1 day
   ○ 6 months
   ○ 7 days
   ○ 2 years

2. José rode his bike for 60 minutes. Which is the same amount of time as 60 minutes?
   ○ 1 hour
   ○ 1 day
   ○ 1 week
   ○ 1 month

Spiral Review

3. What time is shown? (Lesson 11.9)

   ○ 9:58
   ○ 10:58
   ○ 11:10
   ○ 11:48

4. What is the sum? (Lesson 4.3)

   $$\begin{array}{r} 28 \\ + 54 \\ \hline \end{array}$$

   ○ 72
   ○ 82
   ○ 84
   ○ 712

5. Which number completes this number sentence? (Lesson 3.9)

   ___ + 5 = 7 + 6

   ○ 18
   ○ 13
   ○ 8
   ○ 6

6. Which of the following is another way to write seventeen? (Lesson 1.3)
   ○ 70
   ○ 17
   ○ 11
   ○ 7

Name _____

Chapter 11 Extra Practice

Lessons 11.1–11.2 (pp. 473–480)

Count on to find the total value.

1.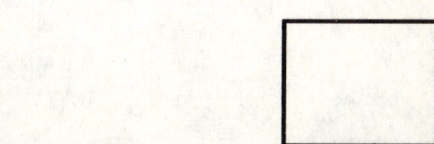

total value

2.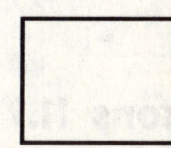

total value

Lesson 11.3 (pp. 481–484)

Draw and label the coins from greatest to least value. Find the total value.

1.

_____

Lesson 11.4 (pp. 485–488)

Find a pattern. Complete the table.

1. Rob has 5 dimes. He wants to trade them for nickels. How many nickels should he get?

dimes	1	2	3	4	5
nickels					

Rob should get _____ nickels.

Chapter 11   two hundred forty-five **P245**

Lesson 11.5 (pp. 489–491)
Circle coins to make $1.00.
Cross out the coins you do not use.

1.

Lessons 11.7 – 11.9 (pp. 497–508)
Look at the clock hands. Write the time.

1.

2.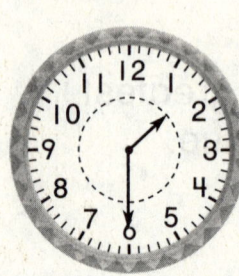

3.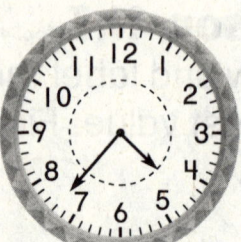

4.

5.

6.

Chapter 12
School-Home Letter

Dear Family:

My class started Chapter 12 this week. I will learn about three-dimensional and two-dimensional shapes. I will also describe and extend growing patterns.

Love, _____

Vocabulary

quadrilateral

pentagon

hexagon

cone

cylinder

cube
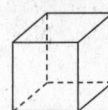

Home Activity

Name a two-dimensional shape: triangle, quadrilateral, pentagon, or hexagon. With your child, look for an object that has that shape.

Repeat the activity using a three-dimensional shape: cube, rectangular prism, square pyramid, sphere, cylinder, or cone.

Literature

Reading math stories reinforces learning. Look for these books at the library.

Shape Up! by David Adler. Holiday House, 1998.

The Village of Round and Square Houses by Ann Grifalconi. Little, Brown and Company, 1986.

Capítulo 12
Carta para la casa

Querida familia:

Mi clase comenzó hoy el Capítulo 12. En este capítulo, aprenderé acerca de las figuras bidimensionales y tridimensionales. También aprenderé a describir y a seguir patrones que se incrementan.

Con cariño, _____

Vocabulario

cuadrilátero

pentágono
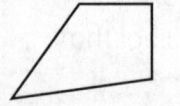

hexágono
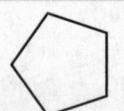

cono

cilindro

cubo
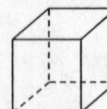

Actividad para la casa

Nombre alguna figura bidimensional, como triángulo, cuadrilátero, pentágono o hexágono. Juntos, busquen una figura que tenga la misma forma.

Repitan la actividad con una figura tridimensional, como cubo, prisma rectangular, pirámide cuadrada, esfera, cilindro o cono.

Literatura

Leer cuentos de matemáticas refuerza el aprendizaje. Busquen estos libros en la biblioteca.

Shape Up! por David Adler. Holiday House, 1998.

The Village of Round and Square Houses por Ann Grifalconi. Little, Brown and Company, 1986.

Lesson 12.1

Name _____

Three-Dimensional Shapes

Circle the objects that match the shape name.

1. cube
2. cone
3. sphere
4. cylinder

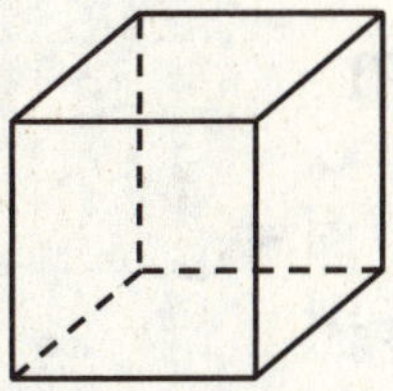

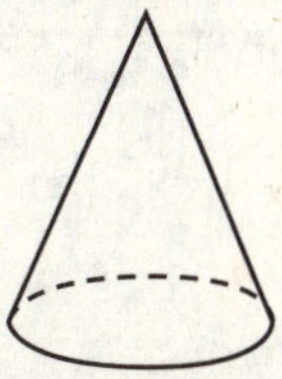

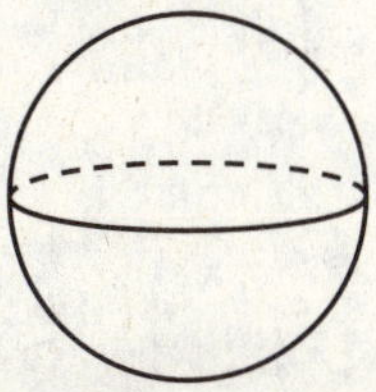

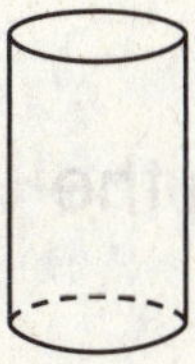

PROBLEM SOLVING · REAL WORLD

5. Lisa draws a circle by tracing around the bottom of a block. Which could be the shape of Lisa's block? Circle the name of the shape.

cone   cube   square pyramid

Chapter 12   two hundred forty-nine **P249**

Lesson Check

1. What is the name of this shape?

   ○ cube
   ○ cone
   ○ cylinder
   ○ sphere

2. What is the name of this shape?

   ○ rectangular prism
   ○ cube
   ○ square pyramid
   ○ cone

Spiral Review

3. The string is about 6 centimeters long. Which is the best estimate for the length of the crayon? (Lesson 9.12)

   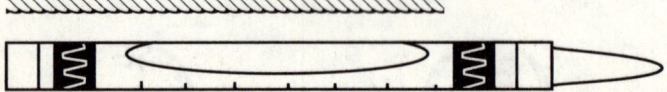

   ○ 3 centimeters   ○ 9 centimeters
   ○ 4 centimeters   ○ 12 centimeters

4. What is the total value of the coins? (Lesson 11.1)

   ○ 3¢
   ○ 11¢
   ○ 15¢
   ○ 16¢

5. What time is shown on the clock? (Lesson 11.7)

   ○ 6:00
   ○ 10:06
   ○ 10:30
   ○ 11:00

P250 two hundred fifty

Name _____

Lesson 12.2

Two-Dimensional Shapes

Write the number of sides and the number of vertices.

1. triangle	2. square	3. pentagon
____ sides ____ vertices	____ sides ____ vertices	____ sides ____ vertices
4. quadrilateral	5. hexagon	6. rhombus
____ sides ____ vertices	____ sides ____ vertices	____ sides ____ vertices
7. rectangle	8. pentagon	9. trapezoid
____ sides ____ vertices	____ sides ____ vertices	____ sides ____ vertices

PROBLEM SOLVING REAL WORLD

10. Oscar is drawing a picture of a house. He draws a pentagon shape for a window. How many sides does his window have?

____ sides

Chapter 12   two hundred fifty-one **P251**

Lesson Check

1. How many sides does this hexagon have?

   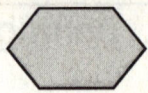

   - ○ 3 sides
   - ○ 4 sides
   - ○ 5 sides
   - ○ 6 sides

2. How many vertices does this quadrilateral have?

   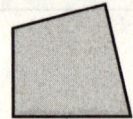

   - ○ 6 vertices
   - ○ 5 vertices
   - ○ 4 vertices
   - ○ 3 vertices

Spiral Review

3. Use a centimeter ruler. What is the length of the ribbon to the nearest centimeter? (Lesson 9.11)

   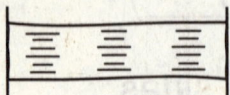

   - ○ 3 centimeters
   - ○ 6 centimeters
   - ○ 10 centimeters
   - ○ 12 centimeters

4. Which is most likely the weight of an orange? (Lesson 10.1)

   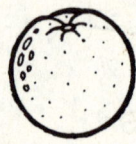

   - ○ 1 ounce
   - ○ 10 ounces
   - ○ 5 pounds
   - ○ 20 pounds

5. What is the difference? (Lesson 5.1)

   73 − 7 = ____

   - ○ 63
   - ○ 66
   - ○ 76
   - ○ 80

6. What is the sum? (Lesson 7.2)

   646
   + 335

   - ○ 311
   - ○ 971
   - ○ 981
   - ○ 1,081

Name _____

Lesson **12.3**

Sort Two-Dimensional Shapes

Circle the shapes that match the rule.

1. Shapes with fewer than 5 sides

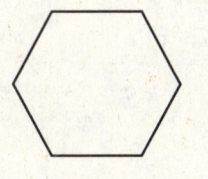 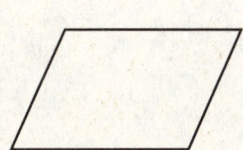

 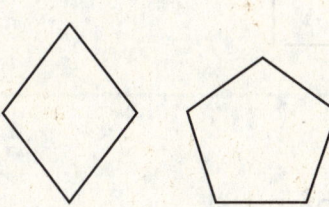

2. Shapes with more than 4 sides

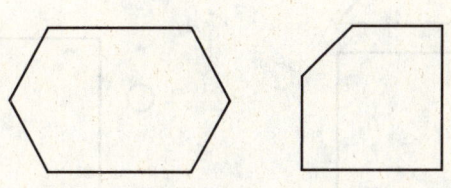

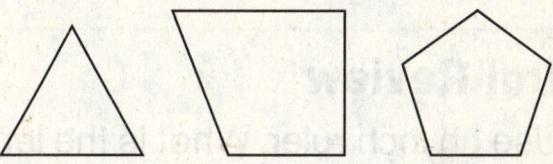

3. Shapes with 4 vertices

 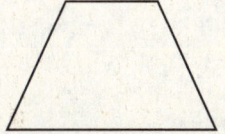

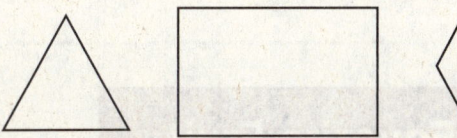

4. Shapes with fewer than 6 vertices

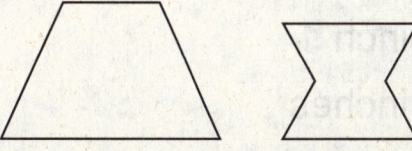

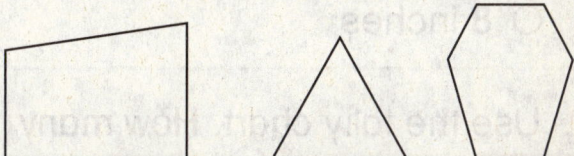

PROBLEM SOLVING  REAL WORLD

Circle the correct shape.

5. Tammy draws a shape. It has more than 3 vertices. It is not a hexagon. Which shape did Tammy draw?

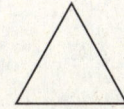 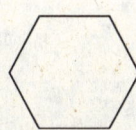  

Chapter 12   two hundred fifty-three **P253**

Lesson Check

1. Which has fewer than 4 sides?

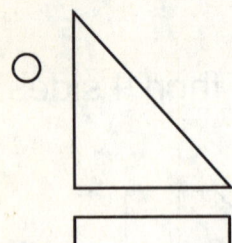 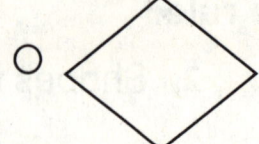

 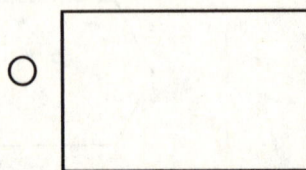

Spiral Review

2. Use an inch ruler. What is the length of the pencil to the nearest inch? (Lesson 9.6)

   ○ 1 inch
   ○ 2 inches
   ○ 6 inches
   ○ 8 inches

3. Use the tally chart. How many children chose grapes as their favorite fruit? (Lesson 6.3)

   ○ 4
   ○ 5
   ○ 6
   ○ 7

Favorite Fruit	
bananas	|||||
grapes	||||| ||
apples	||||

Name _____

Angles

Essential Question How can you compare the sizes of angles?

Lesson **12.3A** Dig Deeper

Activity • A corner of a shape is an **angle**. You can compare the sizes of angles.

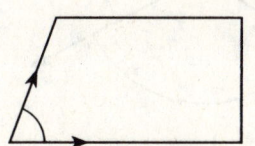

Use the corner of a sheet of paper to help you.

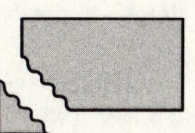

Right Angle	Greater than a Right Angle	Less than a Right Angle
A square corner is a right angle.		

Practice

Is the angle greater than or less than a right angle?
Circle **greater** or **less**.

1.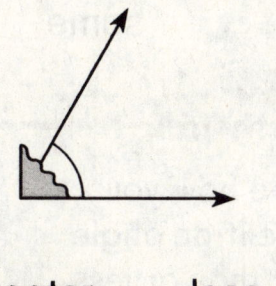

   greater   less

2.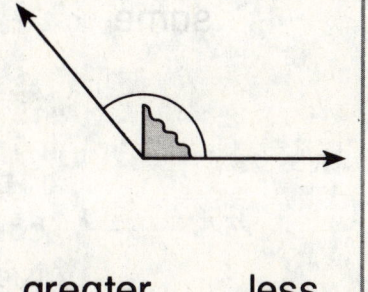

   greater   less

3.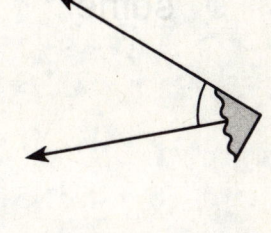

   greater   less

Chapter 12

Is the angle greater than or less than a right angle? Circle **greater** or **less**.

Use the corner of a sheet of paper to help you.

4.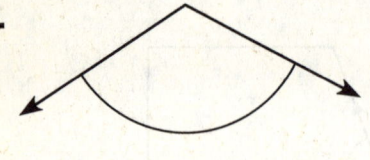

greater   less

5.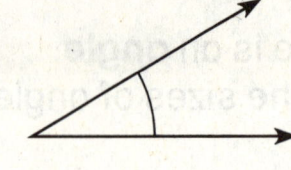

greater   less

6.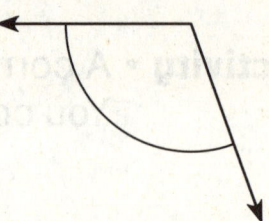

greater   less

7.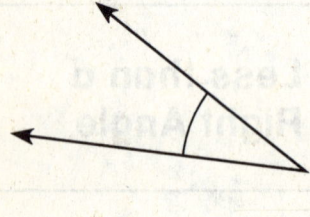

greater   less

8.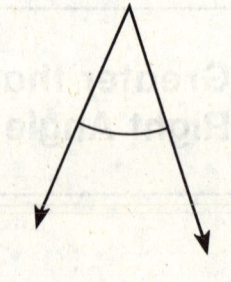

greater   less

9.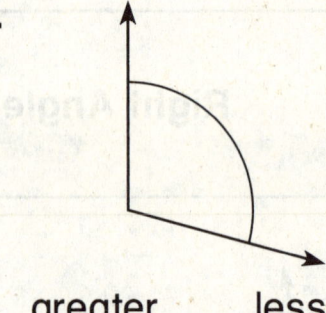

greater   less

Is the angle greater than, less than, or the same as a right angle? Circle **greater**, **less**, or **same**.

10.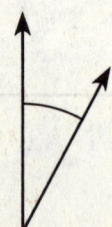

greater   less
     same

11.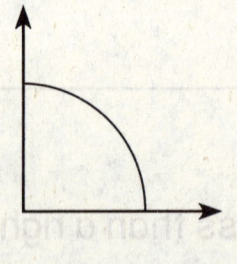

greater   less
     same

12.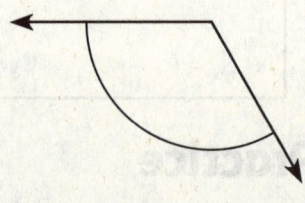

greater   less
     same

Math Talk

Describe how you can decide if an angle is greater than or less than a right angle.

P254b two hundred fifty-four

Name _____

Angles in Shapes

Essential Question How can you describe shapes by their sides and angles?

Lesson 12.3B Dig Deeper

Activity • You can describe a shape by looking at its sides and its angles.

Shape	Sides	Right Angles	Angles Greater than Right Angle	Angles Less than Right Angle
◇	4	0	2	—

Practice

Look at the shape. Complete the table.

	Shape	Sides	Right Angles	Angles Greater than Right Angle	Angles Less than Right Angle
1.	△	3	1	—	—
2.	⬠	—	—	—	—

Chapter 12   two hundred fifty-four

Draw a shape that matches the numbers in the chart.

Shape	Sides	Right Angles	Angles Greater than Right Angle	Angles Less than Right Angle
3.	3	0	0	3
4.	5	2	2	1
5.	4	0	2	2

6. Brianna drew a shape with 4 equal sides and 4 right angles. Draw a shape that could be Brianna's shape.

   Write the name of the shape. _____

Math Talk

Describe how all triangles are alike. **Describe** how they can be different.

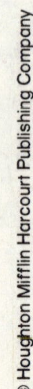

Name _____

Lesson 12.4

Symmetry

Does the shape have a line of symmetry?
If yes, draw the line.

1. (arrow) yes / no	2. (shape) yes / no	3. (triangle) yes / no
4. C yes / no	5. (square with curve) yes / no	6. M yes / no
7. F yes / no	8. ⊢ yes / no	9. L-shape yes / no

PROBLEM SOLVING

10. The dashed line is a line of symmetry. Draw the matching part.

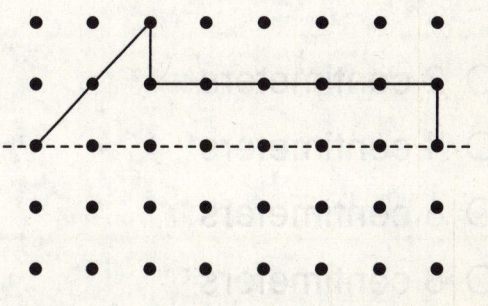

Chapter 12

two hundred fifty-five P255

Lesson Check

1. Which shape has a line of symmetry?

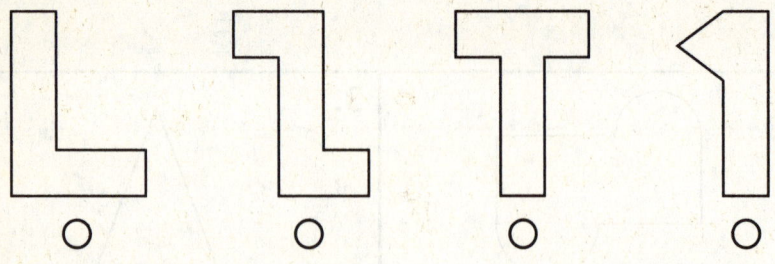

○   ○   ○   ○

Spiral Review

2. Which shape has 4 vertices? (Lesson 12.3)

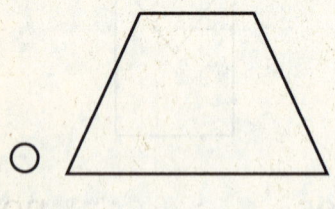   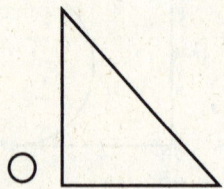

○   ○

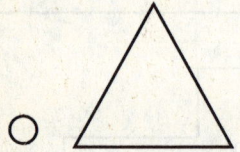   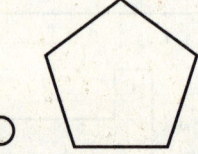

○   ○

3. Use a centimeter ruler. What is the length of the string to the nearest centimeter? (Lesson 9.11)

―――――――

○ 2 centimeters
○ 4 centimeters
○ 6 centimeters
○ 8 centimeters

4. What time is it? (Lesson 11.8)

○ 5:35
○ 4:35
○ 4:30
○ 4:25

Name _____

Lesson 12.4A Dig Deeper

Equal Parts

Essential Question How do you know if a shape is divided into equal parts?

Activity • **Equal parts** of a whole are the same size.

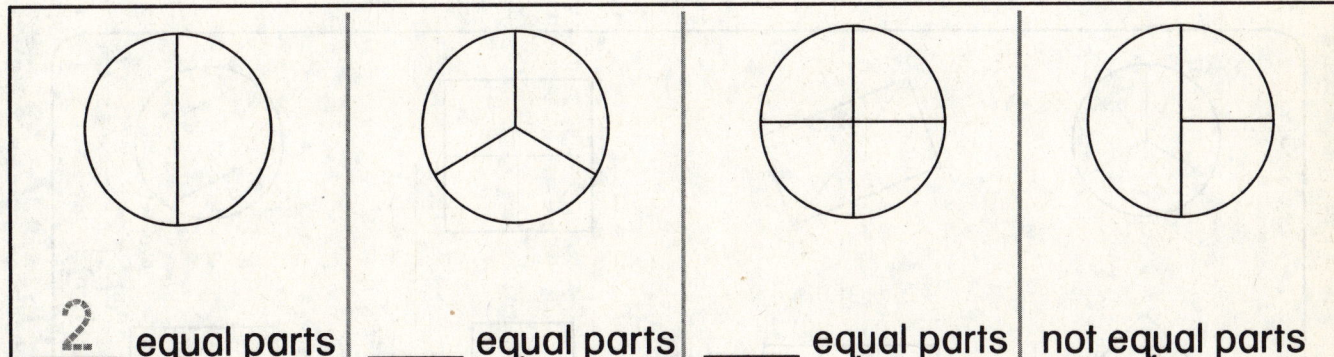

__2__ equal parts   ____ equal parts   ____ equal parts   not equal parts

Practice

Write the number of equal parts.

1.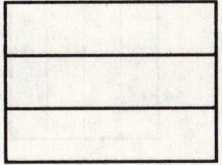

__3__ equal parts

2.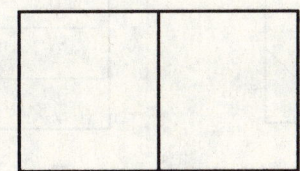

____ equal parts

3.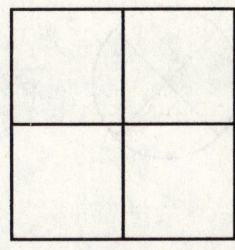

____ equal parts

4.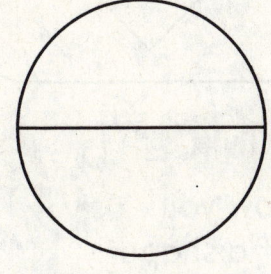

____ equal parts

5.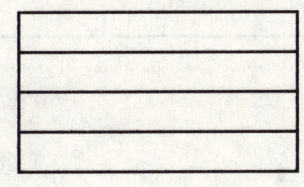

____ equal parts

6.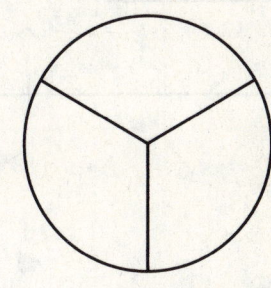

____ equal parts

Chapter 12   two hundred fifty-six **P256a**

7. Color red the shapes that are divided into 2 equal parts.

8. Color yellow the shapes that are divided into 3 equal parts.

9. Color blue the shapes that are divided into 4 equal parts.

10. Draw an X on the shapes that are **not** divided into equal parts.

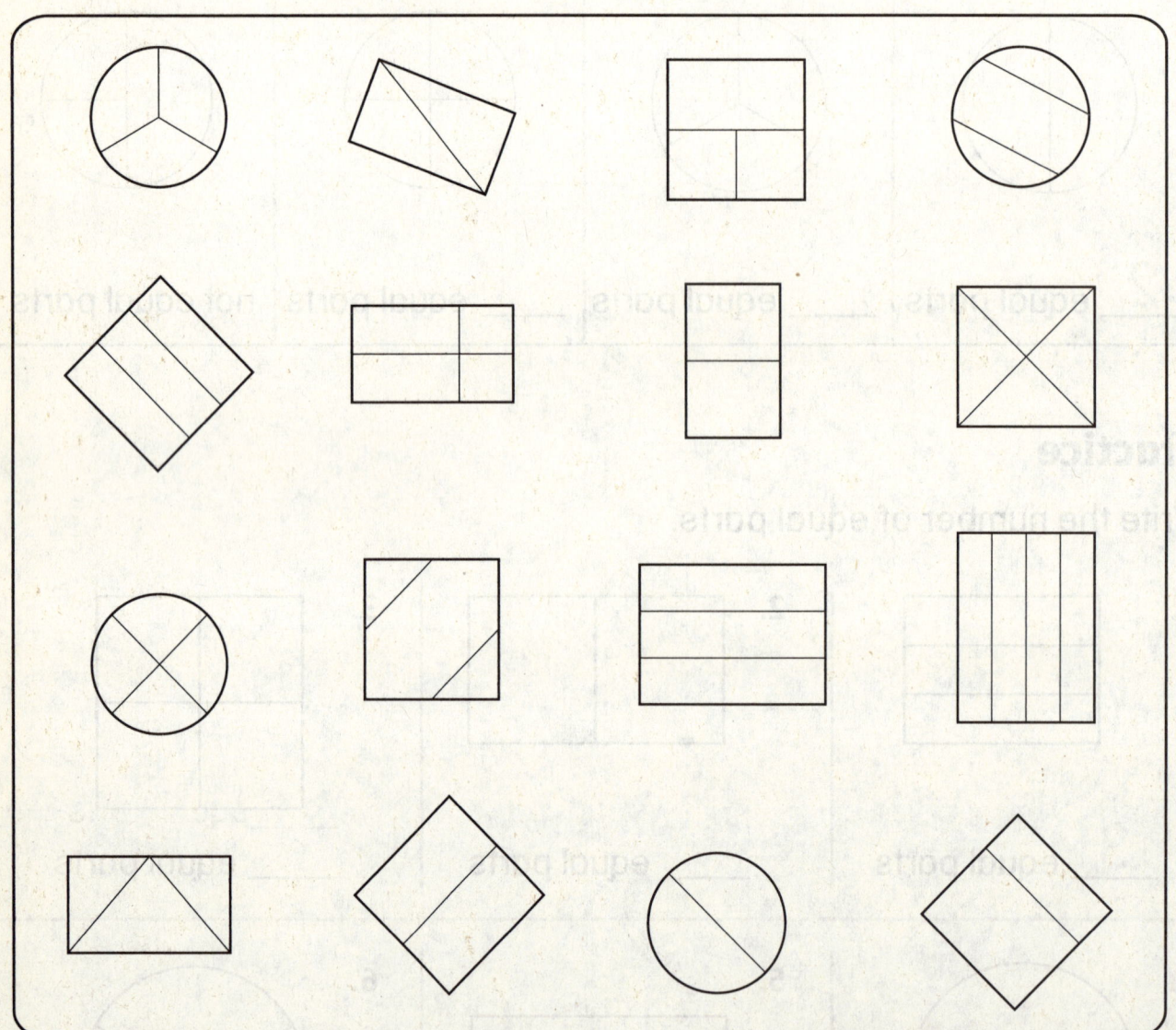

Math Talk

Explain how you can decide if a shape is divided into equal parts.

Name _____

Name Equal Parts

Essential Question What are halves, thirds, and fourths of a whole?

Lesson 12.4B Dig Deeper

Activity • This rectangle is the whole. It can be divided into equal parts.

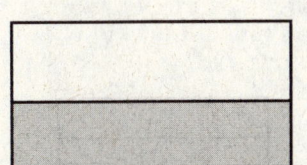
These are 2 **halves**.
I half is shaded.

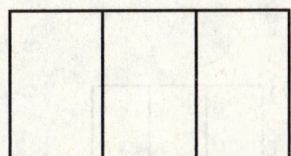
These are 3 **thirds**.
Color I third yellow.

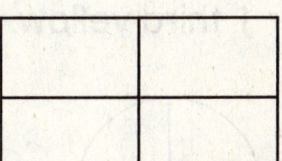
These are 4 **fourths**.
Color I fourth blue.

Practice

Write how many equal parts there are in the whole.
Write **halves**, **thirds**, or **fourths**.

1.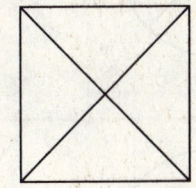

   __4__ equal parts

   __fourths__

2.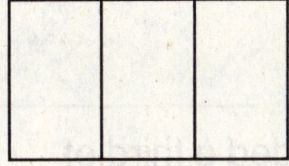

   __3__ equal parts

   _____

3.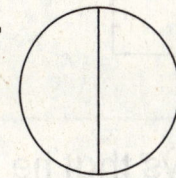

   ____ equal parts

   _____

4.

   ____ equal parts

   _____

5.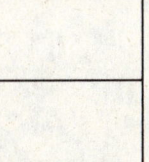

   ____ equal parts

   _____

6.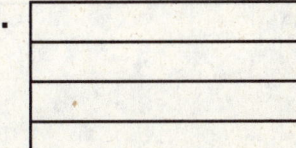

   ____ equal parts

   _____

Chapter 12   two hundred fifty-six **P256c**

Color 1 half red.

7.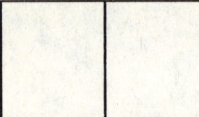
8.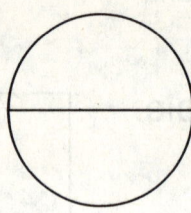
9.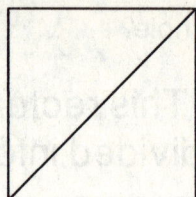

Color 1 third yellow.

10.
11.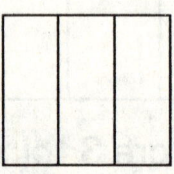
12.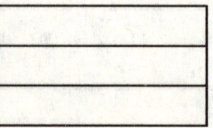

Color 1 fourth blue.

13.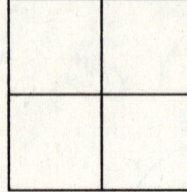
14.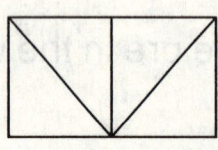
15.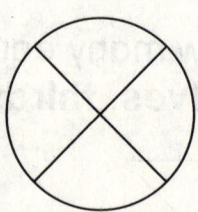

16. Jake says that he has shaded a third of the circle. Is Jake correct? Explain.

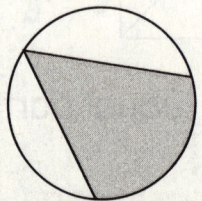

_____

_____

Math Talk

How many fourths make up 1 whole? **Explain** how you know.

P256d two hundred fifty-six

Name _____

Lesson 12.5

Algebra: Extend Growing Patterns

Draw what might come next in the pattern.

1.

_____

2.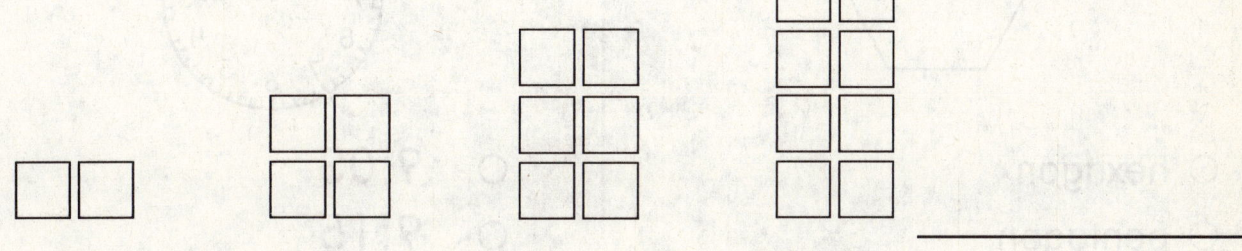

_____

3.

_____

4.

_____

PROBLEM SOLVING

5. Ms. Lennox is building a display of soup cans in her store. Draw what might be the next row in the pattern.

Chapter 12   two hundred fifty-seven P257

Lesson Check

1. What might come next in this pattern?

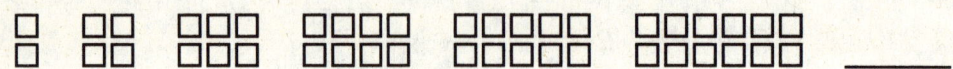

○   ○   ○   ○

Spiral Review

2. What is the name of this shape? (Lesson 12.2)

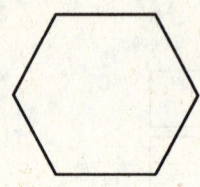

- ○ hexagon
- ○ pentagon
- ○ rectangle
- ○ triangle

3. What time is shown on the clock? (Lesson 11.8)

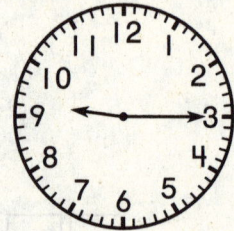

- ○ 9:03
- ○ 9:15
- ○ 9:45
- ○ 10:15

4. Which shows a line of symmetry? (Lesson 12.4)

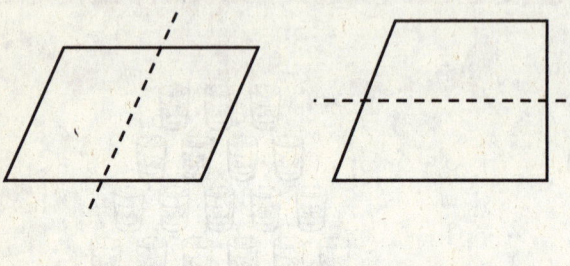 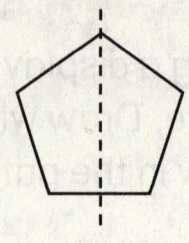 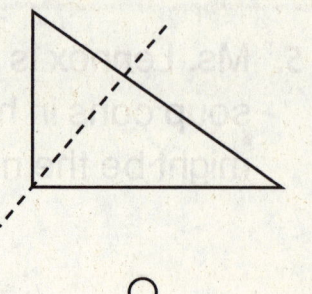

○   ○   ○   ○

Name _____

PROBLEM SOLVING
Lesson 12.6

Find a Pattern • Number Patterns

Solve. Draw to show what you did.

1. Marci likes to put her bears in a pattern. She has 2 bears in the first row, 4 bears in the second row, and 6 bears in the third row. How many bears should Marci put in the fifth row?

_____ bears

2. Darnell stores pencils in a pattern in his desk. The first box has 3 pencils, the second box has 6 pencils, and the third box has 9 pencils. How many pencils should be in the sixth box?

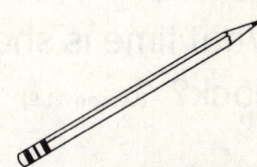

_____ pencils

3. Rena put her star stickers in a pattern. The first row has 3 stickers, the second row has 5 stickers, and the third row has 7 stickers. How many stickers should Rena have in the fifth row?

_____ stickers

Chapter 12   two hundred fifty-nine **P259**

Lesson Check

1. Zach made a pattern with 3 dimes in the first row, 5 dimes in the second row, and 7 dimes in the third row. How many dimes should he put in the sixth row?

   ○ 6
   ○ 9
   ○ 11
   ○ 13

2. Emily drew a pattern with 4 squares in the first row, 7 squares in the second row, and 10 squares in the third row. How many squares should she draw in the fifth row?

   ○ 12
   ○ 13
   ○ 16
   ○ 21

Spiral Review

3. What time is shown on this clock? (Lesson 11.9)

   ○ 12:15
   ○ 12:17
   ○ 1:15
   ○ 1:17

4. What is this shape? (Lesson 12.1)

   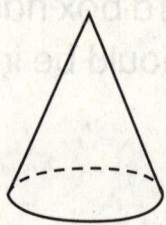

   ○ cone
   ○ square pyramid
   ○ cylinder
   ○ cube

5. Which group of coins has a total value of 35¢? (Lesson 11.5)

   ○   ○   ○   ○

Lesson 12.7

Name _____

Algebra: Find a Rule • Growing Patterns

Write a rule for the growing pattern.

1. oo ooo oooo ooooo oooooo
   oo ooo oooo ooooo oooooo

   Rule: _____

2.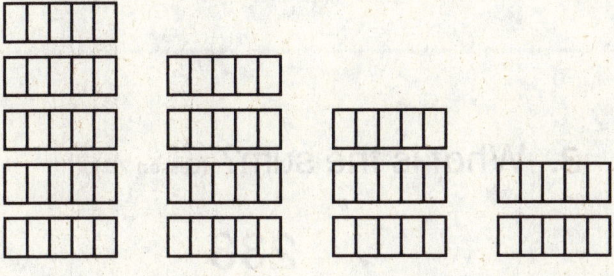

   Rule: _____

3.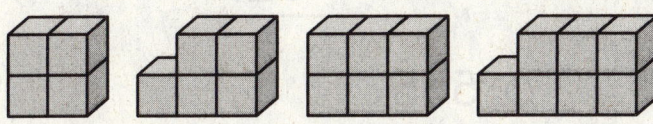

   Rule: _____

4. XX   XXXX   XXXXXX   XXXXXXXX
   XX   XXXX   XXXXXX   XXXXXXXX
   XX   XXXX   XXXXXX   XXXXXXXX

   Rule: _____

PROBLEM SOLVING  REAL WORLD

5. John planted some flowers in this pattern. He wants to continue this pattern when he plants another row. How many flowers should he plant in the bottom row?

   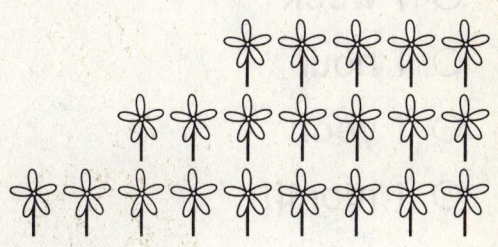

   _____ flowers

Chapter 12   two hundred sixty-one **P261**

Lesson Check

1. Which is a rule for this growing pattern?

   - ○ Add 2.
   - ○ Add 3.
   - ○ Add 4.
   - ○ Add 6.

Spiral Review

2. What is the difference? (Lesson 5.6)

   $$73 - 58$$

   - ○ 131
   - ○ 25
   - ○ 21
   - ○ 15

3. What is the sum? (Lesson 7.2)

   $$238 + 327$$

   - ○ 555
   - ○ 565
   - ○ 585
   - ○ 665

4. Tom visited his aunt for 7 days. Which is the same amount of time as 7 days? (Lesson 11.10)

   - ○ 1 week
   - ○ 1 hour
   - ○ 1 year
   - ○ 1 month

5. Which of the following is the name of this shape? (Lesson 12.1)

   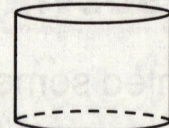

   - ○ square pyramid
   - ○ cone
   - ○ cylinder
   - ○ cube

Lesson 12.8

Name _____

Algebra: Explain Rules for Patterns

Write a rule for the growing pattern.
Explain how you found the rule.

1.

   ___ ___ ___ ___ ___

   Rule: _____

   _____
   _____

2. ```
   xxxxx    xxxxx    xxxxx    xxxxx
            xxxxx    xxxxx    xxxxx
                     xxxxx    xxxxx
                              xxxxx
   ```

   Rule: _____

   ___ ___ ___ ___

   _____
   _____

PROBLEM SOLVING

3. Keenan made a pattern with block towers. He used 3 blocks for his first tower. He used 5 blocks for the next tower. He used 7 blocks for the third tower. How many blocks should he use for the fifth tower?

   _____ blocks

Chapter 12   two hundred sixty-three   **P263**
   ```

Lesson Check

1. What is a rule for this growing pattern?

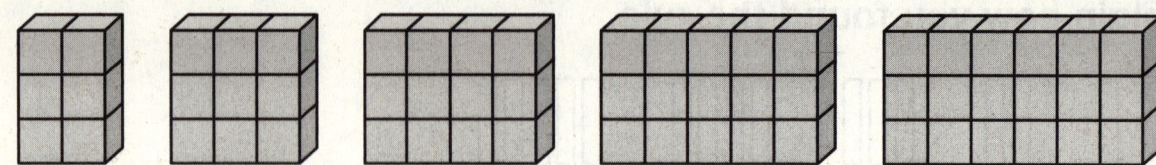

- ○ Add 9.
- ○ Add 6.
- ○ Add 3.
- ○ Add 1.

Spiral Review

2. Use a centimeter ruler. What is the length of this pencil to the nearest centimeter? (Lesson 9.11)

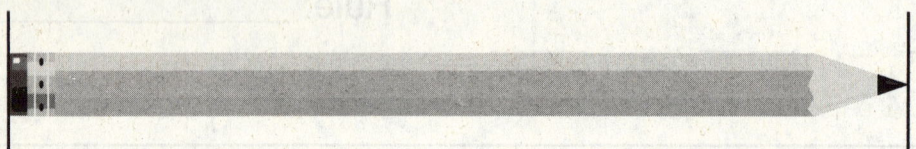

- ○ 5 centimeters
- ○ 11 centimeters
- ○ 10 centimeters
- ○ 12 centimeters

3. What is the difference? (Lesson 5.6)

```
  68
- 17
```

- ○ 51
- ○ 52
- ○ 61
- ○ 85

6. What time is shown on this clock? (Lesson 11.7)

- ○ 2:06
- ○ 3:30
- ○ 2:30
- ○ 6:13

Lesson 12.9

Name _____

Algebra: Find Missing Terms for Patterns

Write the missing term. Then write a rule.

1. 24   26   28   ____   32   34

   Rule: _____

2. 256   266   276   286   ____   306

   Rule: _____

3. 50   53   56   ____   65

   Rule: _____

4. 50   46   ____   38   34   30

   Rule: _____

5. 115   110   105   ____   95   90

   Rule: _____

PROBLEM SOLVING — REAL WORLD

Write or draw to explain.

6. The lockers in Rachel's school have a number pattern. One of the numbers is missing. What is the missing locker number?

148	146	144		140

locker number _____

Lesson Check

1. What is the missing term?

   21 23 25 ____ 29

   - ○ 26
   - ○ 27
   - ○ 28
   - ○ 30

2. What is the missing term?

   81 85 89 ____ 97

   - ○ 93
   - ○ 91
   - ○ 90
   - ○ 88

Spiral Review

3. What is the sum? (Lesson 7.4)

   $$\begin{array}{r} 536 \\ +456 \\ \hline \end{array}$$

   - ○ 80
   - ○ 892
   - ○ 982
   - ○ 992

4. What is the difference? (Lesson 7.7)

   $$\begin{array}{r} 489 \\ -137 \\ \hline \end{array}$$

   - ○ 252
   - ○ 343
   - ○ 352
   - ○ 625

5. What is the total value of this group of coins? (Lesson 11.2)

   - ○ 80¢
   - ○ 75¢
   - ○ 71¢
   - ○ 57¢

Name _____

Chapter 12 Extra Practice

Lesson 12.1 (pp. 521–524)
Circle the objects that match the shape name.

Lesson 12.2 (pp. 525–528)
Write the number of sides and the number of vertices.

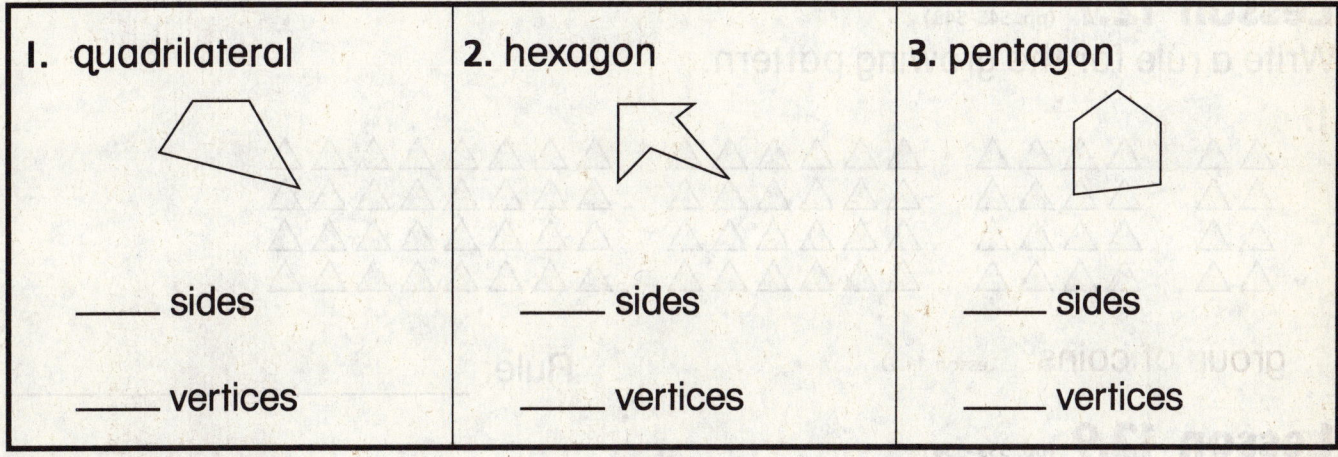

1. quadrilateral

___ sides

___ vertices

2. hexagon

___ sides

___ vertices

3. pentagon

___ sides

___ vertices

Lesson 12.4 (pp. 533–535)
Does the shape have a line of symmetry? If yes, draw the line.

1.

yes   no

2.

yes   no

Lesson 12.5 (pp. 537–540)

Draw what might come next in the pattern.

1. 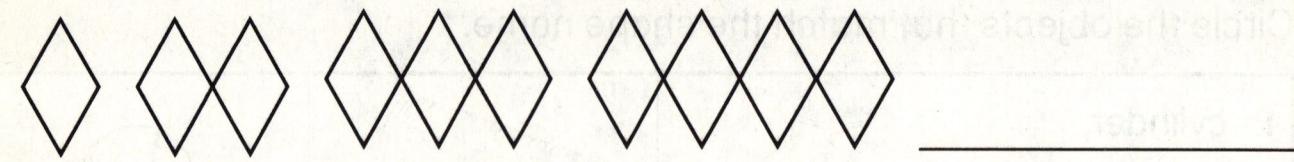 _____

Lesson 12.6 (pp. 541–544)

Solve. Draw to show what you did.

1. Charles is putting all the baseballs in a pattern. He put 2 baseballs in the first row, 5 baseballs in the second row, and 8 baseballs in the third row. How many baseballs should Charles put in the fourth row? _____ baseballs

Lesson 12.7 (pp. 545–548)

Write a rule for the growing pattern.

1.

Rule: _____

Lesson 12.9 (pp. 553–556)

Write the missing term. Then write a rule.

1. 18   15   12   9   ____   3   Rule: _____
2. 110 120 130 ____ 150   Rule: _____
3. ____ 38   42   46   50   54   Rule: _____

P268 two hundred sixty-eight

Name _____

Thousands

Lesson 1

Essential Question How are hundreds grouped as thousands?

Model and Draw

There are 10 ones in 1 ten.

There are 10 tens in 1 hundred.

There are 10 hundreds in 1 thousand.

There are __10__ hundreds in __1,000__.

Share and Show

Count. Write how many hundreds. Then write the number.

A comma (,) goes between the thousands place and the hundreds place.

1.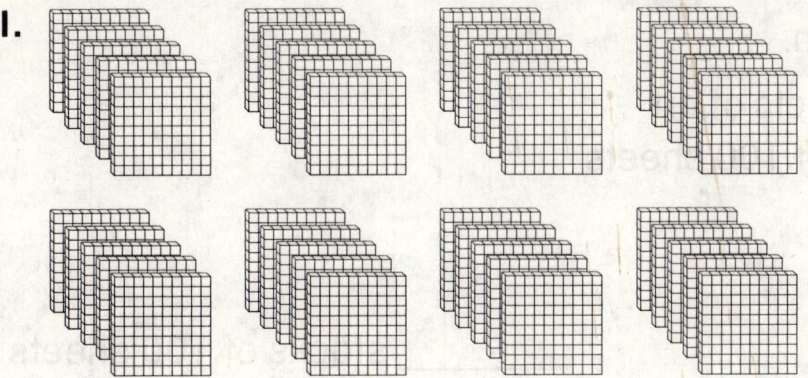

____ hundreds = ____,____

 **Math Talk** How many hundreds are there in 8,000? **Explain.**

Getting Ready for Grade 3

On Your Own

Count. Write how many hundreds.
Then write the number.

2.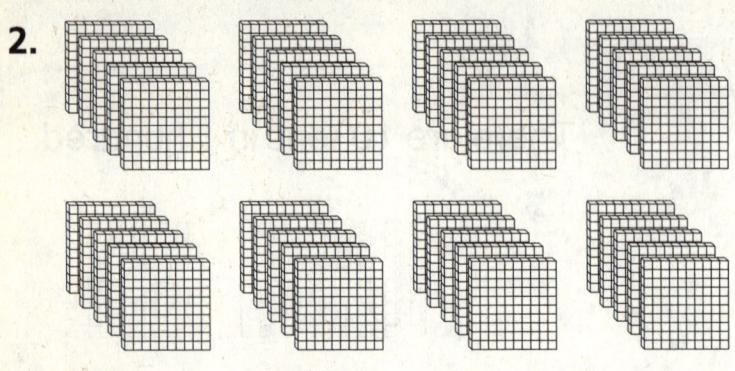

_____ hundreds = _____,_____

3.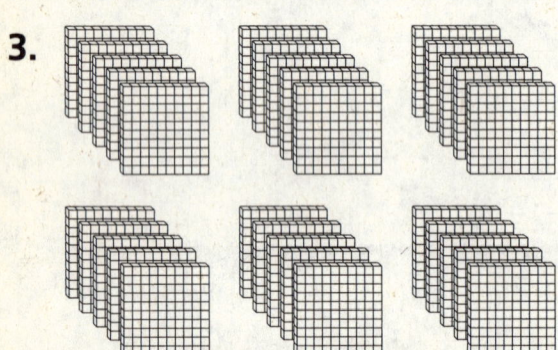

_____ hundreds = _____,_____

PROBLEM SOLVING · REAL WORLD

Solve. Write or draw to explain.

4. Ms. Adams has 6,000 sheets of art paper. How many stacks of 100 sheets can she make?

_____ stacks of 100 sheets

TAKE HOME ACTIVITY • Ask your child: If you have 3 hundreds, how many more hundreds do you need to have 1,000?

Name _____

Lesson 2

Place Value: 4-Digit Numbers

Essential Question How do you know the value of a digit in a 4-digit number?

Model and Draw

You know the value of a digit by its place in a number.

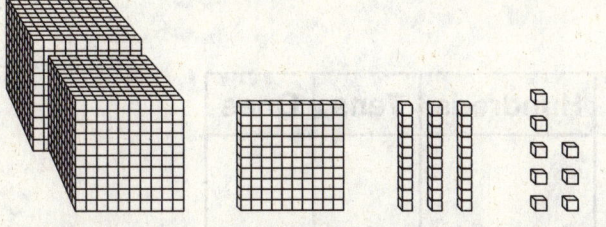

Thousands	Hundreds	Tens	Ones
2	1	3	8

2,000   100   30   8

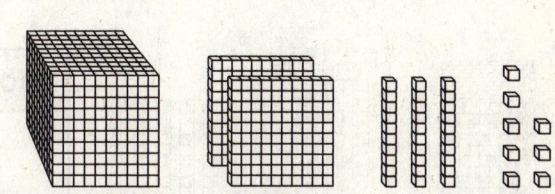

Thousands	Hundreds	Tens	Ones
1	2	3	8

1,000   200   30   8

Share and Show

Write how many thousands, hundreds, tens, and ones. Write the number.

1.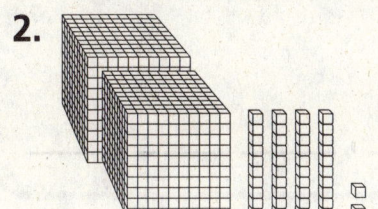

Thousands	Hundreds	Tens	Ones

_____

2.

Thousands	Hundreds	Tens	Ones

_____

 **Math Talk** How is the value of 2,000 different than the value of 200?

Getting Ready for Grade 3   two hundred seventy-one **P271**

On Your Own

Write how many thousands, hundreds, tens, and ones. Write the number.

3.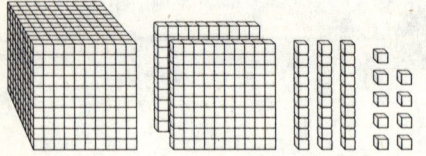

Thousands	Hundreds	Tens	Ones

_____

4.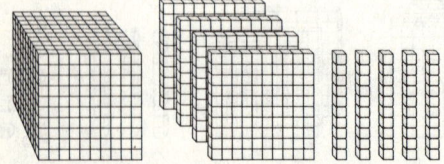

Thousands	Hundreds	Tens	Ones

_____

Circle the value of the underlined digit.

5.	<u>8</u>,310	8	80	800	8,000
6.	5,4<u>9</u>2	9,000	900	90	9

PROBLEM SOLVING

Write the number that matches the clues.

7. My number has the same number of thousands as tens. It has three hundreds and no ones. The sum of its digits is 11. What is my number?

_____ , _____ _____ _____

TAKE HOME ACTIVITY • Write a 4-digit number on a piece of paper. Ask your child to tell the value of each digit in that number.

Name _____

Lesson 3

Different Forms of 4-Digit Numbers

Essential Question What are different ways to write a 4-digit number?

Model and Draw

You can write numbers in different ways.

two thousand, four hundred thirty-five

__2__ thousands __4__ hundreds __3__ tens __5__ ones

__2,000__ + __400__ + __30__ + __5__

__2,435__

Share and Show

Write the number in different ways.

1. six thousand, two hundred three

   _____ thousands _____ hundreds _____ tens _____ ones

   _____ + _____ + _____ + _____

   _____

2. two thousand, six hundred twenty-seven

   _____ thousands _____ hundreds _____ tens _____ ones

   _____ + _____ + _____ + _____

   _____

Math Talk In the number 4,528, what digit is in the thousands place? What is its value?

Getting Ready for Grade 3

two hundred seventy-three **P273**

On Your Own

Write the number in different ways.

3. five thousand, two hundred seventy

_____ thousands _____ hundreds _____ tens _____ ones

_____ + _____ + _____ + _____

_____

4. eight thousand, nine hundred forty-one

_____ thousands _____ hundreds _____ tens _____ one

_____ + _____ + _____ + _____

_____

5. one thousand, five hundred twenty-eight

_____ thousand _____ hundreds _____ tens _____ ones

_____ + _____ + _____ + _____

_____

PROBLEM SOLVING

Write the number.

6. 40 + 3,000 + 7 + 600

_____

TAKE HOME ACTIVITY • Ask your child to write 4,392 in different ways.

Name _____

Lesson 4

Algebra: Compare 4-Digit Numbers

Essential Question How does the value of each digit help you compare numbers?

Model and Draw

Compare numbers by looking at the greatest place first.

1,342

1,461

THINK: The thousands are the same.
3 hundreds < 4 hundreds

1,342 is less than 1,461.

1,342 < 1,461

Share and Show

Compare. Then write >, <, or =.

1. 1,254

    2,307

    1,254 ◯ 2,307

2. 1,262

    1,095

    1,262 ◯ 1,095

 **Math Talk** Use **is greater than** to compare 248 and 2,408. **Explain.**

Getting Ready for Grade 3

two hundred seventy-five **P275**

On Your Own

Compare. Then write >, <, or =.

3. 3,250 ◯ 2,508

4. 9,841 ◯ 9,841

5. 672 ◯ 6,536

6. 1,356 ◯ 3,165

7. 6,768 ◯ 6,768

8. 999 ◯ 5,678

PROBLEM SOLVING

Use the information in the table to solve.

Fruits at the Fruit Stand	
Fruit	Number
apples	1,262
pears	1,304
bananas	1,258
plums	1,293

9. Use > or < to compare. Are there more plums or more apples at the fruit stand?

_____ ◯ _____

There are more _____ at the fruit stand.

TAKE HOME ACTIVITY • Ask your child to explain how to compare numbers to find which number is greater.

P276 two hundred seventy-six

Name _____

Lesson 5

Algebra: Order 4-Digit Numbers

Essential Question How does place value help you order numbers?

Model and Draw

Compare the digits to write the numbers in order.

Thousands	Hundreds	Tens	Ones
3	2	5	6
3	4	1	8
3	2	1	9

The thousands digits are all the same. → 3,418 has the most hundreds. ____ < ____ < 3,418 → 1 ten < 5 tens, so 3,219 is the least number. 3,219 < ____ < 3,418

3,219 < 3,256 < 3,418
least   greatest

Share and Show

Compare the digits. Write the numbers in order.

1.
| 4,576 |
| 3,402 |
| 3,813 |

_____ < _____ < _____
least   greatest

 **Math Talk** When comparing numbers, which digits should you look at first?

Getting Ready for Grade 3   two hundred seventy-seven **P277**

On Your Own

Compare the digits. Write the numbers in order.

2.
6,521
7,039
4,804

_____ < _____ < _____
least   greatest

3.
9,484
9,375
9,702

_____ < _____ < _____
least   greatest

PROBLEM SOLVING REAL WORLD

Read about the class trip. Then solve.

Our class went to the insect zoo. We learned that 1,287 bees are at the zoo. We also learned that 959 ants and 1,216 butterflies are at the zoo.

4. Order the numbers of bees, ants, and butterflies from greatest to least.

_____ > _____ > _____
greatest   least

TAKE HOME ACTIVITY • Write 3,870 < _____ < 4,295 on a sheet of paper. Have your child write a number to make this true.

P278 two hundred seventy-eight

Name _____

✓ Checkpoint

Concepts and Skills

Count. Write how many hundreds.
Then write the number. (pp. P269–P270)

1. 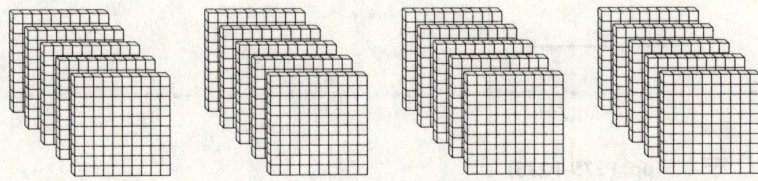 ____ hundreds = ____,____

2. 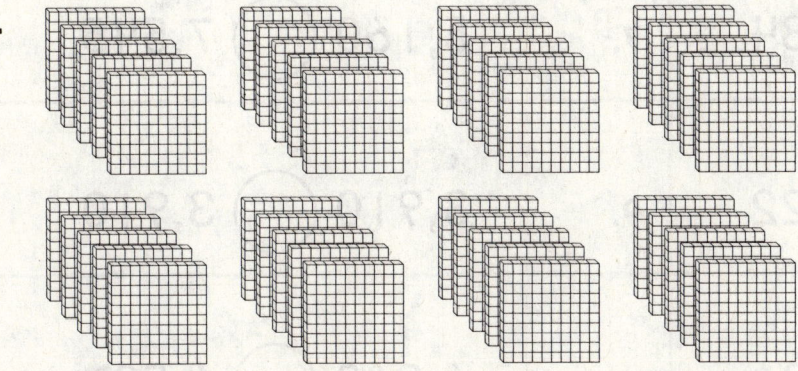 ____ hundreds = ____,____

Write how many thousands, hundreds, tens,
and ones. Then write the number. (pp. P271–P272)

3.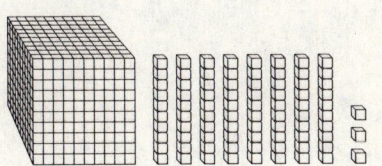

Thousands	Hundreds	Tens	Ones

4.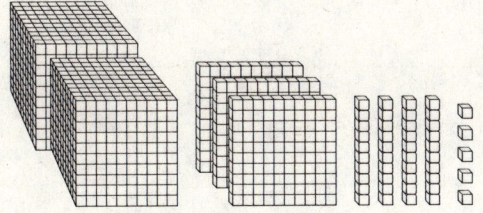

Thousands	Hundreds	Tens	Ones

Getting Ready for Grade 3   two hundred seventy-nine **P279**

Write the number in different ways. (pp. P273–P274)

5. three thousand, two hundred ninety-one

_____ thousands _____ hundreds _____ tens _____ one

_____ + _____ + _____ + _____

_____

Compare. Then write >, <, or =. (pp. P275–P276)

6. 2,423 ◯ 1,934 | 7. 5,160 ◯ 7,545

8. 4,137 ◯ 4,622 | 9. 3,910 ◯ 3,910

10. 953 ◯ 9,136 | 11. 6,812 ◯ 6,537

12. At the store, there are 5,315 strawberries, 5,720 raspberries, and 4,862 blueberries. Which shows the numbers of berries in order from least to greatest? (pp. P277–P278)

○ 5,720 < 4,862 < 5,315

○ 5,315 < 5,720 < 4,862

○ 4,862 < 5,315 < 5,720

○ 4,862 < 5,720 < 5,315

Name _____

Lesson 6

Estimate Sums: 2-Digit Addition

Essential Question How can you estimate the sum of two 2-digit numbers?

Model and Draw

Estimate the sum of 24 + 38.
Find the nearest ten for each number.

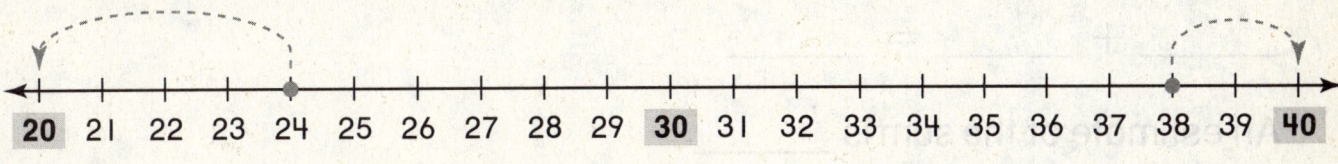

__20__ + __40__ = __60__

An estimate of the sum is __60__.

Share and Show

Find the nearest ten for each number.
Add the tens to estimate.

1. Estimate the sum of 17 + 29.

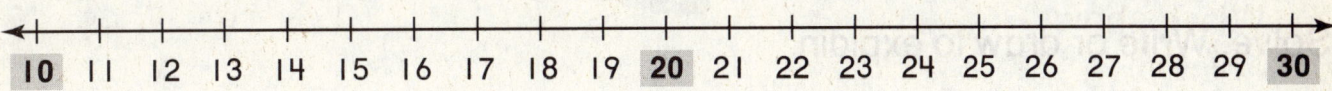

____ + ____ = ____

An estimate of the sum is _____.

Math Talk How did you know which ten is nearest to 17?

Getting Ready for Grade 3

two hundred eighty-one **P281**

On Your Own

Find the nearest ten for each number.
Add the tens to estimate.

2. Estimate the sum of 13 + 28.

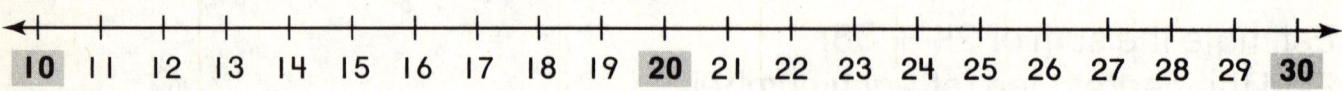

_____ + _____ = _____

An estimate of the sum is _____.

3. Estimate the sum of 34 + 22.

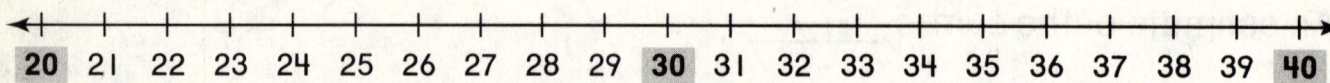

_____ + _____ = _____

An estimate of the sum is _____.

PROBLEM SOLVING REAL WORLD

Solve. Write or draw to explain.

4. Mark has 36 pennies. Emma has 47 pennies. About how many pennies do they have altogether?

about _____ pennies

TAKE HOME ACTIVITY • Ask your child to describe how to estimate the sum of 57 + 21.

Name _____

Lesson 7

Estimate Sums: 3-Digit Addition

Essential Question How can you estimate the sum of two 3-digit numbers?

Model and Draw

Estimate the sum of 274 + 168.
Find the nearest hundred for each number.

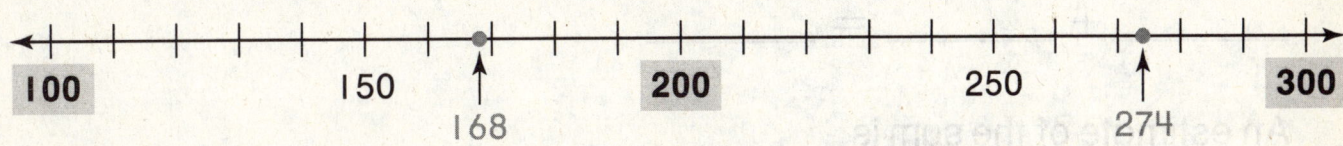

__300__ + __200__ = __500__

An estimate of the sum is __500__.

Share and Show

Find the nearest hundred for each number.
Add the hundreds to estimate.

1. Estimate the sum of 229 + 386.

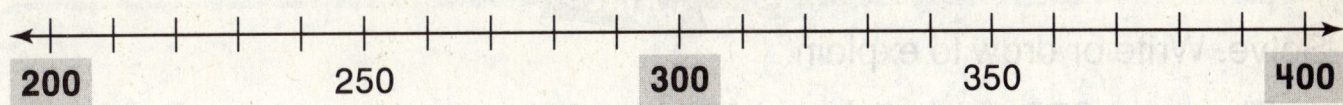

_____ + _____ = _____

An estimate of the sum is _____.

Math Talk How do you know which two hundreds a 3-digit number is between?

Getting Ready for Grade 3

two hundred eighty-three **P283**

On Your Own

Find the nearest hundred for each number.
Add the hundreds to estimate.

2. Estimate the sum of 342 + 238.

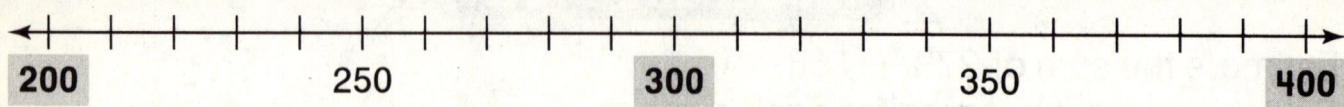

_____ + _____ = _____

An estimate of the sum is _____.

3. Estimate the sum of 468 + 439.

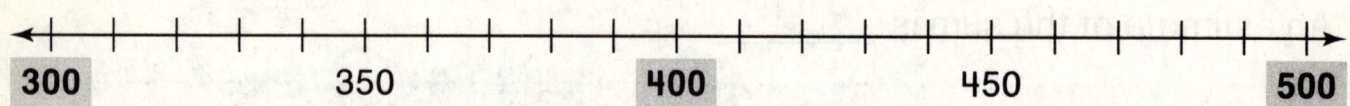

_____ + _____ = _____

An estimate of the sum is _____.

PROBLEM SOLVING

Solve. Write or draw to explain.

4. There are 375 yellow fish and 283 blue fish swimming around a coral reef. About how many fish are there altogether?

about _____ fish

TAKE HOME ACTIVITY • Ask your child to describe how to estimate the sum of 215 + 398.

Name _____

Lesson 8

Estimate Differences: 2-Digit Subtraction

Essential Question How can you estimate the difference of two 2-digit numbers?

Model and Draw

Estimate the difference of 62 − 48.
Find the nearest ten for each number.

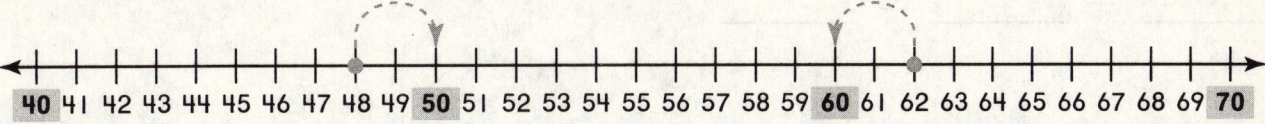

__60__ − __50__ = __10__

An estimate of the difference is __10__.

Share and Show

Find the nearest ten for each number.
Subtract the tens to estimate.

1. Estimate the difference of 42 − 29.

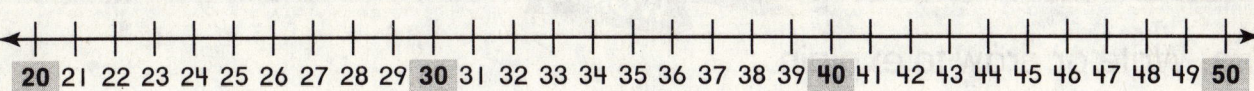

_____ − _____ = _____

An estimate of the difference is _____.

 **Math Talk** How do you know which two tens a number is between?

Getting Ready for Grade 3

two hundred eighty-five **P285**

On Your Own

Find the nearest ten for each number.
Subtract the tens to estimate.

2. Estimate the difference of 54 − 37.

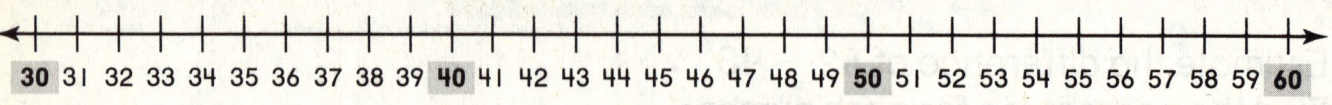

_____ − _____ = _____

An estimate of the difference is _____.

3. Estimate the difference of 79 − 56.

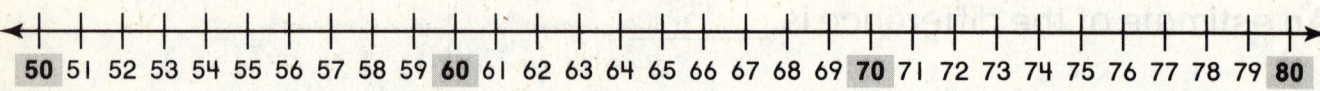

_____ − _____ = _____

An estimate of the difference is _____.

PROBLEM SOLVING REAL WORLD

Solve. Write or draw to explain.

4. A farmer has 91 cows. 58 of the cows are in the barn. About how many of the cows are not in the barn?

about _____ cows

TAKE HOME ACTIVITY • Have your child estimate the difference of 57 − 41.

Name _____

Estimate Differences: 3-Digit Subtraction

Lesson 9

Essential Question How can you estimate the difference of two 3-digit numbers?

Model and Draw

Estimate the difference of 382 − 265.
Find the nearest hundred for each number.

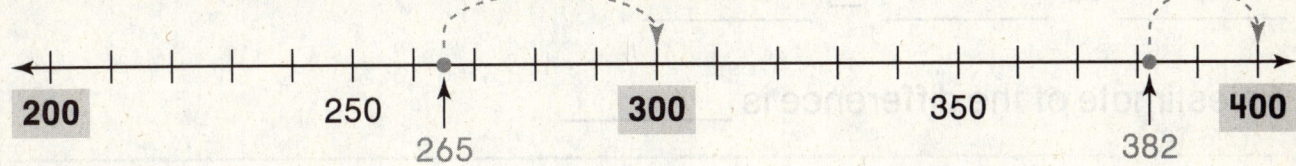

$\underline{400} - \underline{300} = \underline{100}$

An estimate of the difference is $\underline{100}$.

Share and Show

Find the nearest hundred for each number.
Subtract the hundreds to estimate.

1. Estimate the difference of 682 − 565.

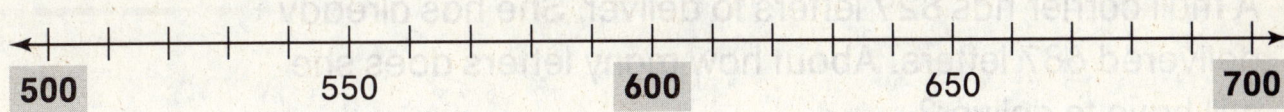

_____ − _____ = _____

An estimate of the difference is _____.

 **Math Talk** How did you know which hundred was nearer to 682?

Getting Ready for Grade 3   two hundred eighty-seven **P287**

On Your Own

Find the nearest hundred for each number.
Subtract the hundreds to estimate.

2. Estimate the difference of 781 − 612.

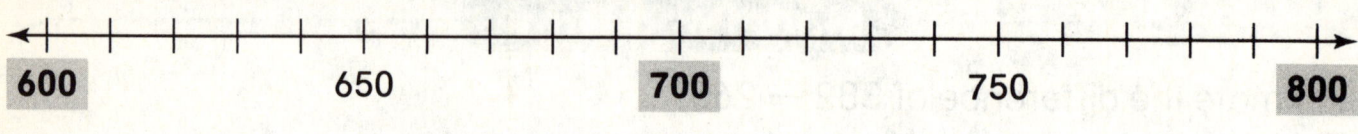

_____ − _____ = _____

An estimate of the difference is _____.

3. Estimate the difference of 467 − 312.

_____ − _____ = _____

An estimate of the difference is _____.

PROBLEM SOLVING

Solve. Write or draw to explain.

4. A mail carrier has 829 letters to deliver. She has already delivered 687 letters. About how many letters does she still have to deliver?

about _____ letters

TAKE HOME ACTIVITY • Ask your child to describe how to estimate the difference of 569 − 235.

Name _____

Concepts and Skills

Find the nearest ten for each number.
Add the tens to estimate. (pp. P281–P282)

1. Estimate the sum of 22 + 37.

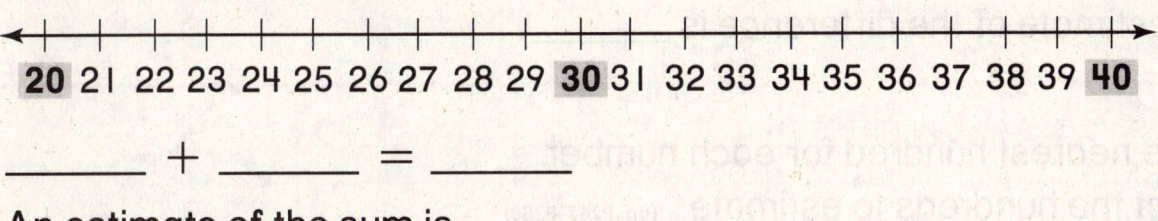

_____ + _____ = _____

An estimate of the sum is _____.

Find the nearest hundred for each number.
Add the hundreds to estimate. (pp. P283–P284)

2. Estimate the sum of 487 + 378.

_____ + _____ = _____

An estimate of the sum is _____.

3. Estimate the sum of 267 + 310.

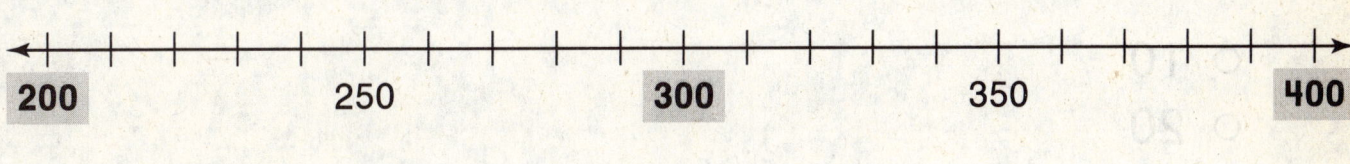

_____ + _____ = _____

An estimate of the sum is _____.

Getting Ready for Grade 3   two hundred eighty-nine **P289**

Find the nearest ten for each number.
Subtract the tens to estimate. (pp. P285–P286)

4. Estimate the difference of 34 − 11.

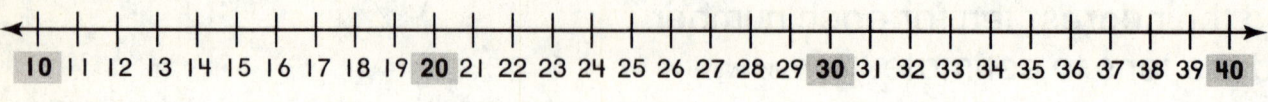

_____ − _____ = _____

An estimate of the difference is _____.

Find the nearest hundred for each number.
Subtract the hundreds to estimate. (pp. P287–P288)

5. Estimate the difference of 873 − 769.

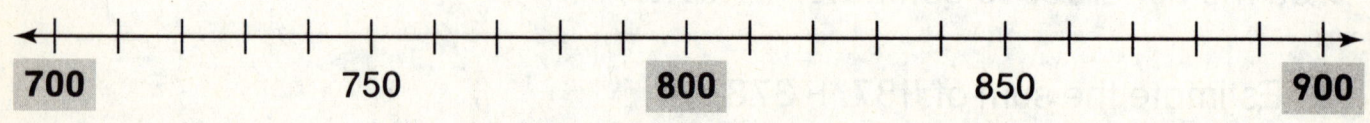

_____ − _____ = _____

An estimate of the difference is _____.

6. Which is the best estimate for the sum of 28 + 37? (pp. P281–P282)

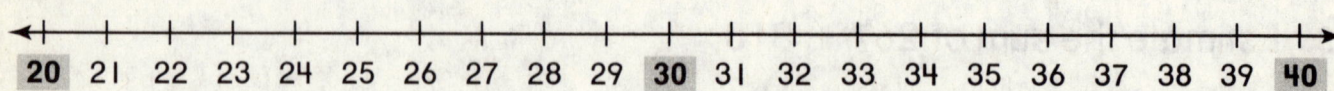

○ 10
○ 20
○ 30
○ 70

Name _____

Equivalent Amounts

Essential Question How do you choose coins to show a money amount in different ways?

**HANDS ON
Lesson 10**

Model and Draw

Here are two ways to show 30¢.

Look at Matthew's way. If you trade 2 dimes and 1 nickel for 1 quarter, the coins will show Alicia's way.

Count the cents.
10, 20, 25, 30

Count the cents.
25, 30

Share and Show

Use coins. Show the amount in two ways.
Draw and label the coins.

1.

61¢

 **Math Talk** Can you show 10¢ with 3 coins?
Explain how you know.

Getting Ready for Grade 3

two hundred ninety-one **P291**

On Your Own

Use coins. Show the amount in two ways.
Draw and label the coins.

2.

55¢

3.

91¢

PROBLEM SOLVING · REAL WORLD

Use coins to solve.

4. Lee wants to buy a pen for 50¢. Draw coins to show two different ways to pay 50¢.

TAKE HOME ACTIVITY • With your child, take turns drawing different collections of coins to show 67¢.

P292 two hundred ninety-two

Name _____

Lesson 11

Compare Amounts

Essential Question How do you compare amounts of money?

Model and Draw

Compare the values of the two groups of coins.
Then write >, <, or =.

10¢ < 11¢   31¢ > 22¢

Share and Show

Write the total value of each group.
Then write >, <, or =.

1.

   _____ ◯ _____

 **Math Talk** Compare 46¢ and 64¢. Use **is greater than** to tell about these amounts.

Getting Ready for Grade 3

On Your Own

Write the total value of each group.
Then write >, <, or =.

2.

   _____ ◯ _____

3.

   _____ ◯ _____

PROBLEM SOLVING · REAL WORLD

Read the clues. Draw the coins.

4. Jake has 3 coins.
   He has no half dollars.
   He has more than 55¢.
   What coins can Jake have?

 **TAKE HOME ACTIVITY** • Draw two groups of coins, each with a total value of less than 75¢. Have your child compare the groups.

P294 two hundred ninety-four

Name _____

Lesson 12

Make Change to 50¢

Essential Question How can you make change for amounts up to 50¢?

Model and Draw

When you pay more money than the price, you get **change**.

Lee buys:	Lee pays:	Make change. Count on from the price to the amount Lee paid.
 38¢	 50¢	 1¢ 1¢ 10¢ 39¢ 40¢ 50¢ The change is __12¢__.

Share and Show

Write the amount paid.
Draw coins and count on to find the change.

	Price	Amount Paid	Draw coins to count on.	Change
1.	24¢ (toy car)	 30¢		

 **Math Talk** Mimi says that Lee can subtract the price of the toy robot from the amount paid to find the change. Is she right? **Explain**.

Getting Ready for Grade 3

two hundred ninety-five **P295**

On Your Own

Write the amount paid.
Draw coins and count on to find the change.

	Price	Amount Paid	Draw coins to count on.	Change
2.	34¢ (basketball)	quarter, dime		_____
3.	29¢ (bunny)	quarter, quarter		_____
4.	32¢ (doll)	dime, dime		_____

PROBLEM SOLVING • REAL WORLD

5. 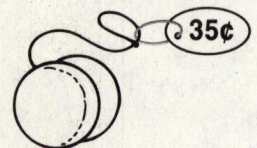 35¢ (yo-yo) Cleo pays for this toy with 50¢. She gets back 3 coins as change. What coins does she get?   Draw or write to solve.

TAKE HOME ACTIVITY • Role play going to the market. Have your child pretend to be the clerk and help him or her practice making change up to 50¢.

P296 two hundred ninety-six

Name _____

Lesson 13

Make Change to $1.00

Essential Question How can you make change for amounts up to $1.00?

Model and Draw

Ann buys:

84¢

Ann pays:

$1.00

Make change.
Count on from 84¢.

1¢	5¢	10¢
85¢	90¢	$1.00

Count the change.

The change is __16¢__.

Share and Show

Write the amount paid.
Draw coins and count on to find the change.

Price	Amount Paid	Draw coins to count on.	Change
1. Yogurt 69¢	 75¢		

Math Talk Ashok says that Ann can subtract the price of the popcorn from the amount paid to find the change. Is he right? **Explain.**

Getting Ready for Grade 3

On Your Own

Write the amount paid.
Draw coins and count on to find the change.

	Price	Amount Paid	Draw coins to count on.	Change
2.	55¢ (muffin)	3 dimes		_____
3.	63¢ (orange juice)	2 quarters		_____
4.	60¢ (bagels)	$1.00 bill		_____

PROBLEM SOLVING • REAL WORLD

5.  Josh pays for this sandwich with $1.00. He gets back 2 coins as change. What coins does he get?   Draw or write to solve.

 **TAKE HOME ACTIVITY** • Role play going to the market. Have your child pretend to be the clerk and help him or her practice making change up to $1.00.

P298 two hundred ninety-eight

Name _____

Money Amounts Over $1.00

Essential Question How can you count money amounts over $1.00?

Lesson 14

Model and Draw

Circle the money that makes $1.00.
Count on. Write how much money in all.

75¢ can be written as $0.75.

$1.75

Share and Show

Circle the money that makes $1.00.
Count on. Write how much money in all.

1.

_____

2.

_____

Math Talk **Explain** how you counted to find the total value.

Getting Ready for Grade 3

On Your Own

Circle the money that makes $1.00.
Count on. Write how much money in all.

3.

_____

4.

_____

PROBLEM SOLVING Real World

5.   Todd has a dollar bill and a dime. How much more money does he need to buy the toy?

Write the answer two ways.

_____ _____

TAKE HOME ACTIVITY • Put 5 quarters, 4 dimes, 5 nickels, and some pennies on the table. Have your child show one way to count how much money in all.

Name _____

Lesson 15

$5, $10, and $20 Bills

Essential Question How can you find the total value of a group of bills?

Model and Draw

Look at the number in the corners of a bill. The number tells you how many dollars the bill is worth.

five dollars — ten dollars — twenty dollars

$5 — $10 — $20

Count on to find the total value.
Start at $10. Count on by tens.

$10, $20, $30 _____ $30
_____
total value

Share and Show

Count on to find the total value.

> Write the dollar sign ($) before the number.

1.

_____
total value

 **Math Talk** How are a $5 bill, a $10 bill, and a $20 bill different?

Getting Ready for Grade 3 — three hundred one P301

On Your Own

Count on to find the total value.

2.

_____ total value

3.

_____ total value

4.

_____ total value

PROBLEM SOLVING

Solve. Write or draw to explain.

5. Travis gave two $10 bills and two $5 bills to the clerk for a new pair of shoes. How much money did he give to the clerk?

_____

 **TAKE HOME ACTIVITY** • Have your child draw and label $20 bills, $10 bills, and $5 bills to show a total value of $75.

Name _____

✓ Checkpoint

Concepts and Skills

Use coins. Show the amount in two ways.
Draw and label the coins. (pp. P291–P292)

1.  72¢

Write the total value of each group.
Then write >, <, or =. (pp. P293–P294)

2.

_____ ◯ _____

Write the amount paid.
Draw coins and count on to find the change. (pp. P295–P296)

	Price	Amount Paid	Draw coins to count on.	Change
3.	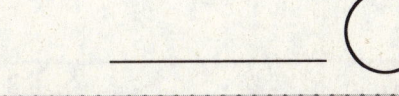 29¢			

Getting Ready for Grade 3   three hundred three   P303

Write the amount paid.
Draw coins and count on to find the change. (pp. P297–P298)

	Price	Amount Paid	Draw coins to count on.	Change
4.	87¢	$1		

Circle the money that makes $1.
Count on. Write how much money in all. (pp. P299–P300)

5.

_____

6. Suneet has exactly three bills in his wallet.
The total value of the bills is $20.
What bills are in Suneet's wallet? (pp. P301–P302)

○ one $10 bill, two $5 bills

○ one $20 bill, two $1 bills

○ three $10 bills

○ two $10 bills, one $5 bill

Name _____

Lesson 16

Multiply with 3

Essential Question How can you multiply with 3?

Model and Draw

Skip count by threes to multiply with 3.

There are 4 plates of counters.
Each plate has 3 counters.
How many counters are there in all?

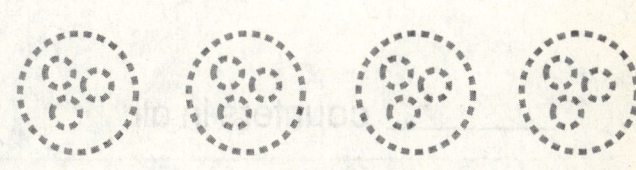

Skip count by threes 4 times to find how many.

___3___, ___6___, ___9___, ___12___

There are ___12___ counters in all. $4 \times 3 =$ ___12___

Share and Show

Draw to show your work.
Write how many counters in all.

1. 8 plates. 3 counters on each plate.

_____ counters in all $8 \times 3 =$ _____

Math Talk   Explain how you can use skip counting to find 9×3.

Getting Ready for Grade 3

On Your Own

Draw to show your work.
Write how many counters in all.

2. 3 plates. 3 counters on each plate.

   _____ counters in all $3 \times 3 =$ _____

3. 6 plates. 3 counters on each plate.

   _____ counters in all $6 \times 3 =$ _____

4. 5 plates. 3 counters on each plate.

   _____ counters in all $5 \times 3 =$ _____

PROBLEM SOLVING REAL WORLD

Draw to show your work.

5. There are 7 waiters. Each waiter has a tray. Each tray has 3 plates. How many plates do the waiters have in all?

   _____ plates

TAKE HOME ACTIVITY • Ask your child to explain how to find the number of wheels on 5 tricycles.

Name _____

Lesson 17

Multiply with 10

Essential Question How can you multiply with 10?

Model and Draw

Skip count by tens to multiply with 10.

There are 3 friends. They each have 10 fingers. How many fingers do they have in all?

Skip count by tens to find how many.   __10__ , __20__ , __30__

They have __30__ fingers. $3 \times 10 =$ __30__

Share and Show

Skip count by tens to find how many fingers in all.

1.

__10__ , __20__ , __30__ , __40__ , __50__

_____ fingers in all $5 \times 10 =$ _____

 **Math Talk** How does skip counting by tens help you multiply with 10?

Getting Ready for Grade 3 three hundred seven **P307**

On Your Own

Skip count by tens to find how many fingers in all.

2.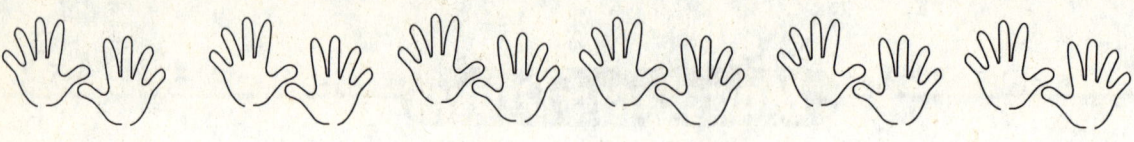

_____, _____, _____, _____, _____, _____,

_____ fingers in all $6 \times 10 =$ _____

3.

_____, _____, _____, _____, _____, _____,

_____, _____

_____ fingers in all $8 \times 10 =$ _____

PROBLEM SOLVING — REAL WORLD

Draw a picture or skip-count to solve.

4. Jane has 7 dimes in her pocket. How many cents is 7 dimes?

_____

TAKE HOME ACTIVITY • Ask your child to figure out how many fingers there are altogether on 8 pairs of gloves.

P308 three hundred eight

Name _____

**HANDS ON
Lesson 18**

Size of Shares

Essential Question How can you place items in equal groups?

Model and Draw

When you divide, you place items in equal groups.

Joel has 12 carrots. There are 6 rabbits. Each rabbit gets the same number of carrots. How many carrots does each rabbit get?
Place 12 counters in 6 equal groups.

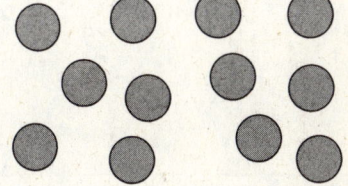

__2__ counters in each group   So, each rabbit gets __2__ carrots.

Share and Show

Use counters. Draw to show your work.
Write how many in each group.

1. Place 10 counters in 2 equal groups.

_____ counters in each group

2. Place 6 counters in 3 equal groups.

_____ counters in each group

 **Math Talk** How did you know how many counters to place in each group for Exercise 2?

Getting Ready for Grade 3

On Your Own

Use counters. Draw to show your work.
Write how many in each group.

3. Place 9 counters in 3 equal groups.

   _____ counters in each group

4. Place 12 counters in 2 equal groups.

   _____ counters in each group

5. Place 16 counters in 4 equal groups.

   _____ counters in each group

PROBLEM SOLVING  REAL WORLD

6. Mrs. Peters divides 6 orange slices between 2 plates. She wants to have 4 orange slices on each plate. How many more orange slices does she need?

   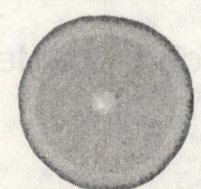

   _____ more orange slices

 **TAKE HOME ACTIVITY** • Ask your child to place 15 pennies into 3 equal groups.

P310 three hundred ten

Name _____

Number of Equal Shares

**HANDS ON
Lesson 19**

Essential Question How can you find the number of equal groups that items can be placed into?

Model and Draw

There are 12 cookies. 3 cookies fill a snack bag. How many snack bags can be filled?

Place 12 counters in groups of 3.

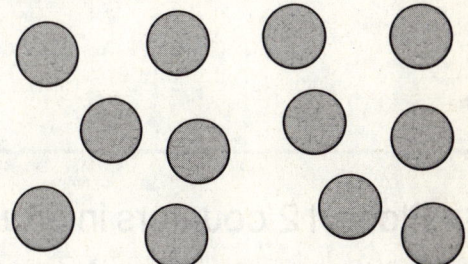

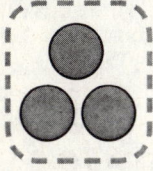 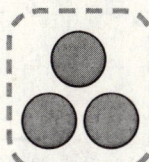 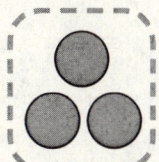 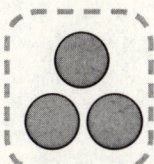   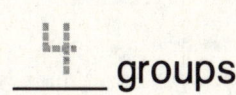

____4____ groups

So, ____4____ snack bags can be filled.

Share and Show

Use counters. Draw to show your work.
Write how many groups.

1. Place 8 counters in groups of 4.

_____ groups

2. Place 10 counters in groups of 2.

_____ groups

Math Talk   Describe how you could find the number of groups of 2 you could make with 12 counters.

Getting Ready for Grade 3

On Your Own

Use counters. Draw to show your work.
Write how many groups.

3. Place 4 counters in groups of 2.

_____ groups

4. Place 12 counters in groups of 4.

_____ groups

5. Place 15 counters in groups of 3.

_____ groups

PROBLEM SOLVING REAL WORLD

Draw to show your work.

6. Some children want to play a board game. There are 16 game pieces. Each player needs to have 4 pieces. How many children can play?

_____ children

TAKE HOME ACTIVITY • Have your child find out how many groups of 5 are in 20.

Name _____

Lesson 20

Connect Subtraction and Division

Essential Question How does counting back on a number line help you divide?

Model and Draw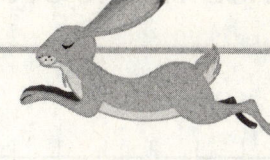

A number line can help you divide by equal groups.
How can you divide 8 into equal groups of 4?

Start at 8.
Count back by fours until you reach 0.
Count the number of hops.

Each hop subtracts 4.

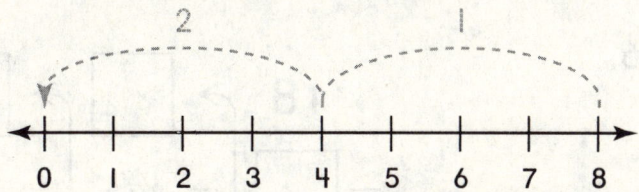

$$\begin{array}{r}8\\-4\\\hline 4\end{array} \quad \begin{array}{r}4\\-4\\\hline 0\end{array}$$

__2__ groups of 4 in 8

Subtract four __2__ times.

Share and Show

Use a number line to show equal groups.
Complete the repeated subtraction.

1. Divide 15 into equal groups of 5.

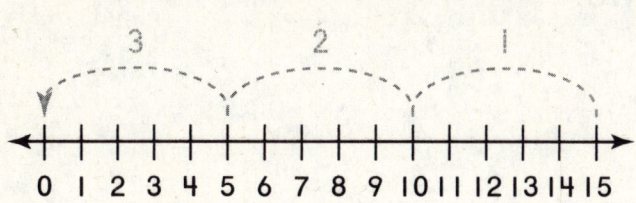

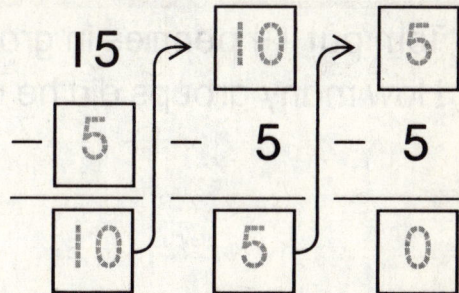

____ groups of 5 in 15

Subtract five ____ times.

 **Math Talk** How do you know where on the number line to begin and how big the hops should be?

Getting Ready for Grade 3

On Your Own

Use a number line to show equal groups.
Complete the repeated subtraction.

2. Divide 12 into equal groups of 3.

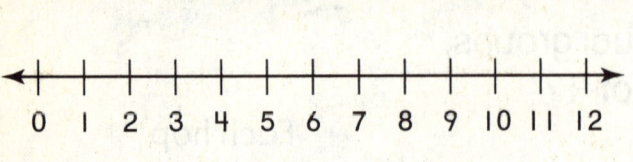

____ groups of 3 in 12

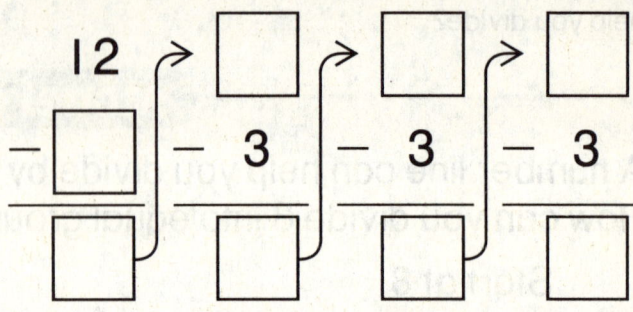

Subtract three ____ times.

3. Divide 18 into equal groups of 6.

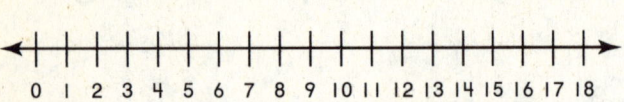

____ groups of 6 in 18

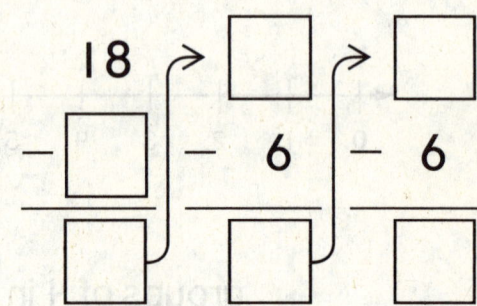

Subtract six ____ times.

PROBLEM SOLVING REAL WORLD

Draw or write to explain.

4. Tom put 14 pennies in groups of two. How many groups did he make?

____ groups of pennies

TAKE HOME ACTIVITY • Give your child 15 pennies. Take turns taking away 3 pennies at a time. How many groups of 3 are there?

Name _____

✓ Checkpoint

Concepts and Skills

Draw to show your work.
Write how many counters in all. (pp. P305–P306)

1. 7 plates. 3 counters on each plate.

   _____ counters in all $7 \times 3 =$ _____

Skip count by tens to find how many
fingers in all. (pp. P307–P308)

2.

   _____ , _____ , _____

   _____ fingers in all $3 \times 10 =$ _____

Use counters. Draw to show your work.
Write how many in each group. (pp. P309–P310)

3. Place 18 counters in 3 equal groups.

   _____ counters in each group

Getting Ready for Grade 3   three hundred fifteen **P315**

Use counters. Draw to show your work.
Write how many groups. (pp. P311–P312)

4. Place 16 counters in groups of 8.

_____ groups

5. Place 9 counters in groups of 3.

_____ groups

6. Keri uses this number line to help her divide.

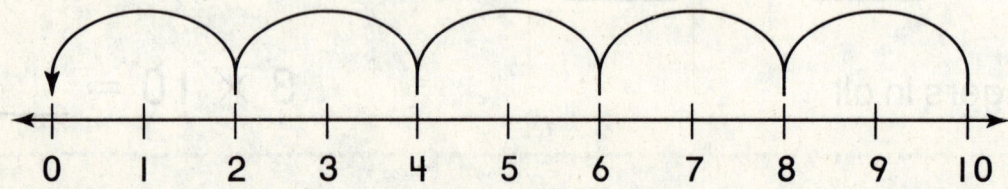

Which of these sentences
does Keri's number line show? (pp. P313–P314)

○ There are 2 groups of 4 in 8.
○ There are 3 groups of 3 in 9.
○ There are 5 groups of 2 in 10.
○ There are 4 groups of 3 in 12.